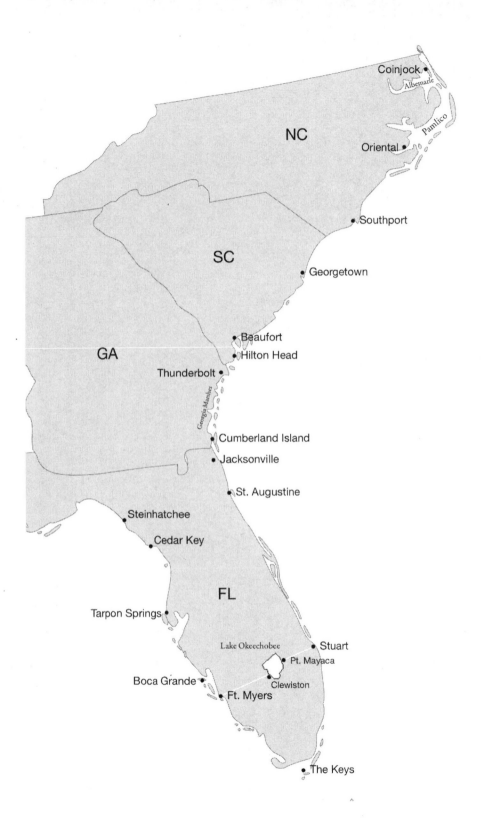

Fair Winds!

An Unlikely Voyage
2000 Miles Alone in a Small Wooden Boat

John Almberg

9 Apr 2016

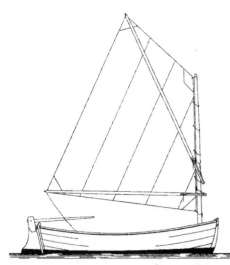

Unlikely Voyages
Books for the Adventuresome Mind

Published by
Unlikely Voyages, 249 Lenox Rd, Huntington Station, NY 11746

First Edition 2016
* * * * * * * * * *

Images of John Atkin's "Cabin Boy" used with permission of Mrs. Pat Atkin.
www.atkinboatplans.com

Unless credited otherwise, all images by John Almberg

ISBN-13: 978-0692601433
ISBN-10: 0692601430

For Helena, who has always said, "Just go for it", no matter how crazy the idea.

Moreover, I, on my side, require of every writer, first or last, a simple and sincere account of his own life, and not merely what he has heard of other men's lives; some such account as he would send to his kindred from a distant land; for if he has lived sincerely, it must have been in a distant land to me.
— Henry David Thoreau

CHAPTER 1

I DECIDE TO BUILD A BOAT

And you, you will come too, young brother, for the days
pass, and never return. Take the Adventure, heed the call,
now ere the irrevocable moment passes! 'Tis but a banging of
the door behind you, a blithesome step forward, and you are
out of the old life and into the new! Then some day, some day
long hence, jog home here if you will, when the cup has been
drained and the play has been played, and sit down by your
quiet river with a store of goodly memories for your company.
— Kenneth Grahame "The Wind In the Willows"

I could have titled this chapter 'I decide to go to the moon'.
That's how difficult building a boat seems to me, even after forty
years of sailing. More difficult than building furniture, for example.
Furniture is mainly sticks joined together at right angles, but there
are few right angles in a boat. Wooden boats aren't built, they are
carved—each plank bent and beveled and hollowed to fit the constantly changing shape of the hull. And unlike your average Chip-
pendale, cosseted in a cozy bedroom, a boat needs to keep the sea
out while an enraged King Neptune kicks in her ribs.

There's another problem.

People have been telling me that I'm unhandy since I was a
small boy. My brother was the handy one. He had a good eye. He
was tall and strong. He looked good holding tools, and he could
whip up a tree house or interplanetary space ship in no time. I
was the bookish one. I preferred *reading* about people who built
tree houses or interplanetary space ships. Tools felt awkward in my

hands, and I guess they looked awkward, too, because my poor old dad was forever shaking his head at me, and telling the neighbors over the fence that my brother was the handy one.

But somehow, in the middle of middle age, I've decided to build a wooden boat. It's not my fault. As in all good stories, there's a woman at the bottom of it.

The trouble started on the clearest, coldest day you can imagine. For a year, Helena and I had been shopping for a sailboat. To be more precise, I'd been shopping and Helena had been rejecting. She didn't reject the *idea* of sailing. She liked water sports. She liked me. We'd spent the last few years rowing a double scull in Huntington Harbor, and now she seemed ready to try something new and exciting. It was just that none of the boats we'd looked at had struck Helena's fancy. The many, *many* boats we'd looked at, such as the lusty ketch she'd turned thumbs-down on, back in the fall.

"What don't you like about her?" I'd asked while the salty beauty at my feet tugged impatiently at the dock lines—and my heart strings.

"I can't put my finger on it."

"It's the upholstery in the main salon, right? Who likes electric-blue suede, anyway? We could have the settees reupholstered."

"No, that's not it."

"The sail plan? A ketch is a bit different from what we've sailed before, but having a mizzen makes a lot of sense for cruising."

She'd looked at me as if I'd been speaking Japanese. "No, it's *not* the sail plan."

"Well, it would be helpful if you could give me a clue. Just a little one. Exactly what kind of boat are we looking for?"

"Don't worry," she'd said confidently. "I'll know it when I see it."

And that's how we ended up in a frozen marina on the coldest day of the year. As we approached the marina, tires crunching on frozen snow, I began to wonder why we were there at all.

"We're here because it's Sunday and you're restless," said Helena. "And because William invited us."

William, my insane friend from work. The wooden boat fanatic who'd heard we were in the market for a boat; and who, coincidentally, had one he was looking to unload.

"But I have no interest in wooden boats," I said. "I've never even been on a wooden boat. Not one that was floating, anyway."

When I was ten, my dear old dad had bought a massive raised-deck cruiser. He'd had it deposited in our yard and, as I remember it, she was larger than the house we lived in. Her paint was peeling, her seams had opened up, and my little brother—who was then deemed too young to work on boats—could poke his head between the missing planks and stick his tongue out at me as I wasted my summer scraping and sanding, sanding and scraping. That boat was a trial for me. It was a happy day when my father, three years wiser, took a chain saw to the rotting hulk.

"Seeing William's boat will be fun," said Helena. "Oh, there he is."

William stood by the marina's main gate, waving frantically, as if afraid we'd drive by. The wind, blowing off the harbor, picked up snow and whirled it around him like an ice tornado.

Reluctantly, I rolled down the window. The wind tousled the ginger hair on William's hatless head. He seemed immune to the cold.

"Just park over there, by the snow bank," he said with a big smile for Helena.

He cut the greetings short as we climbed out of our warm car.

"Much nicer on board the *Rose!*" he said. "This way! This way! Watch your step!"

He lead us, Pied Piper-like, into the maze of boats. Nice, practical, fiberglass boats, hauled out of the water and wrapped in white plastic to sleep through the winter.

"Which one is yours?" I asked, trying to spot the wooden boat. All I could see ahead were bare blue bottoms.

"Not here! On the dock!"

He led us through the icy boat yard, to a long dock that floated on grey, sullen, half-frozen water. Its slips were empty, except for one boat with a wide deck, and a short but thick wooden mast.

"There she is! The *Rose!*" William pointed at her, as if we could be confused about which boat he meant. "Isn't she beautiful? Wooden boats like to stay in the water year round, you know. Saves you money on hauling. Come along! It's much warmer in the cabin."

He grabbed Helena's arm, steered her carefully down the slippery dock, and handed her onto the *Rose's* deck. After a quick look around, they disappeared into the boat's reputedly warmer cabin. A cheery glow spilled out of her portholes.

"Probably still uses kerosene lamps," I said.

I lingered on the dock, studying the Rose's lines. She wasn't a large boat, maybe thirty-two feet, not including her ridiculously long bowsprit; but she was much beamier—wider—than her modern, plastic cousins, and the planks of her spacious teak deck swept from stem to stern, broken only by a cabin top and the small foot well that served as a cockpit.

Aloft, the Rose's rigging was a maze of lines and blocks that reminded me of an old pirate movie.

"This isn't a boat," I thought, "it's a museum."

And yet, as I walked along her deck to the bow, I felt her solidity, her steadiness. This was a real ship, one that could take you places: to the high latitudes of Labrador, or the Faroe Islands, or down the trades to the South Pacific. Anywhere you dared to go.

A cold blast of wind brought me to my senses. Sure, she'd take you places. As long as you were handy and could keep her afloat long enough to get there. Wooden boats needed a ridiculous amount of maintenance. They demanded skills I didn't have—skills practically no one had anymore. Crazy! I was far too sensible to fall for a white elephant like this. Plastic. That was the future. Time to get Helena out of William's clutches. I walked back to the cockpit and opened the cabin door.

"Welcome aboard!" said William. He was sitting on the port-side settee—a kind of couch that doubles as a bunk. Helena was curled up on the starboard side. An old cast iron stove, much bespattered by ancient chowders, glowed in the galley.

"Is that a wood fire you've got going there?" I asked, worried.

"Coal! Much warmer," said William. "Shut the door!"

The cabin was so warm that Helena had doffed her woolen coat. She held a steaming mug of something in her hands and looked dangerously comfortable.

"Hot cocoa?" William lifted a kettle off the stove and waved it over an empty mug. "Something stronger?"

He splashed a large amount of rum into the mug, while I perched uneasily on the settee next to Helena.

"Isn't she beautiful?" said William, meaning the boat.

I braced myself to resist as William launched cheerfully into his sales pitch, pointing out the *Rose's* various features, such as the mahogany drop-down table, the heavy bronze pumps in the galley ("both fresh and salt water!"), and the hand-carved bench in the forepeak that lifted up to reveal, ta-da!, the head.

Meanwhile, I sniffed. There was something odd about this Rose. Something was missing, but what was it? Ah, I had it. Where was the familiar, though slightly sickening, smell of diesel fuel? I looked aft, and saw nothing behind the companionway ladder but a few coils of rope and an orange life jacket.

"Doesn't this boat have an engine?" I asked, interrupting William's stream-of-consciousness ramble.

"Hell, no!" said William. "She doesn't need one!"

"Isn't that amazing?" Helena said. "No boat smell!"

I started to laugh. A boat with no engine, that was a riot. But my laugh died away when I saw the look on Helena's face. William must have seen it too, because he suddenly leaned back on his settee with a satisfied smile.

"You know," said Helena, looking rather pleased with herself, "this is the first boat we've looked at that I really like."

"Well, yes, but..." I started to say, in my most condescending tone.

"Why aren't we looking at wooden boats?"

* * *

A few minutes later, I maneuvered Helena back into the car. Telling the slightly disappointed-looking William that we would, "certainly think about it!", I sped out of the marina, my tires throwing a larger spray of snow in William's direction than politeness strictly allowed.

"So, why *aren't* we looking at wooden boats?" Helena asked again.

Why? Wasn't it obvious?

"For the same reason no one uses cotton sails anymore," I said. "Or hemp lines, or dial telephones, for that matter. Time moves on. Technology improves. Civilization advances."

But this line of reasoning didn't seem to carry much weight with Helena. Not Helena the Brazilian who insisted we live in a 'real' house made of concrete; who required steam radiators that hissed and gurgled and warmed our clothes so beautifully on cold winter mornings; and who loved the impractical cast iron windows she'd lovingly restored.

"The thing is," she said, "when you touch wood, it feels good. When you touch that powdery fiberglass stuff, it feels horrible." She made a face.

"That's the gelcoat," I explained. "That only happens on older boats and you can clean it up with polish."

"No one does, though, do they? They all have it. It's horrible."

Horrible. I was getting that part of the message. Pretty clearly.

"And then there's the smell," she said with an air of finality.

"That's the diesel engine. Has nothing to do with whether the boat is wood or fiberglass."

"But every fiberglass boat seems to have an engine. And they all smell."

"But we *need* an engine."

"That's silly. Who would want a boat that smells?"

"But..."

"And did you notice the deck? So much space!" She smiled, as if imagining herself sunbathing on that wide, flat deck under a hot July sun. Did I mention Helena is Brazilian?

I'd heard this particular complaint from Helena many times. Even when sailing on large boats, owned by rich friends, there was never a place to sunbathe. Or to even sit comfortably. Every square foot of your modern sailboat is covered by the cabin top, or a cleat, or a sheet track.

"Yes," I said, conceding this minor point to female logic. "But the simple fact of the matter is, I don't know anything about wooden boats. I have no idea how to fix them. And everyone knows that wooden boats require a huge amount of maintenance. In fact, they say you spend more time fixing a wooden boat than you do sailing her."

I smugly rested my case, confident the argument that had satisfied two generations of American sailors would defeat even Helena.

She dismissed it with a wave of her hand. "You can learn!"

"But I'm not *handy*!" I said, suddenly feeling desperate.

"You always say that. It's silly. Who told you that?" She waited for an answer as I floundered, not even knowing where to begin.

"Never mind," she said. "You just need practice. And I have the perfect project for you to start on. You know that door in our bedroom?"

The door that hadn't closed properly for fifty years? The door that generations of previous owners had struggled with—the marks of their futile efforts barely marring the edges of the fiendishly non-fitting, solid oak door? Yes, I knew it. I also knew that nothing I could say about that door would have any effect on Helena, who is rarely swayed by logic and who has a deranged but bracing confidence in my hidden (and even unsuspected) abilities.

Besides, she'd been bugging me about it for months.

"I'll look into it," I grumbled.

* * *

The next weekend, I confronted that balky bedroom door.

Since I'm an unhandy guy, my usual approach to hated, home-handyman jobs is to rush through them as quickly as possible, with lots of huffing, puffing, and "Where's my dang screw driver!?" type dramatics. I inherited this approach from my father, the Huffer-and-Puffer-in-Chief of our whole family.

But for some reason—and I can't say what it was—I took a different tack with this job. Maybe, with four kids still in the house, I was just motivated to have a bedroom door that closed; maybe I started off so stumped on this project (*why* didn't it close???) that rushing through it wasn't an option; or maybe I was just ready for it.

Whatever the reason, I let out a deep breath and decided to give the job as much time as it needed. Little did I know what a turning point this decision would be.

At first, the problem with the door didn't seem complicated. Our house had been built in 1929 by an Italian immigrant who'd made some money in New York City as a master mason, working on the 8th Avenue Madison Square Garden. This man had been an artist in concrete: the house was a minor Art Deco masterpiece, and I have no doubt that the door fit perfectly when he first carried his young bride into the bedroom.

Nevertheless, in the eighty years since, either the door or the door frame had changed shape. They no longer matched. The peg no longer fit the hole.

Since the shape of the door frame was literally fixed in concrete, I swiftly reasoned that I'd have to reshape the door to fit the frame. Slightly dazzled by this unexpectedly brilliant insight, I pushed the door against the frame to see where it stuck. At the top, I saw. It was a quarter inch too tall at the top. If I could take a bit off, maybe with some sort of file.

I actually had a rusty old file in my pitiful collection of hand-me-down tools. I fetched it from the basement and stood on a chair to get a better view of the problem.

The top of the door looked as if it had been chewed by a chipmunk: shallow, grooved tooth marks gnawed into eighty year old oak. The chipmunk hadn't gotten far. I compared the toothed file in my hand with the tooth marks on the door. Apparently, at least one previous owner had had similar tools. And skills.

I climbed off the chair, sat on it, and had a think. Perhaps a saw was a better tool for the job. Yes, I was sure it would be. I climbed back on the chair, measured the amount to be cut three times, then took the door off its hinges and lugged the absurdly heavy monster down to my 'workshop' in the basement.

At that point, my workshop consisted of a rickety table and a handful of rusty tools. Luckily, one of the tools was an ancient handsaw I'd inherited from my grandfather. I didn't know it at the time, but it was a Disston—a saw of noble lineage. This was luck akin to Bilbo finding *Sting* in a troll's cave. Fate? I don't know, but by some magic, the saw's teeth were still sharp.

I laid the door on the table, picked up the saw, eyed the line I'd marked, and then had a moment familiar to every newbie wood-worker. Was the line drawn correctly? Could I follow the line? Or, with one cut, would I ruin a beautiful—and lets face it, valuable—piece of wood? Would I end up the hero who fixed something? Or the damn fool who destroyed it? Helena loved that door, even if it didn't close.

It took a long time to work up the courage, but eventually I consigned my fate to the gods, and started making sawdust. Amaz-ingly, when I rehung the door on its hinges, it closed with a satisfy-ing *snick*. Helena applauded.

"Wow," I said, opening and closing the door, wondering if it really had been fifty years since it last closed properly.

As that door closed, another one opened. *Time.* It was all about *time.* My grandfather—a blacksmith, raconteur, and perennial seeker of rainbows—had a stock of proverbs he loved to repeat. One of them was, "You can climb any mountain, as long as you climb it slowly enough." He's said it a million times, but I'd never really listened. Maybe, with enough time, I could fix or build any-thing.

Such is the delusional power that comes from fixing a door.

"I might even be able to fix a wooden boat," I said, not realizing I'd spoken aloud.

"Of course you can," said Helena, giving me a congratulatory kiss before moving on to the eighty-two other chores she accom-plished that day. Such is the power of women.

"I might even be able to *build* a wooden boat," I said, the idea taking hold. "A small boat," I corrected myself, some remnant of common sense still clinging on. "A dinghy. We'll need a dinghy, anyway. If I can build a small wooden boat, I might be able to maintain a larger one."

Palm trees waving against a blue sky. A pink beach. A gleaming white schooner floating in a turquoise lagoon. A stout dinghy pulled up on the sand. Helena and I picnicking on the beach…

And that was how all the trouble started.

CHAPTER 2

MY PLAN EVOLVES

*If a man must be obsessed by something, I suppose a boat is
as good as anything, perhaps a bit better than most.*
— E.B. White

Unfortunately, enthusiasm, backed by hazy dreams, can only carry you so far. By the next day, skepticism had set in. Could I really learn how to build a boat? It didn't seem likely.

"You need to do some research," said the Engineer in me.

"Books!" I thought. "The answer will be in a book. Somewhere."

"No! Just dive in!" the Adventurer in me cried. "Life is short!"

"Doing your homework is the responsible thing to do," said the Engineer.

"What's responsibility got to do with it?" cried the Adventurer. "This is a boat we're talking about!"

With that, the Adventurer and Engineer set to, wrestling vigorously over the issue as if their very lives depended on it. You'd think the rough, tough Adventurer would beat the nerdy Engineer every time, but no. As usual, the Engineer won.

"He's a dirty fighter," said the Adventurer, nursing a bruised lip. The Engineer just smiled, smugly.

I drove to the library.

Normally, I found our local library a bit useless. Although the building itself was beautiful and meticulously maintained, its collection was packed with old, hopelessly out-of-date tomes such as "DOS 4 for Nitwits" and "The 1968 Ford Fairlane Repair Guide".

But this time, outdated books were just what I was after. I hoped that somewhere in that temple to old books I'd find the information I needed to get started. So, pen and notebook in hand, I walked into the Huntington Library on Main Street, and went straight to the reference desk.

"I'm looking for information on how to build a wooden boat," I said to the rather stately looking woman sitting behind a computer.

"Oh," her look seemed to say. "You're one of *them*."

"Follow me," she said.

I trailed behind her, down the aisles between tall shelves of old books, further and further from the main reading room. In the deepening silence, her skirt rustled, making it sound as though we were walking through piles of dry leaves. We turned right, then left, then right again. The flickering lights seemed to grow darker. There didn't seem to be any other patrons in this part of the library. And still we carried on, deeper and deeper into the trove of old books.

At last we entered what must have been the oldest part of the building, and the aisle came to an end. We faced a blank grey wall. The librarian stopped and motioned towards the very last shelf of books.

"You'll find them about half way down on the left," she said. Then, without waiting for any questions, she rustled off, the sound of her skirt gradually fading away, leaving me in profound silence.

I looked at the end of the shelf. A hand-written card had been inserted into a brass frame: *Stuff Nobody Reads Anymore*, it said.

"Ah-ha," I said. "Perfect."

* * *

Many years ago, when Helena and I first started looking for a house together, we agreed it would be her job to drive around with her real estate agent friend Leslie, visit a bunch of houses, and draw up a list of five or six homes that suited our tastes, needs, and budget. We would then visit them together and make our decision. Very organized and efficient.

So I was a bit surprised when Helena returned early from her first day's house-hunting with a big smile on her face.

"I found it!" she said. "It's perfect!"

"You can't have found it," I said, hardly looking up from my computer.

"It was the first house we looked at," Helena said. "Leslie wanted to show me a few others, but there was no point. We went and had coffee instead. You're going to love it!"

"Darling," I said, very patiently. "That's not how it works."

"Why?"

"Because what if there's something better out there?"

"There isn't," she said confidently. "This is it."

"We can't buy the first house you look at!"

"Why not?"

"I don't know!" I said, sputtering a bit. "It's just wrong!"

So Helena dutifully visited dozens of other houses, each time returning with a sad shake of her head. After a week, I relented, and visited that first house with her. She was right. It was perfect. We still live in it.

My hunt for a dinghy to build was something like that.

* * *

Back in the furthest corner of the library, I discovered two shelves bulging with boatbuilding books, many of them 50 or 60 or 100 years old. I scanned the faded titles, looking for a place to start. Most of them looked highly technical, with titles like *Lapstrake Boatbuilding*. What was a lapstrake? No idea.

One book looked promising: John Atkin's *Practical Small Boat Designs*. 'Practical' and 'small' sounded about right. I pulled the book off the shelf, not expecting much from the first book I looked at.

It almost fell open to a well-thumbed page. Someone in the distant past must have loved the design for the *Florence Oakland*, a twenty-two foot... *schooner?* That was odd. I didn't know much about old boats, but I knew that two-masted schooners were usually big boats. Yet a photo showed the little *Florence Oakland* tear-ing through the water with all sails flying, looking like a miniature tall ship. You had to look closely to see she was a day sailer.

The next design was even odder: *Valgerda*, an eighteen foot Hardangersjekte? This boat looked positively Nordic, with its swooping lines and up-thrust bow. Its square-shaped sail looked straight off a Viking boat. Fascinating.

I slowly paged through the rest of the book, studying each design, each one illustrated by drawings and photographs. Not one looked like what I thought of as a 'normal' sailboat — i.e., a round-bottom, fin-keel, Bermuda-rigged cruiser/racer. The book was a real eye-opener.

There were also five dinghy designs in Atkin's book. Three were prams (flat on both ends), and two were skiffs (pointy in the front). One in particular looked perfect.

The skiff was called *Cabin Boy*. He had a certain sturdy stoutness that made him look capable of sailing around the world, or at least across the emerald green lagoon of my Polynesian dream. There was something about the *Cabin Boy* design that spoke to me. As soon as I saw him, I knew I'd found my dinghy.

"No. You can't choose the first boat you look at," the Engineer in me said. "You need to do more homework."

"Homework, schmoamwork," the Adventurer said. "He's perfect!"

"For all you know, there are a dozen better designs hidden in those old books, just waiting to be built. Go on, keep looking."

Dutifully, I put down Mr. John Atkin's book, and pulled the next one from the shelf. Oddly, it was by another Atkin—a Mr. William Atkin. Flipping through the first few pages, I discovered it was not so odd: William was John's father. I skipped through the first chapter, which was about William's boyhood, and started reading Chapter 2, which started off like this:

> *In the late spring of 1906, if you had by chance been walking or carriage-riding through a most delightful byway which lead from the cozy little hamlet of Cold Spring Harbor to the then pastoral village of Huntington, L.I., NY, you might have noticed two very young men driving a livery horse and buggy.*

Upon reflection, I somehow feel you would have noticed this plodding equipage and its two carefree occupants. — William Atkin, Of Yachts & Men.

Huntington, NY? That's where I was that very minute. Coming from Cold Spring Harbor, they must have driven down Main Street, right past the library, over a hundred years ago. For some reason, I found that amazing. I read on.

The two young men in the buggy were William Atkin and his friend Cottrell Wheeler, and they were on their way to purchase the Red Boat Shop from Charles Sammis, a member of an old Huntington family. For the next thirty years, I read, William and Cottrell built boats in Huntington Harbor. John Atkin had been raised right in the village. How had I never heard of the Atkins? Could the whole town have forgotten them?

Seized by a sudden impulse, I checked the book out of the library and walked down Main Street, determined to find the old Atkin & Wheeler boat shop. Fate seemed to be calling me. I followed the directions printed in the story:

Reaching the intersection of Main Street and New York Avenue, turn left and proceed about one mile; the red building on the waterside will be the boatbuilding shop of Charles G. Sammis & Son.' And so it was. A new building standing on piles; some outbuildings; some boats standing on blocking in the yard; and wood smoke curling from the steam box fireplace; a delightful old-fashioned boatshop. The tide was very high with a soft breeze rippling the salt creek water which washed the little beach upon which the shop was built. — William Atkin, Of Yachts & Men.

But when I reached the spot where the old creek led into the head of the harbor, I realized the little Red Boat Shop was gone. That wasn't surprising, really. Even the creek was mostly gone, dammed and filled to within an inch of its life. I stood on the spot where the old boat shop had been and looked over Huntington Harbor, trying to see it as William had, those many years ago. I felt I almost could.

The call of Fate is strong and it's a foolish sailor who spurns her unsubtle nudges.

I made my decision on the spot: the dinghy I built would be the Atkin skiff, *Cabin Boy*.

Back home, I showed *Cabin Boy's* design to Helena, and she oooh-ed and aaah-ed in all the right places. That confirmed my decision. Maybe this boatbuilding thing wouldn't be so hard, after all. I ordered the plans from Mrs. Pat Atkin, John's widow, who still carried on the family business after John's passing in 1999. She had a website, but preferred more traditional means of payment.

"How appropriate," I said. I dusted off my checkbook and my quill pen, and dispatched my order for *Cabin Boy's* plans via what used to be called the Post.

Choosing a boat design? Done.

Would it be as easy to build?

As I inventoried my collection of half-rusted, hand-me-down tools, I had my doubts.

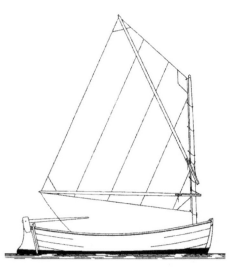

John Atkin's 7'6" Skiff -- Cabin Boy
Used with permission from Pat Atkin
www.atkinboatplans.com

CHAPTER 3

I AM BITTEN

*Houses are but badly built boats so firmly aground that
you cannot think of moving them... The desire to build a house
is the tired wish of a man content thenceforward with a single
anchorage. The desire to build a boat is the desire of youth,
unwilling yet to accept the idea of a final resting place.*
— *Arthur Ransome*

"There is nothing particularly difficult about sailing," my friend John V. mused, as we beat across Peconic Bay into a freezing breeze. "But there are an enormous number of simple skills to be mastered."

At that particular moment, I was trying to master the skill of staying warm under the dodger, while John squinted into the wind like the Ancient Mariner, seemingly unaffected by the ferocious wind-chill.

Still, I took his point. There were the basic sailing skills, like helmsmanship and sail trimming that you learned as a child in a dink or Sun Fish. Then there were the big boat skills you learned at the knee of your father or uncle, such as knot tying, anchoring, docking, putting in a reef without getting blown off the cabin top, and crawling forward to change the headsail in the middle of a Wednesday night race.

Then, when you finally ventured out of your childhood harbor, master of your own little ship, there were the skills of weather forecasting, coastal piloting, and the granddaddy of them all, celestial navigation.

And that is forgetting the domestic skills of getting a hot meal out of a heaving galley, or maneuvering your way into a V-berth without dislocating your hip.

Yes, John was right. Learning to be a proper sailor took longer than getting a Ph.D. So what was I doing, effectively doubling my lifetime course load, by opting for the double major of sailing *and* boatbuilding?

Trying to keep Helena happy, of course.

The night before, I'd been browsing the various boat broker websites on the Internet, and had seen a boat that seemed like the perfect big sister for *Cabin Boy*. She was a *Blue Moon Yawl*—a twenty-three foot sailboat designed by Tom Gilmer—and she was a real beauty. I just couldn't get her out of my mind, even with an ice cold spray pelting my face, but the price! The owner wanted $20,000—even more than William had wanted for the much bigger *Rose*. Far too much for a small boat. I tried to put her out of my mind, but it wasn't easy.

Back on shore, in my warm study, I was quickly learning that boatbuilding, like sailing, wasn't a single skill, but a vast collection of skills, and the first skill I needed to master was lofting.

Lofting, I read, is the black art of translating the small-scale, paper plans you receive from your designer into the full-scale plans you need to build the various pieces of your boat.

In boatbuilding mythology, lofting is the eye of the needle through which all newbie boatbuilders must pass before entering boatbuilding heaven. I was determined to be among the few who succeeded.

To that end, while waiting for *Cabin Boy's* plans to arrive, I studied every lofting book I could get my hands on. It was hard going.

"It's a classic chicken-and-egg problem," I told Helena one evening. "I need experience to loft *Cabin Boy* properly, but I can't get that experience until I loft a boat."

"You've spent twenty-five years doing the most tricky, detailed work possible," Helena said, meaning computer programming.

"True. But this lofting…" I sucked my breath through pursed lips, and shook my head.

She didn't look impressed.

I tried to explain. Every boatbuilding book has a chapter that insists lofting *isn't* a black art—that any damn fool can do it. It then proceeds to demystify the supposed non-mystery with language and diagrams so impenetrably complicated that the mind—at least this mind—boggles.

Even Wikipedia, the giant online encyclopedia that explains Nuclear Fusion with enough detail to threaten national security, sputters out after a few confused sentences when trying to explain the ancient art of lofting. They throw in the towel saying: "Generally, boatbuilding books have a detailed description of the lofting process, beyond the scope of this article."

So when the postman finally delivered the tube containing *Cabin Boy's* plans, my stomach fluttered with a combination of excitement, and fear.

"I'm not sure I can do this," I said, as we unrolled the five sheets of paper, filled with intricate construction drawings and arcane measurements.

"Of course you can," Helena said.

I spread each sheet on the dining room table, and weighed down their curled corners with Helena's collection of small candles. When the plans were laid out flattish, we stood back to admire them.

"Looks complicated," I said.

I pointed to one sheet that was more abstract than the others. Instead of detailed construction drawings, the page contained a simple set of lines. Three sets, actually, encoding *Cabin Boy's* essential dimensions in three views: in profile, as seen from above, and as a series of cross sections.

"I think these are *the lines*," I said, parroting something I'd read in my boatbuilding books. "The lines I need to loft."

"See? You're becoming an expert, already."

I studied them. *Cabin Boy's* lines looked simpler than those for some round-bottom boats I'd seen in books. Just one waterline and no... what were they called? Buttock lines?

"Right, I'll leave you to it!" Helena said, already seeing the tell-

Cabin Boy's Lines
(Not the real dimensions)

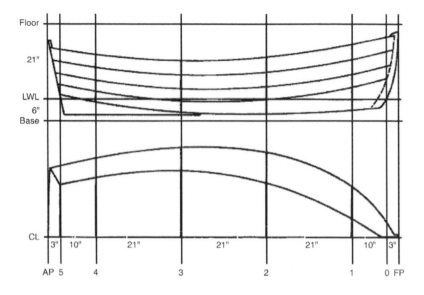

Profile/HalfBreadth Grid with Dimensions

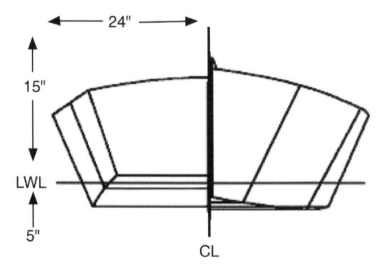

Body Plan Grid with Dimensions

tale signs of a man on a mission. The single mindedness that allowed my caveman ancestors to chase after an antelope for days, until it dropped to its knees in defeat. Victory through persistence: an underrated skill bred into the male human genes. Dormant, perhaps, in me, but slowly awakening, like dawn over the savanna.

"M'mm, right. Thanks," I muttered.

Lines, points, grids. I knew a bit about geometry. In fact, my degree was in Computer Science, but like everyone else, I suffered through high school geometry thinking, "I'm never going to use this stuff," and I was right. For twenty-five years I toiled in the field of mathematics and never used geometry. As I labored to make sense of *Cabin Boy's* plans, I wondered if it was finally going to come in handy.

* * *

Before I could start lofting, though, I needed a surface large enough to hold the full-size plans. Traditionally, lofting was done on the floor of the sail loft over the boat shop. The loft floor was sanded smooth and left open, so it was the perfect place for lofting the boat at the beginning of a project, and for building the sails at the end.

Unfortunately, I didn't have a sail loft over my boat shop. In fact, I didn't have a boat shop at all. What I had was a semi-finished room in my basement—a room half-filled with old furniture: a sofa, TV, rowing machine, and three large bookshelves crammed with books. The castoffs that had made the room cozy were now decidedly in the way.

I was particularly short of floor space. Boats, even small ones, take up a lot of room. First, I'd need room on the floor for a lofting board which, for *Cabin Boy*, would have to be the size of a four-by-eight-foot sheet of plywood. Once I had the plans lofted, I'd need more space for the skiff's eight foot long mold. I'd also need plenty of room on both sides of the mold for bending on long planks and other space-hungry tasks. Finally, I'd need to squeeze in a work bench, tools, stacks of wood, various goops and fasteners and ropes. Not that I had any of these things, yet, but I was *anticipating*.

Unfortunately, the floor wasn't large enough to hold both a sheet of plywood and *Cabin Boy's* mold and a work bench. That was a problem.

Luckily, I'd just picked up an out-of-print book called *Building the Skiff "Cabin Boy": A Step-by-step Pictorial Guide* by Clem Kuhlig. Clem must have had the same space problem I did, because his book contained an intriguing idea: mounting the lofting board on the wall. That would save valuable floor space, and eliminate the need to crawl around on my knees while drawing the plans. As soon as I read this idea, I decided: 'Right, that's for me'.

I immediately drove down to our local Big Box hardware store and purchased the smoothest sheet of ¼ inch plywood I could find, along with a handful of concrete wall anchors. After raising a cloud of dust with an impact drill, my lofting board hung on the wall like a high school blackboard.

As I stood back to admire this sheet of plywood, mounted on the wall with twelve heavy-duty wall anchors, it occurred to me that I had just completed my second woodworking project, and it was pretty trivial.

So why did I feel so good?

Helena came up behind me, put her arm on my shoulder, and helped with the admiring process.

"You've started," she said.

She was right. That was it: I'd cast off the lines to the Pier of Procrastination, and was on my way.

* * *

Like supermodels, boats are mainly skin and bones. Big boats, like models and dinosaurs, carry their bones around inside them for strength and to help them keep their shape. Small boats shed most of their bones before birth to save weight.

In boatbuilding language, the bones are called molds. A mold is something like the rib of an Apatosaurus, only smaller. Like the Apatosaurus's ribs, each mold is a different size and shape. When you bend the boat's skin (planking) around the molds, the molds determine the boat's shape, in the same way that the dinosaur's

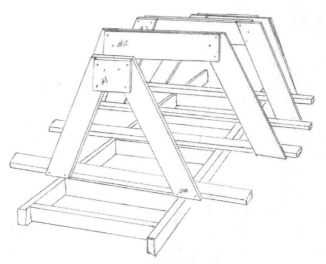

Cabin Boy's Molds
Mounted on Ladder-like Strongback

ribs determine its shape. When the planking is secured and rein-
forced, the molds are removed.

Once I'd lofted *Cabin Boy's* lines on my plywood lofting board—
a tortuous job that took weeks of trial-and-error drawing, erasing,
and redrawing—I was finally able to take measurements from the
full-sized plans, to use them to build the molds out of cheap pine,
and to mount the molds sturdily on a ladder-like structure called
a strongback.

When done, the finished mold assembly looked impressive to
my eyes, but it suddenly occurred to me that *none* of the wood that
I'd carefully selected, measured, cut, and fastened together would
actually end up in the finished boat. They were just *Cabin Boy's*
bones. Eventually, I'd have to pull them out of the hull and throw
them in my junk box.

In short, I hadn't even started building my boat. To do so, I
needed some real wood—not construction grade lumber, but the

half-inch of knot-free planking that would someday be the only thing between my feet and the bottom of the deep blue sea, or at least the bottom of Huntington Harbor.

When John Atkin drew *Cabin Boy*, he didn't bother to draw up a lumber list. I imagine his audience of hearty, do-it-yourselfers would have been insulted if he had. So it was up to me to study the five pages of plans, to visualize every plank and chine and seat riser, to imagine the length and shape of wood it would be cut from, and to add that piece to my wood list.

Cabin Boy, as conceived by John Atkin, was a creature of oak and cedar: oak for the bones, and cedar for the skin. Other woods were used by builders in other parts of the world, but for builders on the East coast of the US—particularly the New England boatbuilders who flourished during the heyday of the wooden boat age—air dried white oak and white cedar were the woods of choice.

White oak is heavy and rugged. It holds fasteners well. When green it can easily be steam-bent into ribs and other structural components. Its cell structure is closed, which stops water from getting inside of it, making it resistant to decay and rot. It's also beautiful when varnished. A better wood for frames and other structural members would be hard to imagine.

White cedar is light, rot resistant, bends well, and shrinks hardly at all. It's the perfect wood for planking.

One problem: where to buy them? If you amble down the aisles of your local BigBox lumber store, you will find kiln-dried red oak and red cedar, which are great for building shelves and decks, but useless for boatbuilding.

To get boat-quality white oak and white cedar, you have two choices. The first choice—if you're the kind of person that thinks ahead and lays down stores for the future—would be to buy your wood green from a small mill nestled deep in the New England forest. You'd take the wet planks right off the saw, truck them home, paint the ends to reduce checking, and stack them outside, inserting stickers between each board to allow air to circulate freely through the stack. In a year or two, you'd have prime boatbuilding wood, worth twice what you paid for it.

On the other hand, if you're like me, you probably don't have stacks of wood drying in your backyard, and don't want to wait a year or two to start building. You want your wood now! In that case, you'll need to start hunting for lumber that someone else had the foresight to cut and dry. I didn't need to fill my entire list—I wasn't that confident, yet. No, what I had in my sights were the two pieces of white oak for *Cabin Boy's* backbone—the stem and keelson—and a good-size piece of mahogany for the transom.

I hoped to find a local supplier. As romantic as it might sound to drive up to a small lumber yard in Maine, it wasn't practical to drive a thousand miles every time I needed another piece of wood. So I started the old fashioned way—with the phone book. There were two local yards that sounded promising. Both mentioned the word 'hardwoods' in their listings, which most didn't, and both were short drives away. Optimistically packing my lumber list and American Express card, I drove off through the suburban wilderness to bag my wood.

The first yard shattered my confidence almost immediately. It was nestled by the side of the railroad tracks in a space that seemed too small for a sawmill. It consisted of a main yard, surrounded by barn-like sheds on three sides. The office was in front, by the main gate, but the door was locked and no one answered the bell.

I left Helena's tiny Honda Fit out front and wandered, hesitantly, through the open gate, wondering where everyone was. The central yard was piled high with two-foot thick, uncut logs. A dusting of snow lay on the frozen ground and on the logs themselves. Somewhere, hidden in one of the barns, a saw screamed.

What to do? Follow the sound of the saw? Crack open the door and wave to a burly sawyer who was, no doubt, half-deafened by the work of slicing gigantic logs into massive planks? Get him to shut down the line so he could hear my pathetic request for a few toothpicks?

He'd either laugh me out of the shed, or strap me to a log to teach me a lesson. I started walking backwards. No... perhaps not... best not to bother him.

"Can I help you, sir?"

Rather than the tall, austere Yankee I'd expected to find, I found myself talking to a rather short, smiling Central American.

"I'm looking for a couple pieces of white oak," I said apologetically, as if white oak was some rare, exotic wood. "Got anything like that?"

"Sure, sure," he said, waving me in the direction of a door I hadn't seen, clearly marked 'Hardwoods'. "How much you looking for?"

Inside the shed were shelves containing random lengths of various woods. One shelf was labeled "White Oak".

"We don't have too much," he confessed, as we looked at his stock, which consisted of a few rather narrow boards.

He helped me pick through the stock, looking for a piece that was wide enough for my keelson, or thick enough for the stem, but it was clear that he didn't have either. Hopes dashed.

"Red oak no good?" he asked, pointing to the next rack which was stacked high with long, thick boards.

"No good," I said. "I'm building a boat."

"Ah," he said gravely, looking me up and down again, as if re-measuring me for something. "That is hard, building a boat."

"Yes," I said. "Yes it is."

* * *

The next place was situated in a modern industrial park, right off the highway. Its front office had the windows, high ceilings, and open space of an auto dealership. And the chief salesman had obviously spent some time selling used cars.

"White oak?" he said in a loud voice. "Definitely. Got a few beautiful slabs. Gorgeous stuff."

"Slabs?"

"Flitch sided, vertical grain. You said you're building a boat, right?"

"Yes," I said. I was about to tell him it was only a seven foot boat, but talking to him was like talking back to a firehose.

"Just the thing, then. Got them in from Pennsylvania last night.

Won't last long. Name's Josh, by the way," he said, sticking out his hand. "Come and take a look!"

He led me through a half-mile of warehouse stacked high with plywood and particle board and lumber. Enough to rebuild a whole village from scratch, it looked like. Forklifts zoomed up and down the aisles and Josh kept up such a steady stream of sales patter that I couldn't squeeze in a question.

Then he stopped, waved his hand, and said, "Here they are."

I looked where he was pointing, but didn't see any boards.

"What am I looking at?" I asked.

"These, right here." He smacked his hand against a monolith that towered over my head; a slab so monumental, it could have been a stunt-double in *2001—A Space Odyssey*.

"There are three of them, as you can see. Just let me know which one you want," he said. "Take your time. I'll be in the office."

With that, he pulled out one of those push-to-talk phones, and strode off into the labyrinth of aisles, beeping and barking.

I remained, gaping at the three slabs, as he called them. They were twelve feet tall and four feet wide, sawn right through the tree, about four inches thick, with bark on both edges.

They were massive, rough sawn, and beautiful.

I'd never seen such a thing. Never imagined you could buy a hunk of wood like that on Long Island. And yet, as Josh had said, here they were. I could have them forklifted onto the roof of my Fit, and drive away with enough white oak to last a life time. Assuming the little car wasn't squashed flat, of course. I wondered if they delivered.

Like an eighteen year old virgin, I lusted after these blond beauties for a while; then, like the mature, adult male that I was, I gradually came to my senses. Sure, *Cabin Boy's* stem and keelson were hidden in those slabs, somewhere, but how to get them out? Leaving aside the impracticality of buying a three thousand pound piece of wood, I had no idea how to turn one of these monsters into usable pieces of lumber.

I was shopping for a tasty bit of steak, neatly wrapped in plastic; these were enormous sides of beef. They were out of my league.

Regretfully, I slunk away, careful not to retreat through the front office.

* * *

This went on for a couple weeks. I asked every amateur boat-builder I could find for recommendations, and got several: a company in Brooklyn that reclaimed wood from 200 year old buildings; a yard in New Jersey that sawed planks from white cedars that fell into swamps during the Jurassic period; and any number of small mills hidden away in the dark hollows of New England.

One lumberyard appeared—with positive or negative comments attached—on nearly everyone's list. The positive comments tended towards the "they have everything" sort. The negatives focused on their outrageous prices and BMW-driving, Brie-eating, yuppie clientele.

Now, some of my best friends used to be yuppies, before the Great Recession. For that matter, I didn't mind a tasty bit of Brie, myself. But the rumors of high prices… now that was discouraging.

Even worse, the place sounded intimidating and I was already intimidated by the whole wood buying process. I'd learned just enough from my lumber yard visits to realize I had no idea what I was doing. Oh, I'd picked up a bit of the jargon from books—enough to fool Helena, anyway—but my confident façade crumbled under the fire of one or two questions from a real lumber guy. I was a fraud, and they could smell it.

So mad butterflies clawed at the pit of my stomach as I pulled up to the so-called lumber boutique. But I carried on. I persevered. I needed that wood.

I don't remember if bells jingled as I walked in through the front door. If they didn't, then they should have, because the main office had that sort of old-fashioned feel. There was a long main counter, and behind the counter, several rows of desks with four or five men and women working. By then, I was used to being ignored by such people—particularly the men—so it was a pleasant surprise when one of the more senior-looking guys looked up, smiled, and asked, "Can I help you?"

"Yes…" I said, a bit flummoxed. I really thought I'd have a few more minutes to gather my thoughts. "I'm looking for some wood."

Well, duh, I thought, and waited for the usual wisecrack, but the man just got up and came to the desk, with a look of sincere interest on his face. I wasn't sure what to make of it.

"Do you have a list?" he asked.

"I do, actually…"

I pulled my much creased, much marked-up list out of my pocket, and unfolded it on the counter top. He studied it with furrowed brow.

"I just need the first two pieces of white oak for now," I said, apologetically. "Plus the mahogany for the transom."

"Building a boat, I see," he said.

"Yes," I said.

"What are you building?"

"John Atkin's *Cabin Boy*."

"Ah," he said, knowingly. "The little skiff. Good first boat."

"Yes, I thought so!" I said, warming to him.

"I remember building my first boat…" He shook his head, fondly recalling those distant days. Then he studied the first three items on my list as if they were the first of ten articles etched into stone tablets. "I'm sure we can help you with these. Let me call Matt to help you."

He picked up a phone, pressed a few buttons, spoke a few words, and put the phone back down.

"He'll be right up."

Right, I thought. In a half-hour or so. I sighed, prepared, stoically, to wait.

"Ah, here he is," he said, indicating a young man who'd magically appeared at my elbow. "Matt, this gentleman is looking for some white oak and mahogany for a boat he's building."

He handed Matt my list. "Just the first three items, for now."

Matt studied the list as intently as his boss had.

"No problem," he said. "Right this way."

Feeling as though I'd fallen into an alternate universe, I followed Matt down some steps and into the lumber yard. The yard was small, but neatly arranged, with a number of buildings around an open courtyard. He led me into a shed in which tiers of racks held neatly stacked lumber.

Not only was the lumber neatly stacked, it was neatly labeled. Each shelf had a name written on a white sticker, so even a newbie could see that here was the Sitka Spruce, here the Ash, and there the Cherry and Walnut. The end of every piece was marked with its length, so you could tell a board was twelve feet long without pulling it out.

As I surveyed the two long tiers of shelves, packed to the rim with wood, I thought, they do have everything! At least, everything I could imagine at the moment.

"This place is amazing," I said, sounding slightly more gushy than is strictly allowed in a lumber yard.

Matt didn't seem to notice. Probably happened all the time.

"Here's the white oak," he said, stopping in front of a large shelf.

For the next ten or fifteen minutes, Matt pulled out planks for my inspection, patiently helping me find the two pieces that 'spoke' to me. As he patiently pulled out plank after plank, I became acutely aware that I was a very small fry. I only wanted two tiny pieces of white oak. I felt guilty for wasting Matt's time. But he didn't seem to mind, so…

I finally settled on two pieces that looked about right. Then it was over to the mahogany section. The choice there was simpler, because the boards were more uniform. I picked out one that had nice grain. It was just a bit thicker than I needed, but I could plane it down to the right thickness in an hour or two, probably. If I could figure out how to sharpen my new plane.

"Want me to mill that down to the right size for you?" Matt asked. "It's just a few bucks more."

"Sure!" I said. "Can you do that?"

He carried the board across the courtyard to another building filled with big iron—heavy duty tools that could mill lumber as fast as you could feed it through. He made some adjustments to something called a thickness planer, ran my board through it a couple of times, and then handed it to me, exactly the size I needed.

"That will save you some work," he said.

Just a little.

In the end, the prices were about the same as those I'd seen in other places. More importantly, Matt and his boss had gotten me over a difficult hump. Not only did they have what I needed, they'd made it accessible to a newbie like me, without a single snide remark.

My first Quest for Wood had ended successfully. I had real boat-quality lumber strapped to the roof of my car. I could start my build. I was on my way.

Maybe next time they'd serve me the Brie.

* * *

That night, I just happened to be cruising around eBay. For some reason, I searched for 'wooden boats', just to see what would come up.

I blinked at the first item on the list.

"Can't be…" I muttered.

I clicked on the listing, studied the photos, read the description.

It was true. The *Blue Moon Yawl* I'd seen listed a few weeks ago on a brokerage website for $20,000 was now listed on eBay, with no reserve, and no bids.

"Helena?" I called. "Can you come here for a minute?"

Tom Gilmer's Blue Moon Yawl

CHAPTER 4

PLAN B

It's a dangerous business… going out of your door. You step into the Road, and if you don't keep your feet, there is no knowing where you might be swept off to. — *Bilbo Baggins*

I write software for a living. To write software, you think about the problem, invent a solution, and make a plan to implement that solution. This plan—call it Plan A—almost never works. Unexpected hitches develop, the problem changes, new opportunities emerge. These events, and many more, conspire to make Plan A obsolete or unattainable.

For many years, I found this frustrating. I went to the Rensselaer Polytechnic Institute to study *engineering*. I graduated out of the State University of New York at Albany's *math* department. What project managers like me searched for was a better Plan A. One that you could follow like a road map: start at the beginning, keep going, and when you're done, you've got a useful new program.

This, as the software world discovered many years later, was the wrong approach. Building software is not like building a bridge. It is not an engineering process that can be managed with Gantt diagrams or PERT charts. Writing software is more like a voyage of discovery. It requires energy, resourcefulness, creativity, and a large dollop of positive thinking. In other words, for better or for worse, writing software is like life—a messy, unpredictable, and often surprising process.

You still need a plan, of course. People are hardwired to need

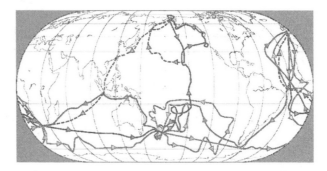

What a real plan looks like—Captain Cook's Voyages

a plan. It's difficult to cook dinner without one. So, whether you keep your plans in your head, or turn your computer screen into a sticky-note fringed checklist, you need a Plan A for whatever you're doing. But, life being the unpredictable mess it is, you'll also need a Plan B. Probably.

* * *

"I'm definitely going to need a Plan B," I thought a week later, as I rowed a dinghy slowly around a scruffy, bedraggled, down-at-the-heels *Blue Moon*.

She was moored in a mud-brown lagoon, on the slow-moving Steinhatchee River, in the part of Florida affectionately known as the Redneck Riviera. Her rigging drooped in a dispirited way. Her white topsides were scuffed and bruised, her peeling deck was painted acid green, and her jaunty sheer line was an inexplicable black. The effect would have been garish, if the colors hadn't faded under the harsh Florida sun.

"Isn't she beautiful?" asked Bob, the *Blue Moon's* octogenarian owner. Bob's eyes couldn't get enough of the boat as I rowed slow circles around her. He could barely keep his seat. "Look at those lines… classic. If I were twenty years younger, I'd sail her down to the islands myself. Gorgeous!"

He was right. Limp rigging and faded paint couldn't hide her beautiful lines. Her sheer swooped up like the crest of a wave. Her long bowsprit jutted out at a jaunty angle. It was easy to imagine her with her five sails flying, heeled down to a trade wind breeze, skimming across a turquoise sea.

"Damn," I thought. "What have I got myself into?"

* * *

A week earlier, back in New York, the eBay auction had looked like a long shot.

"She'll never sell for a price we can afford," I'd told Helena as we studied the *Blue Moon's* eBay listing on my computer. "She's still listed on that brokerage website for $20,000. There are two other *Blue Moon's* listed for twice that. She's a classic. Everyone's talking about her on the forums. The bidding's going to be fierce. We don't stand a chance."

"She's so beautiful," said Helena. "So different. What would you pay for her?"

I considered our meager bank balance. The Great Recession had taken a toll on my computer business. Fully a third of my clients had gone belly up. The rest were hunkered down and spending as little as possible. It was insane to buy a boat in a recession. Maybe that was why the *Blue Moon* had ended up on eBay.

"The listing says she has a brand-new set of sails from Gambell and Hunter: hand-sewn, leathered grommets, all the rest. That kind of workmanship doesn't come cheap. The sails, alone, are worth $5,000. If we could get her for that…"

"Give it a try, then."

"I'd have to sail her home. That could take months."

"You've been talking about going on a big sailing adventure since the day we met."

"Yes, but…"

"Business is slow. You always say you can work from anywhere. It's the perfect time."

She was right. It was a once in a lifetime opportunity. And if we could steal her for a crazy low price…

I shook my head. "We won't get her, anyway. She'll go for $10,000, at least."

"Give it a try," said Helena. "What's the worst that could happen?"

"Maybe," I said, doubtfully.

Three days later, I again sat at my computer. Helena was cleaning up in the kitchen. The *Blue Moon's* auction was due to end in a few minutes. For some reason, she had only attracted a few bids. The high bid was just $2,300.

Helena came in to check on the action.

"It's crazy," I said. "The lead in her keel is worth more than $2,300."

"Still no new bids?"

"No, but that doesn't mean anything. The smart bidders are doing the same as I am, lying low. They'll flood in at the last minute."

There is only one sensible way to buy something on eBay: decide in advance how much you want to pay, and then make one bid at the end of the auction, at the last possible moment. By lying low, you don't show your interest to the other bidders, don't bid up the item prematurely, and don't get caught up in the emotions of bidding. If you win, you get a bargain; if you lose, you probably saved yourself a lot of money. I had decided that the *Blue Moon* would be a steal at $5,000. But I probably wasn't the only one.

"Someone else wants this boat," I said. "He's thinking there's someone like me, who's going to bid $5,000, so he's going to be smart and bid $5,100."

I typed my bid into the box on the screen: $5,300.

"Why $5,300?" asked Helena.

"Just in case he's *extra* smart and bids $5,200. I'd kick myself if we lost by $100," I said. "Not that it's going to matter. Someone will bid $10,000, I'm sure."

As 10 pm approached, an onscreen timer ticked down. 50 seconds... 40 seconds...

"Don't wait too long," Helena said, nervously.

30 seconds... 20... 15... I clicked the 'Confirm Bid' button. The mouse ball twirled...

"Come on!" I said. The mouse ball just hung there, spinning. Had I waited too long?

No. The page refreshed with just seconds to spare. The new

page said, "You are the high bidder."

"Wow!" I said. "So far, so good. But now you'll see the bids flood in."

Three seconds later, the page again refreshed and flashed the words "Congratulations! You have won!"

I looked up at Helena, my eyes and mouth wide open. She looked down at me with exactly the same expression.

"We won?" she asked.

"We won," I said. But I was thinking, "Oh, my God. Now what?"

* * *

Back in the dinghy, Bob said: "You were pretty clever with your bidding."

Bob held the oars as I inspected a particularly rough scuff on the *Blue Moon's* port side. He nodded at the long, black abrasion. "That's no big deal. She dragged her anchor and went aground last summer. Laid on her side for a tide. It happens."

I grunted at that.

"I never saw your bid coming," he said. "Neither did the guy who bid $5,100. I bet he's still kicking himself. You stole it from him, bidding like that at the last second. Didn't give him a chance to up his bid."

I fingered the scuff. Bob was right. It was no big deal. The whole boat needed painting, anyway.

"All right," I said. "Let's haul her out and see what the bottom looks like."

The *Blue Moon's* bottom was my biggest worry. She had been moored in this brackish lagoon for a couple years, neglected and unsailed. Bob and his wife Susan were experienced blue water cruisers and lovers of wooden boats. They had roamed all over the Caribbean in their younger days, but now Bob's hip needed replacing and the little yawl was too much for him to take care of.

Sailed boats are happy boats, and the *Blue Moon* looked exceedingly unhappy. I worried that her bottom was rotten or full of shipworms—the termites of the sea, notorious for boring into and eventually destroying wooden ships. As Henry David Thoreau, philosopher and boatbuilder, once wrote:

The vessel, though her masts be firm,
Beneath her copper bears a worm;
Around the cape, across the line,
Till fields of ice her course confine;
It matters not how smooth the breeze,
How shallow or how deep the seas,
Whether she bears Manilla twine,
Or in her hold Madeira wine,
Or China teas, or Spanish hides,
In port or quarantine she rides;
Far from New England's blustering shore,
New England's worm her hulk shall bore,
And sink her in the Indian seas,
Twine, wine, and hides, and China teas.

I hoped the *Blue Moon* wasn't bored through with worms, but the sale was contingent on inspection. If her hull was rotten, the sale was off. I wasn't experienced enough to deal with serious problems like that. I just hoped I was smart enough to find any fatal flaws. There were no wooden boat surveyors left in Florida to lean on. I had to survey her myself.

Boarding the *Blue Moon*, we started the engine and threw off her mooring lines. She responded sluggishly to the throttle, as if her keel was dragging through thick mud. We didn't go far, just up the river to a small marina, with an even smaller travel lift. A travel lift is machine shaped like an inverted 'U', designed to lift boats out of the water. This was a particularly small, old, and rusty one. After we jockeyed into the lift's slings, I wondered if it was *too* small and old.

"I can't lift her all the way out," said the operator nervously, as the crane-like machine groaned under the *Blue Moon's* 8,000 pounds.

"Just lift her as high as you can," said Bob, waving his hand up.

We stood on the dock, watching, as the machine lifted the *Blue*

Moon out of the water, slowly revealing a bottom covered with a thick crust of snails, mussels, and black gunk.

"That does not look good," I said.

"A power washer will take that all off," said Bob. The marina operator—probably a good friend—nodded in agreement.

As the lift ground away, the *Blue Moon's* long, full keel slowly emerged. Despite my horror at the creeping, crawling infestation, I could not help admiring her shape. That long keel would help keep her on course. I imagined skimming over Sarasota Bay, on our way home, a glass of cold beer in my hands, a clear blue sky overhead. Adventure, with a twist of lime. Ah!

The keel just lifted out of the water, and the travel lift clattered to a stop.

"That's it," said the operator. "I don't dare go any higher."

"But how can I inspect her?" I asked. She was still hanging over the mud-brown water.

"You'll have to do it from the dinghy," said Bob.

"Under there?" I asked. "You don't dare lift her any higher, but you want me to go under her in a dinghy?"

"Sure, the lift will hold," said Bob. "Probably."

The operator nodded. "Probably."

"Great," I said, but there was no other way to do it.

A few minutes later, I crept under the boat's looming, dripping hull in the dinghy. I had an awl to poke with, a putty knife to scrape with, and a hammer. I wasn't sure what the hammer was for.

For the next hour, I scraped and poked and tapped, looking or feeling or listening for signs of rot or worm or damage. Port and starboard I searched, but surprisingly, all seemed well. The *Blue Moon* was encrusted with sea life, but under the gunk, a thin layer of bottom paint still clung to her hull. That, and perhaps her brackish berth, had protected her. In another year, she might have succumbed, but Fate had brought me to her side in time. She was still sound, and I was her new protector. I'd do right by her.

"I think she's okay," I said, finally. I'd already checked her insides, poking every plank and rib with my awl. "Sound as a drum."

"I told you," said Bob, though he clearly looked relieved. "She's a good little boat."

We motored the *Blue Moon* back to the mooring, tidied her up a bit, and rowed away. My brain was already thinking about scraping and painting. It was going to be a big job.

"You going to truck her back to New York?" asked Bob.

"No, I mean to sail her home," I said, handing Bob a large check.

"It's a hell of a long way to New York," he said, looking surprised.

And he was right about that.

* * *

After a busy month home, I drove back down to Florida in my old Jeep, its cargo area filled with scrapers, sanders, paint brushes, rollers, epoxy paste, bottom paint, two colors of topside paint, several suits of old clothes, dust respirator, safety goggles, 147 things I've forgotten, my favorite painting cap, and camping gear. At the end of the long drive, I pulled into a campground, about a mile outside of Steinhatchee.

"We don't get many tenters down here," said the manager as we walked through the nearly deserted RV park.

"I'm old-school, I guess. My grand parents spent every summer in a big green army tent, out at Wildwood State Park, and so did my parents. I still like it."

"Mostly get snowbirds down here, in big RVs."

"I've got a boat. Down here to fix her up."

"Too early for the snowbirds, though." He waved his hand at the mostly empty sites. "Too cold. You gonna be warm enough in a tent?"

"I'll be fine," I said, remembering some stone cold nights in the mountains of Massachusetts. This was Florida. Sure it was winter, and we were in northern Florida, but how cold could it get? "I've got a good sleeping bag."

He showed me the small grassy area set aside for picnicking and the occasional tenter. There were some tables and a big fire pit surrounded by short stools. Just on the other side of the fire pit was the edge of a swamp. I was glad it was too cold for mosquitoes.

"One good thing, anyway," the manager said, eyeing the swamp. "Too cold for 'gators. Probably."

The next morning, fog lay heavily on the river as Bob and I rowed out to the *Blue Moon*. We hoped to get her anchors up quickly and make an early start, but in this we were thwarted. One of the anchors had made a close acquaintance with what Bob called a redneck mooring. If you'd like to build one, here's the recipe:

First, steal a plastic milk crate from the back of your local supermarket. One bought legitimately from Walmart will not work—it must be stolen.

Jam into this box an oversized grapnel: one of those vicious, three-pronged hooks typically thrown over walls by commandos. The prongs must be sharp and rusty, and at least two of the prongs must stick through the openings in the box, so they can grab other boats' anchor lines.

Next, loosely fill the rest of the box with scrap metal—the type doesn't matter, so long as it is sharp-edged and rusty.

Mix up a batch of cement and fill the plastic box to its rim. Yes, a certain amount will ooze through the large holes in the plastic box. This is not a flaw but a feature—it gives the mooring its essential character.

When the cement has set, attach a mooring line to the grapnel's eye with a granny knot. At the other end of the mooring line, tie on several plastic bleach bottles. These make an ideal mooring ball. When ready, motor out to your favorite spot on the river, and tip the whole mess over the side. It will drag a bit at first, but as soon as the grapnel hooks onto several other people's mooring lines, it will hold just fine.

Bob had moored the *Blue Moon* properly with two 50 lb. anchors. One of them, a plough, had become entangled with one of these redneck moorings.

Now, lifting a 50 lb. anchor by hand is no fun in the best of circumstances; lifting an anchor and a block of concrete, wrapped round and around by snagged anchor lines, bristling with twenty or thirty fish hooks, and liberally coated with foul-smelling river mud, was a nightmare.

But somehow, after much exertion and many curses, we managed to get the anchor and mooring into the dinghy. I took great pleasure in cutting the anchor free with a sharp knife. I wanted to drop the blasted mooring back in the water, but Bob said that was bad manners, so we left it in the dinghy to dump ashore. It was nearly noon by the time we motored to the marina—not the marina with the undersized lift, but a larger one downstream with a travel lift powerful enough to haul a fifty foot schooner. The efficient marina crew made short work of pulling the *Blue Moon* out of the water. Before I could even start to fret, she was on 'the hard' (what sailors call dry land) and blocked up on jack stands.

After using a power washer to remove the inch-thick layer of oysters, barnacles, and thick black ooze, I slowly walked around the *Blue Moon*, finally able to give her bottom the complete inspection that had been impossible before.

"Not bad," I said. Unlike many old fiberglass boats I'd seen, her bottom was pretty smooth.

"She should sand up nicely," Bob agreed.

"Only thing I'm worried about are these holes."

Bob studied the line of narrow-bore holes closely, before uttering a grave, "H'mmm. Might be worms in there. Gotta get them out, somehow."

H'mmm, indeed. Of all the monsters in the mythology of the sea, from Jonah's Whale, to Moby Dick, to Jules Verne's giant squid, none are as feared by sailors as much as the lowly marine boring worm, and for good reason. It wasn't a giant squid that sank Christopher Columbus's fleet on his 4th voyage to the New World. It was the worm. In fact, worms plagued all the great wooden ships during the Age of Exploration, until someone discovered that covering their bottoms with sheets of copper—using the same techniques then used to make copper-sheathed roofs—would protect ships from the voracious worm.

So as we scraped and sanded our way through that long hot day, I worried about those worm holes. Were they empty? Or did foot-long worms still hide in my hull?

That night, back in my tent, I opened my laptop to do some research. The Internet teemed with shipworm horror stories and equally horrifying remedies. Some of the best cures included:

• Drilling small holes into the hull and injecting noxious mixtures guaranteed to kill shipworms. The best traditional mixtures tended to include chemicals now banned by the Geneva Conventions.

• Traveling up a fresh water river. Shipworms hate fresh water, and will abandon ship at the first taste of the stuff. Unfortunately, the fresh water reaches of the Steinhatchee weren't navigable by sailboat.

• Flushing the worms out with fire. Traditional methods of burning them out have given way to the modern propane torch. Optional equipment included welding gloves and a fire extinguisher.

The legends described holes extending as far as six feet into the planking.

"Six feet?!" I said, my stomach suddenly churning with anxiety. Perhaps the *Blue Moon's* shapely hull was riddled with worm holes, her planking more like bundles of hollow straw than solid wood. There were pictures of such things. *On the Internet!*

After the panic induced by this research subsided, I decided I didn't need to theorize about the damage. I could look at the boat tomorrow morning with my own two eyes, and see for myself how bad the damage was. There was no point fretting about it now.

With that somewhat comforting thought, I turned off my computer, and zipped myself into my sleeping bag. Tomorrow was another day.

The next morning, I found a stiff wire in my toolbox. Holding my breath, I plunged it into one of the worm holes.

The wire went in a quarter inch. I removed the wire and looked into the hole, half expecting to see two eyes (or however many eyes shipworms have) staring back at me. But no, all I saw was the back of the hole.

I poked into the other holes. All were about the same depth. All were vacant. The worms hadn't liked the taste of the *Blue Moon*, apparently. Since they were southern worms, maybe they preferred their planking deep fried.

After all my fretting, it was a bit of a let down. I blew out my propane torch with a sigh. Other sailors have all the fun. I mixed up some epoxy paste and filled the holes.

For the next two weeks, Bob and I scraped and sanded and painted the *Blue Moon's* bottom and topsides. As we progressed, word got around. People started coming out to the marina to watch us. Some brought their lunch and sat on makeshift stools in the shade of a big power cruiser, watching, commenting, and offering advice. The funny little boat that looked like it might meet its end in this southern backwater had been given a reprieve. She was coming back to life—to youth, even—and these old people were rooting for her. The day we finished, they took pictures. We even had a little party to celebrate.

"Now that's a good looking boat," said one old timer. "Used to have a boat like that, back in the fifties, in Connecticut. A good New England boat. She don't belong down here."

"That's why I'm sailing her home, to Long Island Sound."

The others—all old timers, all Northerners who had somehow washed up in this backwater bayou—nodded. That was fitting. That was where she belonged.

"It's a long way, though," one white-haired old lady said. "I sailed down with my Harry, a long time ago. It's a long way."

After all the work we'd done on the *Blue Moon*, I didn't dare leave her on a mooring for the rest of the winter. Despite Florida's sunny reputation, winter in the state's northwest corner was no day at the beach. Storms blew in from the Gulf of Mexico and I didn't want her dragging across the lagoon when I wasn't around to save her. So I arranged to leave the *Blue Moon* at a marina a few hundred yards down the river.

After the big travel lift hoisted her up and put her back in the water, Bob and I motored the *Blue Moon* down to the new berth, and tied her to the dock with a spiderweb of dock lines and fenders. I was a bit nervous about leaving my little ship on her own, but Bob waved my misgivings aside.

"She'll keep," he said.

* * *

Back home in New York again, the weeks sailed by. There were decisions to be made and supplies to be ordered from far-flung mail order houses that catered to the wooden boat cult.

The most urgent task was finishing *Cabin Boy*. Plan A called for building *Cabin Boy* at a leisurely pace. Now that I was preparing for a 2000 mile voyage, I needed a dinghy, and I needed one fast.

Everyone said to forget *Cabin Boy*, to just buy a cheap plastic dinghy for the trip and be done with it. But that wasn't the plan. It wasn't just my big adventure, it was *Cabin Boy's*, and I wasn't going to leave him behind.

So I worked feverishly on my little boat. Progress was slow— agonizingly slow. Mistakes were made, lessons were learned, but I would not leave until *Cabin Boy* was done.

* * *

Two months later, Helena and I drove back into Steinhatchee with the newly painted *Cabin Boy* strapped to the roof of my old Jeep. We set up headquarters in the best motel in town (which wasn't saying much), and unloaded 1500 lb. of supplies. Just before the sun set, we ran down to the dock to check on the *Blue Moon*.

"Wow," said Helena. "She looks great. But look at that deck!"

The *Blue Moon* floated merrily alongside the dock, her blue topsides smooth and gleaming, but her peeling deck was a reminder of how much work there was before I could set sail. I hoped the ugly green deck paint didn't hide a bunch of problems.

"Yup. A lot to do."

"Can we finish in time?" Helena only had a week before she had to rush back to her piano students.

"Probably," I said.

First thing next morning, we were down at the dock with tools, old clothes, lots of sunblock, and hats.

"How much of this paint do you want to scrape off?" Helena

asked, picking at the pea-green deck paint.

"As little as possible," I said, "But as much as we need to."

"Gosh, what an ugly color!"

She got the scraper under the paint and peeled off a patch as large as my hand.

"It's in really bad shape," she said.

I finished the last gulp of coffee, crumpled the cup, and threw it in the trash.

"Right," I said. "Let's get to it."

A few hours later, we had most of the deck paint off. At least the green layer. Under the green paint was white paint, and under that was Bristol Beige—the same paint we'd picked out for her 'new' color scheme.

"Looks like we're restoring her to her original glory," I said, after Helena showed me this archeological discovery. It was hot, dirty work, but it went fast with both of us working.

As usual, the *Blue Moon* attracted lots of dock-side interest. A

Cabin Boy under construction

steady trickle of watchers drifted down the dock and—this being the south—conversation was not only inevitable, but required for etiquette's sake.

The conversations tended to repeat themselves. They went along these lines:

"Where you from?"

"New York."

For some reason, this always provoked a look of stunned disbelief, though practically everyone in Florida is from New York: "Really? How you going to get her back?"

"Sail her."

"No! That's a long way!"

I got tired of responding to that one.

"How long is it gonna take you to finish painting? A month or so?"

"No, just a few days, I hope."

"Ha-ha. You almost had me fooled there, boy. A few days, ha-ha, that's a good one!" The watcher would walk off, laughing, telling the next one coming down the dock, "Hey, you should talk to those guys down there, painting! They're a riot!"

But in fact, it took exactly three days. One day to scrape, sand, and prime; and two days to give the deck two coats of paint.

When we finished, Bob—who's bum hip was the only thing that had kept him from getting down on his hands and knees next to us—was impressed.

"She looks good," he said, looking her up and down with a critical eye. "Real good." He pointed up to the top of the mast. "But what are you going to do about those missing halyards?"

The next day, we rigged the bosun's chair. That's a broad term for a range of devices, all having the same purpose: to lift a sailor to the top of the mast and return him safely to the deck, hopefully by the end of the decade.

I'd chosen the simplest system: a bosun's chair made from a thick plank of wood, and a block and tackle with a six-to-one mechanical advantage. People said that with a tackle like that, you could pull yourself up the mast. That seemed to break the laws of

Helena painting

physics, but I was willing to give it a try.

After reeving 200 feet of rope through two triple-blocks, I hoisted the fixed block to the masthead with the main halyard, attached my homemade bosun's chair to the moving block, clipped a safety harness around the mast, and prepared to ascend, hopefully not all the way to heaven.

"Are you sure this is safe?" Helena asked.

"Absolutely. The tackle is strong enough to hoist a small car up the mast. My weight won't even take the stretch out of the rope."

I sounded confident, but would I really be able to pull myself up the mast? That sounded unlikely. I handed the end of the rope to the person I trusted most in the world.

"You tail me," I said to Helena. "Just keep a little tension on the end of the rope. If I have to let go of it at the top of the mast, you should be able to hold me up there."

I took a deep breath, looked up the mast, and prepared to put theory to the test.

I pulled down on the tail end of the rope. My seat rose by a couple inches. Effortlessly. Almost by magic.

"This might actually work," I said.

I pulled some more, and away I went. Because of the six-to-one ratio, to lift myself twenty-five feet, I had to pull down 150 feet of rope. That wasn't a problem. I wasn't in a hurry. I'm not generally afraid of heights, but I must admit twenty-five feet seemed like a lot when swinging from the end of a rope. I kept my eyes glued to the mast in front of me.

"How's it going?" Helena asked.

"Fine. Almost there."

Once at the top, it was easy to thread the new halyard (the end of which I'd remembered to tie to the bosun's chair) through the sheave at the top of the mast. First halyard done. A few minutes later, my feet touched the deck.

"Easy-peasy," I said, hoping I didn't sound too relieved, since I needed to go back for the second halyard.

"That looked like fun," Helena said. "Mind if I try?"

Sweeter words of love have never been spoken.

* * *

The week sailed by and pretty soon, we were done. The *Blue Moon* was as ready as Helena and I could make her. Even *Cabin Boy* was now in the water, tied up to the dock by his big sister's side, looking ready and eager for the adventure to come.

Helena was scrubbed free of paint, packed, and ready to drive back to New York. We stood, one last time, on the dock, admiring our work.

"Good luck, my darling," Helena said.

"Thank you for helping. I couldn't have done it without you."

"Be safe. Take as long as you need, but try to be home in time for Thanksgiving, if possible."

Thanksgiving? It was April 7th. I said, laughing, "I'll be home *long* before that."

"I hope so, but don't rush; enjoy the trip."

One last kiss, and she was gone.

I stood on the dock, alone. The world seemed quiet. The air

was still. The river flowed under the *Blue Moon's* keel, and down towards the sea. The same sea that flowed down the west coast of Florida, through the emerald blue Keys, and up the east coast of the United States, all the way to New York.

"Only one way home, now," I said.

Cabin Boy tugged on his painter. "Let's go!" he seemed to say.

"Tomorrow morning," I said.

It was indeed a long way home.

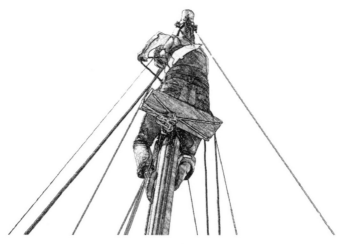

Helena at top of mast

CHAPTER 5

TAMING THE LIZARD

The obstacle is the path — Zen proverb

The next morning, I woke to the tinny ring of my old fashioned, mechanical, windup alarm clock. I groped in the dark to shut it off, surprised to find it not on my bedside table, but perched on the *Blue Moon's* companionway ladder.

"Oh," I thought. "I'm here."

It was my first night aboard. The six glass portholes in the cabin top were still black with night. I lay back down. It was cold outside the sleeping bag. Really cold. My muscles ached from a week of scraping and painting, stooping and carrying.

"Just another hour, maybe," I thought. I deserved a rest, didn't I? Why not sleep in a bit, even linger at the dock for another day? What was the rush? Who would know, or care? I could sleep late, fix a few more things, stroll down to the hardware store to buy a few more batteries...

Groaning, I swung my bare feet out of the bunk and planted them firmly on the cold cabin floor.

"I'm not that easily fooled," I said.

I lit the kerosene lamp. The *Blue Moon's* cabin looked like the cramped hold of a freighter. In the six feet between companionway ladder and mast was a small living space, with a bunk to starboard and a simple galley to port. The galley was no more than a small, cedar locker holding a ready supply of food, a few small pots and pans, two plastic plates, two coffee cups, two glasses, and two sets of cutlery. A one-burner, gimbaled stove swung on the locker's side. The locker and bunk were the only furniture in the boat. The rest was empty.

Forward of the mast and aft of the boarding ladder, the *Blue Moon's* hold was crammed with boxes of equipment, books, food, spare parts, and sundry supplies. On both sides of the cabin swung Brazilian hammocks filled with onions and cabbages, shorts and sweaters, bedding and spare lines, binoculars, flashlights, safety harness, watch cap—things I wanted to be able to get at quickly if I needed them.

Groggily, I wondered if I'd forgotten anything. I filled the kettle and put it on the stove to boil.

I'd spent the night on board to get an early start. My first stop, Cedar Key, was over fifty nautical miles away. If I wanted to arrive before dark—which I most assuredly did—I'd have to leave soon. Malingering was not acceptable.

The water boiled and I began a new routine: I used half the water to make tea in a ceramic Brown Betty teapot I'd bought long ago in England, and the other half to make oatmeal studded with dried cranberries. While they brewed, I stowed sleeping bag and pillow in the port-side hammock, put the book I'd fallen asleep with on the small shelf next to my bunk, and pulled on some clothes, including an Irish wool sweater.

"It's Florida," I complained. "It's supposed to be warm." But it was only the 9th of April—early spring—and it was going to be chilly on deck until the sun came up.

Housekeeping complete, I opened the hatch and ate my breakfast sitting on the companionway steps. It was still dark; stars still winked over the Steinhatchee; but in the east, the rose fingers of dawn rimmed the horizon. Across the river, I could just make out the buoy that marked the channel. That meant it would soon be light enough to head down river. Time to get a move on.

A quick rinse of mug and bowl, a hurried wash-up, and I was ready to face the day. Just the thought made mad butterflies churn in my stomach. I ignored them.

I glanced over the stern at *Cabin Boy*, who had pestered me through the night, thudding his oaken stem against the *Blue Moon's* transom, waking me repeatedly.

"We'll have none of that tonight," I said. "Bad *Cabin Boy*!"

He looked unrepentant. Shaking my head, I started the engine—an old two-stroke outboard of indeterminate make. The fierce Florida sun had bleached the name right off the cowling. I didn't entirely trust it. The engine smoked a bit, but maybe all two-strokes did that. I'd never actually owned an outboard, so I didn't know.

"It'll be okay," I told *Cabin Boy*. "Probably."

Leaving the engine to warm up, I stepped off the *Blue Moon* onto the dock. I untied the web of dock lines and threw them aboard, leaving only a doubled stern line. That left the cockpit a tangle of ropes, so I spent some time rearranging the lines on the cleats, removing the dock lines which I didn't expect to need for a few days.

"That's good enough for now," I thought, tossing the coiled dock lines down below. I'd clean up a bit more when we were sailing south. It was time to get going.

I stood in the cockpit and took one last look around. I felt a bit nervous about handling the *Blue Moon* around docks. For a small boat, she was awfully big. It would take awhile to learn how she moved in the water.

"Right," I said, taking a deep breath, feeling the adrenaline flowing in my veins. "Let's see how we do."

I untied the doubled stern line, pulled it free of the dock cleat, and brought the line aboard. I put the outboard in gear and the *Blue Moon* moved forward slowly, with *Cabin Boy* tagging behind at the end of a short tether. We motored out of the slip without a touch and—just like that—we were on our way.

I pointed the *Blue Moon's* nose towards the channel buoy which, by now, had changed from dark grey to bright green in the clear, just-dawn light. We were the only ones on the water. Small cottages lined the bank, with just a few lights showing in their windows: a quiet and peaceful scene.

"Neatly done, eh?" I asked *Cabin Boy*, when we were nearly across the river and my heart had stopped pounding so hard.

"A hundred feet down; just two thousand miles to go."

Maybe this wouldn't be so hard, after all, I thought. The *Blue Moon* moved well with her smooth, newly painted bottom. The morning felt a bit warmer, now the sun was up. I glanced over my shoulder to admire my smart little skiff, again. It was worth all the work, I thought, just to see that amber varnish gleaming in the morning light. He looked great. Much better looking than the usual white plastic dinghy.

But as I watched, *Cabin Boy's* tether quickly untangled itself from the mass of other lines, wriggled up and over the transom, and dropped with a small splash into the water behind us. I never had a chance to grab it.

"Blast!"

Untied from his big sister, *Cabin Boy* quickly fell behind, turned aside, and drifted—no, sped!—towards the shallows.

"Double blast!" The ingrate was making a break for it!

Uttering a few more salty phrases, I put the tiller over and raced back up river. I grabbed my long boathook off the cabin top. If I could grab him before he escaped into the shallows...

I eased the *Blue Moon* towards the edge of the channel, reached out with the boathook, stretched a bit further while still holding the tiller...

No! He was just out of reach.

"Come back here!" I shouted, shaking my fist futilely as we swept past.

I turned the *Blue Moon* around again, then throttled down. *Cabin Boy*—apparently riding a branch of the flood tide—headed up a small creek. A quick glance at the chart showed the creek was only two or three feet deep. I could not follow in the deep-keeled *Blue Moon*.

There was only one thing to do. As we approached the creek entrance again, I put the engine in neutral, went forward, and dropped the anchor for the first time, not a hundred yards from the dock we'd just left. Suppressing a small howl of frustration, I went down below and returned with oars and a life jacket.

I looked over the side at the mud-brown water. It looked cold.

Too cold for 'gators, I hoped. I peeled off my cozy sweater, stripped down to t-shirt and swimsuit, buckled myself into the life jacket, and tossed the oars into the water.

"This is a damn silly way to start a 2,000 mile voyage."

I jumped in and began swimming, laboriously, in pursuit. Wearing a bulky life jacket and pushing the oars in front of me, I couldn't keep up with *Cabin Boy* who sped up the creek. Where did the creek go? How long was it? And were there any waterfalls in Florida?

I didn't think so.

The creek was twenty or thirty feet wide, lined with houses, docks and small fishing boats. I rapidly fell behind, but hoped the dinghy would get hung up on something before my puff ran out. I just hoped there were no witnesses to this fiasco.

For awhile, it was a race to see if I could catch *Cabin Boy* before he crossed the Georgia border, but finally he bumped into a dock and got stuck, at least momentarily. I clambered up the muddy bank onto someone's back lawn and ran down to the dock before he could escape. When I grabbed his tether, I checked the end of it, half expecting to see it chewed through.

But no, it wasn't. I must have untied it myself while rearranging the tangled lines in the cockpit.

"That's no excuse for running away!" I said.

I rowed back to the *Blue Moon*, climbed aboard, and tied *Cabin Boy's* leash to a ring bolt on the transom. It was less convenient than a cleat, but at least I wouldn't make the same mistake again. First lesson learned.

"It could have been worse," I thought, with a sick feeling in my stomach. Only luck caused me to turn around at the right moment. If I hadn't, I wouldn't have noticed *Cabin Boy's* escape. It might have been half an hour before I noticed he was missing. By that time, it would have been too late. I never would have found him. That would have been a real disaster.

I restarted the engine. The sun was well up by then and there were people about, including a few burly marina guys who stood on a dock just across the river with their hands on their hips, watching. I gave them a hurried wave, then turned to the manly work of pulling up the anchor.

Somehow, I didn't have another chance to look back until we'd motored down the river, out of the sight of their scornful eyes.

* * *

The Steinhatchee flowed around several 'S' bends, growing wider all the time, but its width was deceptive. Outside the narrow dredged channel, the river was only a foot or two deep.

"One lesson a day is my limit," I said. So I steered a careful line between the red and green buoys that marked the channel.

The sun was up and its warm rays quickly dried my T-shirt and swim suit. I was barefoot in my own little ship and we were off on an amazing voyage. What more could a man ask for? I waved cheerfully to a white-haired fisherman in a flat-bottom skiff. He waved back, though not so enthusiastically.

A few minutes later, we (meaning the *Blue Moon*, *Cabin Boy*, and I) turned the last bend on the river. A sandy spit marked the end of the Steinhatchee River. Beyond that, the Gulf of Mexico opened under a clear blue sky. My heart picked up a beat. It suddenly struck me that this was the first time I'd ever sailed beyond the narrow, protected waters of Long Island Sound.

"Am I really going to do this?"

That question came into my mind without invitation. With it, the mad butterflies in my stomach took flight again, clawing at my innards. I found it hard to catch my breath. Was that chest pain? A heart attack? My God, what was I doing?

Fighting the overwhelming urge to turn the *Blue Moon* around and catch a sensible plane home, I pushed through the mouth of the river and out onto the beautiful blue Gulf.

A double line of buoys, red on the left, green on right, marked the channel. It stretched in an arrow-straight line clear to the horizon. When I looked at the line of buoys through binoculars, they seemed to disappear over the curve of the earth.

"No, that can't be…"

I'd studied the chart many times, so knew the channel was

long, but the chart had not prepared me for that view.

"Go one mile offshore for every foot of water you want under the boat," the locals had advised me. The shallows off Steinhatchee weren't quite that bad, but the one fathom (six foot) line—where the channel ended—was three nautical miles away: about the same distance as the horizon.

"It's okay." I told *Cabin Boy*. "That's not the edge of the world out there."

My heart still raced. I had trouble catching my breath. But it was no heart attack, it was just excitement, just butterflies, and I knew all about butterflies.

When I was a boy, I'd wanted to join the Cub Scouts. To join the Scouts, all you had to do was memorize an oath and swear it in a little ceremony.

I <name> promise to do my best
To do my duty to God and my country,
To help other people, and
To obey the Law of the Pack.

Even I could memorize a few lines, but when the time came to put on that crisp blue uniform, to tie on that yellow bandana, and to say my piece, the butterflies came. I cried, and my mother—bless her heart—pitied me, and let me off the hook.

"You don't have to do it if you don't want to," she said.

I did want to, but I was scared and I lunged at the offered life preserver like a drowning rat.

I never did join the Scouts and to this day I regret it. So, as the butterflies flew in formation around my small intestines, I pushed them down where they belonged, opened the throttle a bit, and carried on, between that long line of buoys, into the Gulf of Mexico.

* * *

It took nearly an hour to putter to the end of the channel. The outboard struggled to push the *Blue Moon's* eight-thousand pounds through the water. We couldn't seem to make more than four knots and once the engine stalled. That was a bit awkward in a narrow channel with a cross breeze, but luckily it restarted quickly enough to avoid running aground.

At long last, we passed the final red buoy and entered the deeper waters of the unfortunately named Deadman Bay. By that time, the sun was well up and with the sun had come the wind: a north wind blowing ten to fifteen knots, with the promise of more to come. I hoisted the *Blue Moon's* main and foresail and headed south. She seemed thrilled to be free of the muddy prison that had nearly been her grave. She leaned into her work, took the white bridle in her teeth, and ran downwind for all she was worth.

Cabin Boy, leaping lightly from wave top to wave top, followed joyfully behind.

* * *

All day, we followed the one fathom line south, three to five miles off the west coast of Florida. The land to our left was low, dark green, and featureless. With no evidence of human habitation in sight, I might have been an early Spanish explorer like Alonso Álvarez de Pineda, coasting down a savage, unknown shore.

The wind picked up in the afternoon and I pulled a reef down in the mainsail. Except for a small fishing boat or two, we had the whole Gulf to ourselves, but I still kept a sharp lookout while trying to teach the *Blue Moon* to steer herself.

I had John S. Letcher, Jr.'s famous book, *Self-Steering for Sailing Craft*, as well as a canvas bag full of the light lines, blocks, and rubber tubing required to construct a sheet-to-tiller steering system. Experimenting with various tiller and sail trims kept me occupied for most of the day. A very long but interesting day.

By late afternoon, I began worrying that we wouldn't reach the Cedar Key anchorage before dark. Repeated calculations with chart and pencil confirmed my fears. Unlike the arrow-straight channel off the Steinhatchee, the Cedar Key channel twisted and turned around low-lying islands. It would be no fun at all in the dark.

Even worse, I hadn't planned on sailing at night so soon in the voyage, so I'd put off an important item on my to-do list: "install running lights." Without lights, we'd be invisible to other boats as we wound our way through the dark into Cedar Key. That sounded like a recipe for disaster.

As we approached Cedar Key's northwest channel, the sun lingered for a moment on the western horizon, painting the trade wind clouds a pastel pink before plunging into the sea. By the time we reached the mouth of channel, marked by a flashing red buoy, it was dark. Not city dark. Not Long Island Sound dark, where there are so many lights on shore that you can't possibly miss it. No, this was offshore on the west coast of Florida dark. Scary dark, in other words.

By the light of a flashlight, I studied the chart, unsure what to do. The narrow channel to Cedar Key wound more than six miles between a series of shoals, reefs, and islands, most so small they were unnamed on the chart. On either side of the channel, the water was only a foot or two deep. The islands were just patches of sand. They were so low that I couldn't see any of them in the dark. I had a simple GPS, but without a chart plotter, it wouldn't help me run the gauntlet of hazards. The only aids to navigation were the twenty-five mostly unlit buoys that marked the long channel. One of them—the flashing red that marked the end of the channel—flashed brightly, just off the starboard bow. Beyond that, I could see three other flashers, the furthest nearly three miles away, according to the chart. The rest were hidden over the horizon, or by sea mist, or by the numerous islands that lay between us and Cedar Key.

Did I dare?

"Do I have a choice?"

I started the engine and took down the sails. I sure wasn't going to try to sail in. Worried about encountering other boats in the channel, I hoisted my kerosene-fueled cabin lamp to the top of the mast. The single white light wouldn't satisfy the Coast Guard, but it would keep other boats from running us down, I hoped.

"Well, here we go," I said to *Cabin Boy*. He said nothing, but kept close behind.

We motored past the first flashing red buoy, keeping it on our right, and then headed directly for the next one, a flashing green. That buoy marked a shoal. To pass between the shoal and the north end of South Bank—which submerged at low tide, and was completely invisible in the dark anyway—we'd have to leave the green flasher on our left. The area around the buoy was fairly shallow, so I wanted to pass it about a hundred yards off, just to be safe. Easy to say, but it was hard to judge distance across the water, with only a single point of reference. Especially when that point of reference flashed on and off.

"About a football field," I told myself. "A football field with small waves."

It took a half-hour to motor from the red flasher to the green, so I had plenty of time to judge the distance. When we finally passed that much-studied green light, I did think we were about a hundred yards off, but it was hard to say for sure. We might have been a quarter mile, for all I knew. In that case, we'd hit the South Bank soon. I throttled down so if we did run aground, it wouldn't be a complete disaster.

The next flashing red light was a mile away, but between us and the flasher was an unlit red buoy. These two buoys guarded an extensive line of shoals that stretched away on our right. As long as we left *both* buoys close to our right, we'd be okay. The trick was finding that first unlit buoy.

I swept the darkness ahead with a powerful flashlight my son Chris had given me for the trip. At that moment, I would not have traded that flashlight for a bar of gold. Its beam stabbed into the dark, but soon even it was swallowed up by the gloom. There was no sign of the unlit marker.

"Never mind," I told *Cabin Boy*. "We just need to steer this course and eventually we'll find it." Assuming a cross current didn't push us out of the channel, that is.

I pointed the flashlight at the wake behind us, to see if our track was straight, or bending in one direction or the other. If a current was pushing us off course, the wake would show it, but I couldn't see enough of it to see any curve.

I'd only glanced back, but by the time I looked forward again, we were wildly off course. Was *that* the red flasher we were aiming for? Or the other one? For a moment, I was totally disoriented, and the butterflies rose in flurry of adrenaline. I cut the throttle so we wouldn't ram an underwater sandbank, stood in the cockpit, and looked around at all the lights—green and red—that I could see out there in the dark.

Don't panic.

"It's the closest red one," I told myself after a moment—*after* I'd had a chance to gather my wits. I looked at the compass to double-check my theory. Yes, that must be the one. I opened the throttle and pointed us back on course. Another lesson learned.

Another ten minutes passed. It seemed too long.

"Where is that damn buoy?" I said, meaning the unlit one. I strained forward, willing it to appear. I should have already spotted it with the flashlight.

Suddenly, I felt the strong urge to head in a different direction. But which one? Perhaps the buoy was more to the right, or more to the left, or perhaps we'd already passed it. Should I turn around and go back to the green buoy and try again? Head back out to sea? Call the Coast Guard? My mother?

No. I held my compass course. The buoy must be there. But where? Did I have any idea what I was doing? Or was I completely out of my depth? My heart began to thump.

The flashlight picked up something in the distance: a momentary echo of red. I scanned rapidly back and forth, but couldn't pick it out again. I altered my course anyway, slightly to the left, where I thought I'd seen it, and pressed ahead slowly. Soon, I spotted a thin red line in the distance: a strip of red reflective tape.

"That must be it," I told *Cabin Boy*. Again I altered course, this time heading straight for it. Minutes later the red buoy loomed up out of the dark, a ghostly rust-red can. I'd never been so happy to see a buoy in my life, and I suddenly had a lot more confidence in my navigation. I headed straight for the next marker, which was clearly visible thanks to its flashing red light. I took a deep breath, much relieved. Maybe I could do this, after all.

For another anxious hour, we followed the snaking course

of Cedar Key's Northwest Channel, picking out the unlit buoys with my flashlight, steering straight for the lit ones, my confidence growing with each marker found, keenly aware of the low, brooding, unseen shapes of North Key, Piney Point, and Atsena Otie Key as we passed them in the dark.

And finally, at long last, the lights of Cedar Key hove into view.

Approached from the water at night, Cedar Key looked like Lake-town, the wooden town on Long Lake that Bilbo came to after a long voyage on a raft:

> *Not far from the mouth of the Forest River was the strange town he heard the elves speak of in the king's cellars. It was not built on the shore, though there were a few huts and buildings there, but right out on the surface of the lake... A great bridge made of wood ran out to where on huge piles made of forest trees was built a busy wooden town, not a town of elves but of Men, who still dared to dwell here under the shadow of the distant dragon-mountain. — J.R.R. Tolkien's "The Hobbit"*

Like Lake-town, Cedar Key was built on piles over the water. Its dark walls seemed to rise up out of the sea, and on that chilly off-season night, few lights showed. But one window in the wall seemed to open into a different world. Music echoed out of it, and lively figures moved within.

I looked up at that window where happy people seemed to be living normal lives that didn't involve long, tense journeys up dark, twisting channels. What was I doing out here? For a moment, I wanted to be in that cheerful tavern, with other people, instead of out in the dark, on my own.

When the window was abeam, someone spotted us. There were shouts and laughter, and suddenly the *Blue Moon* was caught in the beam of a powerful spotlight. There was more laughter, accompanied by rude, drunken shouts. The shouts were unintelligible from that distance. I held up my hand to shield my night vision from the bright light, and kept on towards the anchorage ahead.

Suddenly, human company didn't seem all that attractive.

A short time later, I spotted the brightly lit boat ramp that marked the anchorage off Cedar Key Beach. There were no other boats. I picked a spot a hundred yards or so off the beach, dropped my anchor, and shut off the engine. I was home for the night.

I went below and found a bottle of rum in one of my storage bins. I poured myself a large ration and tossed it back. Then I called Helena, who was back in New York.

"I made it," I said grimly.

"How was it?" she asked, sounding anxious. "It's late, isn't it?"

I poured another rum, sat on my bunk, and described the fifty mile offshore passage, and its dark culmination, to an appreciative female.

"Weren't you scared?" she asked.

"It was nothing," I said.

She wasn't fooled for a second.

CHAPTER 6

THE HOSTILE SHORE

*Anchoring anywhere in this bight must be prompted by
necessity and not by any hope of tranquility.*
— *The Mediterranean Pilot*

In 1867, a Scottish-born woodworker with some formal training in geology and botany injured himself when a tool he was using slipped and struck him in the eye. When he regained his sight the young man "saw the world—and his purpose—in a new light." He later wrote, "This affliction has driven me to the sweet fields. God has to nearly kill us sometimes, to teach us lessons." This man would become the naturalist, John Muir.

In September of that year, the twenty-nine year old Muir set out on a 1,000 mile walk from Indiana, heading south through the "wildest, leafiest, and least trodden way I could find." He emerged from the wilderness in Cedar Key, Florida.

> *October 23. To-day I reached the sea. While I was yet many miles back in the palmy woods, I caught the scent of the salt sea breeze which, although I had so many years lived far from sea breezes, suddenly conjured up Dunbar, its rocky coast, winds and waves; and my whole childhood, that seemed to have utterly vanished in the New World, was now restored amid the Florida woods by that one breath from the sea.* —*A Thousand-Mile Walk to the Gulf, John Muir*

Muir had aimed for Cedar Key because its lumber trade made it one of the busiest ports in Florida, and thus a likely place to catch a boat to the Caribbean. Mr. Hodgson, the superintendent of one of the lumber mills, told Muir the next schooner would depart in two weeks for "the flowery plains" of Texas…

> *…from any of whose ports, I fancied, I could easily find passage to the West Indies. I agreed to work for Mr. Hodgson in the mill until I sailed, as I had but little money. He invited me to his spacious house, which occupied a shell hillock and commanded a fine view of the Gulf and many gems of palmy islets, called "keys," that fringe the shore like huge bouquets not too big, however, for the spacious waters. Mr. Hodgson's family welcomed me with that open, unconstrained cordiality which is characteristic of the better class of Southern people. — A Thousand-Mile Walk to the Gulf, John Muir*

It was this final sentence from Muir's journal that made me pick Cedar Key as the first stop on my voyage: the famous "open, unconstrained cordiality" of its citizens. It sounded easy to make friends in Cedar Key, and that was something I wanted to practice. In all the famous cruising memoirs, sailors step off their boats into the arms of friendly, helpful strangers. I, too, wanted to make some friends along the way; I just wasn't sure how to go about it. In normal life, you don't just drop into a place you've never been to before and make friends instantly—at least, I don't—but the skill seemed key to an interesting voyage. There must be a way, I thought.

However, the next morning, as I brought my coffee up on deck and looked at the town built on the water, I remembered the welcome I'd received the night before. So far, when it came to cordiality, Cedar Key had been a disappointment, but I couldn't let one experience shape my opinion of the whole town. It was time for some positive thinking.

"Probably those louts were drunken tourists," I reassured *Cabin Boy*. "The locals will be all right."

To practice my cordiality skills, I first had to get ashore. The morning light showed us anchored some 300 yards off the town dock, with a public beach just to the right. I studied both landing places through binoculars. The white sand beach looked wide and inviting. Beach walkers strolled up and down the tide line. It

Bird's eye view of Cedar-Key, Fla., Levy Co. Beck & Pauli, litho.
Public Domain

would be easy to row ashore and drag *Cabin Boy* onto the beach. I could leave him next to the pier, above the tide line, where he'd probably be safe. Unless those drunken thugs from last night were still around. Or some light-fingered urchins...

I turned my binoculars towards the pier. There were four commercial boat slips, only one of which was occupied by what looked like an excursion boat. That left plenty of room to tie up *Cabin Boy*. Maybe I could even find someone to keep an eye on him.

The prospect of leaving the *Blue Moon* on her own and venturing onto a potentially hostile shore got my butterflies working, but I fed them a quick breakfast, double-checked the anchor, and was soon rowing briskly towards the pier. It was a beautiful day under a bright blue Florida sky. The sun warmed my back and a breeze rippled lightly across the water. As I rowed away from the *Blue Moon*, I admired her long bowsprit, and the jaunty angles of her masts, and wondered, how did I get this lucky? Wow.

I rowed between the wooden piles beside the pier. A ladder led down to the waterline. The tidal range was only two or three feet, so if I tied *Cabin Boy* with a bit of slack, he would be good for a few hours. However, I'd been around boats long enough to know that people can be rather touchy about their dock spaces; I couldn't just tie up without permission. I looked around for a dock master, but there was only the crew of the excursion boat—a stout, sullen-looking fellow in a white captain's hat, and a cheerfully dressed woman. I rowed over for a chat.

"Ahoy!" I said, in my most cordial manner. "Okay if I tie up to one of these ladders for an hour or two?"

The captain turned in my direction. His lip twitched with a surly curl, as if I'd interrupted something important. An odd expression for someone who made his living taking carefree vacationers on pleasure cruises.

"You can," he said, looking me up and down, and obviously not liking what he saw. "But a party boat docks there. When he comes back, he won't worry about crushing your dink against the pier." He shrugged. "Your risk."

With that, he turned back to his work.

"Ah, ha," I said. Another sample of Cedar Key's unbridled cordiality. But as brusquely as the information had been delivered, it was still useful. I really couldn't leave *Cabin Boy* in a working slip. Well, there was nothing else to do. I'd have to try the beach. I hoped a lifeguard wouldn't give me a ticket for beaching my boat.

"Thanks anyway," I said, sincerely. I turned *Cabin Boy's* bow towards the beach, when the brightly dressed woman walked up to the captain and slapped his arm sharply.

"Why are you being so rude?" she asked him. "There's plenty of room to tie up. What are you thinking?"

"Just answering the man's question," the captain growled.

"He can tie up to our dock, can't he?"

"Well..."

"There's plenty of room." She turned towards me and waved towards the end of the dock, near the pier. "You can tie up right there," she said.

The captain scowled and shook his head. "No, won't be safe there."

He looked at his wife, then at me, and seemed to relent.

"Tie up alongside us," he said. "We'll be headed out in four hours, though."

"You sure it isn't too much trouble?" I asked.

"No trouble at all," said the wife.

The captain just took my line and tied it to a cleat on his boat. He put over a couple of fenders to keep the two boats apart, then with a final scowl said: "She'll be fine there."

I climbed aboard and thanked him and his wife.

"Don't you mind the captain," she said, patting his arm fondly. "He just misses the snow."

* * *

It felt good to stretch my legs. The Cedar Keys were a cluster of islands of great historical interest. They'd been occupied by people since at least 500 BC. There was a Seminole Indian burial ground not far away. The Spanish had used the port as a watering spot for their great gold ships, back in the 16th century. They'd given the place its name: *Las Islas Sabines.*

There were no deep water, sheltered ports in that part of Florida, so Cedar Key was merely the best of a bad lot. Its openness to the Gulf led to a repeating pattern of settlement and destruction.

In 1839, General Zachary Taylor established the first permanent presence by building a fort during the Second Seminole War. It was blown away by the hurricane of 1842.

Before the Civil War, two sawmills were built to turn the virgin cedar forest into pencil wood. John Muir worked in one of these mills while waiting for his boat to Texas. These mills were demolished by the hurricane of 1896.

But as I wandered down Dock Street, it seemed that hurricanes were nothing compared to the tsunami of generic kitsch which had erased all trace of the Spanish, Seminole, and Yankee pencil makers. I poked into the tourist shops filled with shells and plastic jewelry and cheaply made T-shirts, looking for a knickknack that I couldn't buy in Maine, or Atlantic City, or Miami… or my own home town, for that matter.

As I weighed a box of salt water taffy in my hand, I thought, maybe the town wasn't so different from the one John Muir knew, with its little store *"which had a considerable trade in quinine and alligator and rattle skins."* Maybe the tastes of tourists had just changed with the times.

After walking through the town's historic district, which had been sadly depleted of historic buildings by the twin scourge of storm and developer, I gave up on history and decided to have lunch on the pier. I wanted to check out the bar from which I'd been so warmly greeted the night before.

I strolled out to the pier and inspected the row of restaurants and bars. There was only one, I decided, that could have been the site of the party.

I walked up green painted stairs. It was dark and cool inside—a relief from the glaring sun. I headed straight to the bar. Three couples, obviously together, sat along one side. I ordered a beer and sandwich, and listened to their conversation for a while. They seemed like happy, civilized folk. Not the rowdy, spotlight-wielding crowd of the night before. I thought I'd finally found the fabled unconstrained cordiality that Cedar Key was famous for, until one of the men asked me where I was from.

"New York," I said. "In fact, I'm—"

"New York, eh?" he said.

"Yes, as I was saying, I'm sailing—"

"Never been there," he said.

"Oh, no?"

"Got my own plane. Been all over the country."

"That's cool. You should check out New York, sometime. A real friendly place."

"Never wanted to go to New York," he said, taking a swig of his beer. "Nothing for me there, as far as I can see."

"Huh," I said. "Interesting…"

He turned away to chat with the rest of his friends. I finished my sandwich, but to be honest, it wasn't that good.

* * *

I walked out of the restaurant, turned right, and walked briskly towards the dock where I'd left *Cabin Boy*. I wanted out of that town as quickly as possible. Unconstrained cordiality, indeed.

Back at the party boat, the crew were gone for lunch. I had one chore to do before I left. I fetched my empty water jug from *Cabin Boy* and walked down the dock, looking for a spigot.

At the end of the dock, a guy was renting plastic kayaks to tourists. He was talking on his cell phone, spraying the concrete with a hose. Not wanting to interrupt him, I sat on a bench and waited for him to get off the phone.

He talked loudly, as people do on cell phones. He was obviously a talk-radio fan. He lectured the poor slob on the other end of the line with the latest talking points, driving home his proclamations with a vehemence I thought excessive. I stood up, ready to go looking for another hose, when his conversation came to an abrupt end.

"You're an idiot," the man said to his phone. He flipped the phone shut, stuck it in his breast pocket, and continued spraying.

I weighed the pros and cons of filling up my water jug vs. another dose of Cedar Key hospitality. I decided the water was worth it. Besides, I needed to practice my friendly skills. Life's tough, but I'm tougher.

"When you're done," I said, waving my empty jug at the sprayer. "Do you mind if I fill up?"

"I pay for this water, you know," he said.

He'd sprayed at least 160 gallons of it on the concrete since I'd been watching.

"Ah," I said. "Well then, I'd *really* appreciate it."

He muttered a bit and continued spraying. I wondered if it was something in the drinking water? Something that turned the citizens of Cedar Key into snarling louts. Perhaps I didn't want to fill up here.

"I'm sailing that little boat," I said, pointing to the *Blue Moon*, bobbing on her anchor off the glistening white beach. "Not sure the next time I'll be able to get water."

"That your boat?" He asked. "I've been admiring her all morning. Pretty little thing."

"Thanks. Just bought her."

"She's wood, isn't she?"

"Yes, sir."

"A gaffer?"

"Sure is."

"God, I used to have a boat like that, back in the Seventies." He took the jug out of my hand, opened it up, and started to fill it. "More fun than the dozen boats I've had since. That was back in New York, of course."

"That's where I'm headed."

"Really? Sailing back in that little boat? Good for you. That would be a blast. Would love to do that, myself. Going through the Keys?"

"That's the plan."

We had a long chat about the *Blue Moon*, my plans, Helena, his grandkids… Customers came and rented kayaks, returned, and still we were chatting. Finally, I finished a third beer from his cooler full of ice and beer, and said, thanks, but it was time I got going. I still had a few chores to do on board before dark.

"Well, you have one hell of a time," he said. "And don't let the tourists bother you. They come down here, thinking they're big shots for vacationing in this tourist trap, but mostly they're just jerks. Stick with the locals. They're all right."

"Thanks, I'll remember that," I said, picking up my jug.

"You gonna spend the night anchored there?" he asked, pointing to the *Blue Moon*.

"I was planning on it."

"She's okay now, because there's not much wind. But you don't want to be anchored in that spot with a strong wind blowing, particularly from the southeast. The holding isn't very good. See that boat over there?"

He pointed to a forty foot ketch lying on its side about a quarter mile down the beach. I hadn't noticed her before, she was so far away.

"She was anchored right where you are a few days ago. Dragged her anchor in a blow and been on the beach ever since. A word to the wise."

"Got it," I said. "Thanks for the tip."

"Have fun," he said, shaking my hand. "Wish I was young enough to go with you."

* * *

Back on board, I spent a few hours fixing and organizing, made a light dinner on my one-burner stove, called Helena, set my alarm for daybreak, read for a few minutes, and fell asleep, thoroughly tired out. But it wasn't my alarm that woke me a few hours later. Not an *external* alarm, anyway.

My eyes popped open. I was wide awake. It was still dark in the cabin. I looked out a porthole. The wind had shifted. The *Blue Moon's* stern now pointed directly towards the beach. She was pitching up and down, as if driving into waves.

I hopped out of my bunk and slid open the cabin top. The wind was blowing like stink from the southeast, right towards the beach—just what my friend from Cedar Key had warned against. We were now on a lee shore with a good thirty mile fetch across Waccasassa Bay. If the wind kept up, the waves would get bigger and bigger, the situation more and more dangerous.

I glanced towards the beach. It didn't look like we had dragged yet, but distances could be deceptive in the dark. I pulled out my portable GPS: a simple Garmin 72. No chart plotter, just basic GPS functionality. I studied our coordinates to see if they were changing, which would indicate we were dragging. They were steady. We weren't dragging. Not yet, anyway.

I wondered if I should find a better anchorage. I didn't want to move if I didn't have to. It would be no fun getting that anchor up in the wind. Worse, I worried about my engine. If it died on us, we'd be on the beach in seconds. Would we be safer staying put? But as soon as the words, "I wonder if I should…" formed in my mind, I knew we had to move. It was one of my rules: if I thought those words on a boat, then I had to do it, whatever it was. It was a habit that had saved me a lot of grief in the past. It sure didn't seem a good time to break it.

Groaning, I threw on some clothes, started the engine, and went forward to get in the anchor. The wind was still relatively light—maybe ten or fifteen knots—so I hoped it wouldn't be that difficult. To my surprise, the anchor broke out easily. Too easily. In fact, *broke* out is overstating it. The anchor *slipped* out of the bottom, as if it had been stuck in loose, watery mud. Poor holding, indeed.

I quickly hauled the anchor aboard, went aft, and put the engine in gear. I headed back towards the twisting channel I'd come through last night. There was an anchorage behind Atsena Otie Key that should be protected from the wind. I'd have to navigate part way through that tortuous channel again, but it was the best shelter available. The dangerous part was motoring back past the walled town. Never mind drunken revelers, we were only a few hundred feet off the dark piles upon which the town was built. If the motor quit…

"We won't drift that fast," I told *Cabin Boy*. "I'll be able to get the anchor down before we hit, probably."

We motored away from the beach, in a southwesterly direction, past the walled town on its barnacle-encrusted piers. Despite my fears, the engine chugged along without missing a beat. Once past that danger, I swept my flashlight over the *Blue Moon's* bow, looking for the unlit #36 buoy that marked the channel entrance. It should have been right in front of us, but as usual, it was harder to spot than I expected. Without the buoy to guide us, I couldn't find the mouth of the channel. If we missed it and went aground in this wind, we'd probably never get off. I had to find that buoy.

Eventually, I had to admit we'd passed it, somehow. The wind had probably pushed us too far to the north. I headed more south, away from the shallows, into the wind. I continued to sweep the flashlight across the water. Talk about sailing blind.

The flashlight picked up a faint reflection ahead: a thin red line. I waved the flashlight back and forth until I picked up the buoy's reflection again, then turned and headed straight for it.

It was the #34. I had indeed missed the first buoy, but at least I knew where we were, now. There was a long shoal between us and the anchorage off Atsena Otie Key. To reach the anchorage, we had to head to the next unlit marker, and then to a flasher, about a half mile altogether. Once at the flasher, we could turn around the end of the shoal and work our way into the narrow anchorage.

I pointed the flashlight towards the next marker and immediately picked up its reflection. I headed straight towards it. About half-way there, the wind and waves suddenly subsided. "We must be in the lee of the key already," I thought. A moment later, the outboard died.

It flashed through my mind that I had two choices: try to restart the engine, or get my anchor down. If I chose the outboard and it restarted, we'd be golden. If it didn't, I probably wouldn't have time to get the anchor down. So I ignored the engine, dropped the tiller, and got the hook down in record time. As I let out the anchor line, I waited to feel the telltale thump of the keel that would signal we'd run out of water. But to my relief, we still seemed to be floating when I'd let out enough scope.

When my heart resumed normal operating speed, I wondered if we should just stay put for the night. The water would be calmer in the Atsena Otie Key anchorage, but to reach it, I'd have to re-start the engine, and then hope it wouldn't stall in a worse place.

I listened to the wind whistle overhead. At the top of the mast, just twenty-five feet up, the wind was stronger. The low island didn't deflect the wind much, but it did block the big waves that would soon roll in from the bay. The protection wasn't perfect, but it was good enough.

I made my decision: we'd stay put for now.

I glanced up to make sure my anchor light was still lit. It probably wasn't legal to anchor in the channel, but how many boats would be threading their way down to Cedar Key in the dark? Not many, I figured. We'd be okay, as long as the anchor light stayed lit.

I heard *Cabin Boy's* bottom slapping in the light chop. I tied his painter short, so he'd be in the *Blue Moon's* wind shadow. Then I double-checked the knot to make sure he couldn't get away.

With every conceivable precaution taken, I went below, closed the hatch, climbed back into my bunk, and set my alarm clock to ring in a half hour.

"You're on anchor watch tonight, seaman," the Captain said.

"Aye-aye, sir," the able seaman replied.

It was going to be a long night.

CHAPTER 7

NIGHT PASSAGE

So we made fast the braces, and we rested,
Letting the wind and steersman work the ship.
— Homer's Odyssey

It *was* a long night. I set my alarm to wake me every half hour to take bearings on the two buoys that flanked our position. Each time the alarm rang, I'd drag myself out of my bunk, grab my flashlight, and probe the dark, trying to pick out their etherial red flashes. As long as the buoys flashed back, and as long as their bearings didn't change, I knew we hadn't dragged our anchor. I'd reset the alarm, climb back into my bunk, and try to grab another few winks of sleep.

As morning approached, the two buoys emerged from the dark, gradually soaking up color from the growing light, easing slowly from grey, to grey tinged with red, to a solid, reassuring red.

At dawn, the wild wind swung into the east, then weakened. By the time the sun rose, the wind blew softly at five to ten knots, the waves melted back into the sea, gulls swooped and called, and the world was at peace. Nothing remained of the long, worrying night but my red-rimmed eyes and foggy brain. The poor crew of the *Blue Moon* had earned their tea and crust of bread that morning. The captain gratefully fed them.

The plan was to take the southern exit out of Cedar Key, through the South Bar Channel, and then head south to the Crystal River where my friends, Dewey and Elizabeth, waited. This was a fifty-five mile journey by car, but only thirty-five miles by sea. I hoped to have my anchor down in the clear, calm river by late afternoon, and maybe even spot a manatee or two on the way. Crystal River, my friends reported, was a nature lover's paradise.

The South Bar Channel was a wide boulevard compared to the narrow, twisting Northwest Channel, but I was still on edge from the night before, and not in a mood to take chances. I stuck to the center of the channel and breathed a sign of relief when we cleared the last buoy and left Cedar Key behind.

The wind blew out of the east at ten knots by then. If it stayed in that quarter, the passage would be an easy one: a beam reach all the way. Perfect sailing weather. I hoisted mainsail, staysail, jib and mizzen, and the *Blue Moon* leaned into her work and scudded south. My goal for the day was to get my self-steering gear working properly. I pulled out the Letcher book and—steering with my foot on the tiller—studied the sheet-to-tiller diagram for a beam reach.

This obsession with self-steering may seem odd to the casual day sailor or racer, who probably regards helming his boat—making the most of every luff and puff—as the very essence of sailing. But for the cruiser, steering is a joy that quickly fades. The noble captain is reduced to a lowly crew member, yoked to the tiller with heavy chains that make it difficult to navigate, make a cup of tea, do chores, or—what I was ultimately hoping for—to read. The *Blue Moon* needed a captain as well as a crew, so getting her to self-steer was no luxury—it was a necessity. And I had plenty of time to work on it.

According to Letcher, the first step in getting a sheet-to-tiller system working is balancing the boat, which means adjusting the sails so they pull efficiently with just a *small* amount of weather helm.

I'd spent the previous day trying various sail combinations, reefs, and trims, and had learned how to balance the *Blue Moon* in wind conditions that varied from five knots up to twenty knots. With her long, deep keel, she balanced easily. As long as I had the right amount of sail up, she was both fast and light on the tiller.

I'd read about old, very long-keeled boats that would self-steer with just the tiller tied off, but the *Blue Moon* wasn't one of them, I discovered. Soon after tying her off, the wind would increase or decrease slightly, or a small wave would knock her off course, or I would move my weight to a different position in the boat and, without my hand on the stick to make small adjustments, she'd soon head up into the wind or threaten to gybe.

So, after sailing out of Cedar Key that morning, I sat comfortably in the cockpit, steered with my bare foot on the tiller, and reviewed the instructions on sheet-to-tiller steering on a beam reach (the wind was blowing offshore that morning.)

Briefly, the idea was to use the force generated by the staysail to provide the small amount of weather helm needed to keep the *Blue Moon* on course.

If she wandered off course to windward, the apparent wind would *increase* and thus increase the pressure on the sail. This force would be transmitted to the windward side of the tiller by a control line lead through two small blocks. The increased pressure would pull the tiller (against an elastic control line) slightly to windward, thus putting the boat back on course.

If she then fell off to leeward, the apparent wind would *decrease*, thus decreasing the pressure on the staysail. The elastic control line would then pull the tiller slightly to leeward again, putting the boat back on course.

That was the theory, anyway. Time to see if it worked.

With the steering gear installed, I put the *Blue Moon* back on course and watched to see what would happen. As soon as I took my hand off the tiller, the force exerted by the staysail pulled the tiller to windward and we immediately turned down wind.

"Not enough tension on the elastic," I told *Cabin Boy* confidently. "The book says it takes a bit of fiddling to get this working."

Several hours later, I looked up from my novel to watch the boat steer herself. It was fascinating to watch the tiller twitch back and forth, back and forth, as the elegantly simple system made tiny adjustments to our course.

The secret, I'd discovered after much trial and error, was to keep the tensions on the control lines as light as possible. If the boat was balanced, with the appropriate amount of sail up, then the helm was light and the forces needed to keep her on course were surprisingly delicate. Just a small pull from the staysail would keep her head down in a puff, and the light pressure from the elastic would pull the tiller back when the wind subsided. When I finally got it working—with the wind itself steering the boat—it seemed miraculous, almost unbelievable. At first, I was afraid to leave the cockpit for more than a few seconds at a time, but eventually it dawned on me that the system was actually working. My boat was steering itself. It was thrilling to be unchained from the tiller: to be free to go below for a cup of tea, or to read, or to work on any of the hundred chores on my list.

I finished my cup of tea and put the cup away down below. Yes, we could have sailed south forever, but such carefree sailing would have to wait. It was time to go back to hand-steering, and to head east into the Crystal River.

As soon as we turned east, I realized we had a problem. We had sailed ten nautical miles offshore to avoid a line of spoil islands, and now the mouth of the river was a long, hard slog almost directly to windward. I was already tired from the long, mostly sleepless night, and the prospect of bashing into the wind for the rest of the day was exhausting.

"Never mind," I said, bucking myself up. "It's only noon. You have plenty of time."

An hour later, the wind was blowing even harder and I'd reduced sail to reefed main and staysail. We'd made two miles good to windward and the next leg was a channel that was too narrow to tack in. It was time to strike sails and let the engine take over.

The nameless outboard started right up and I pointed the *Blue Moon*'s bow straight into the wind. With full throttle, we pitched over the short, nasty chop at four knots. At that speed it would take two hours to follow the channel through open water to the river's mouth. Then perhaps another hour to reach a protected anchorage. It seemed a long way, but the prospect of a quiet anchorage and a good night's sleep drew me in.

Before we even reached the channel's mouth, the engine started smoking. Then it seemed to weaken. Our progress through the waves slowed. The smoke increased. Something like panic thumped in my chest. What if the engine burned out? How would I get into one of these narrow, twisting channels without an engine? Would we be doomed to sail the Gulf of Mexico, forever?

By then, great billowing clouds of smoke poured out of the engine. I wondered if I should shut the wretched thing down, which of course meant I must. Immediately. But before I could even reach for the kill button, the engine stalled.

It was all hands on deck, then. A pitching, rolling deck. The crew made short work of hoisting the staysail and reefed main and we were soon hard on the wind again, which settled things down enough to read a chart.

The prospects, I soon discovered, were grim.

We couldn't possibly enter the Crystal River without an engine. Reefed down and tacking every few minutes up that narrow channel, we'd make very slow progress to windward. It would be dark before we reached the river's mouth, and I didn't want to attempt sailing into an unknown river's mouth by flashlight. But what was the alternative? To stay out here forever?

I ran my finger down the map, looking for an anchorage we could reach without an engine. There were several rivers along the coast, but all were at the end of long, narrow channels. I kept looking down the map until my finger reached Tarpon Springs.

Tarpon Springs was over forty miles away. Eight or ten hours, depending on the wind. That meant sailing through the night— something I'd never done. But, according to the weather radio, the wind would stay in the east, making it an easy beam reach. With her self-steering gear, the *Blue Moon* could sail herself. I'd need to keep a careful watch—I didn't know what sort of shipping we might 'run into' at night—but there would be ample time to rest, make a cup of tea, and eat some hot food, which I was desperate for.

More importantly, Tarpon Springs Bay was wide open to the north. There was an anchorage at the south end of Anclote Key that I should be able sail right into, even if I couldn't get my engine started. Not a *great* anchorage, but it might just be the port of refuge I needed to rest, regroup, and call for help if needed.

I considered the long, slightly frightening, offshore passage for a few minutes, then turned the *Blue Moon's* bowsprit away from the Crystal River, and towards Tarpon Springs. It was the only sensible choice, so the decision was easy.

Immediately, the apparent wind lessened. Rather than bashing into the waves, we seemed to glide over them. The howl in the rigging died away and I could again hear the sound of the sea swishing under the *Blue Moon's* bottom. Her motion steadied and felt much safer.

I double-checked to make sure *Cabin Boy* was still behind us. He scuttled along on top of the waves, barely getting his feet wet.

"You okay, back there?"

"*Turning south! Surfing over waves! Best day of my life!*", he seemed to say.

With the wind on our quarter and the *Blue Moon* well snugged down, it was hard not to agree.

* * *

"What have I gotten myself into this time?"

Many hours later, we were fifteen miles offshore. It was dark— really dark. The west coast of Florida was off to the left, far over the horizon, so I couldn't even see shore lights. All I could see was the black night all round us, and the occasional ghostly-white crest of a wave.

And stars—a million stars.

I was wedged into a corner of the cockpit. I was comfortable, but not *too* comfortable. It had been a long time since I'd slept properly, but now wasn't the time to nod off, tempted though I was.

The wind was still blowing hard enough to need a reef in the main, and with fifteen miles between us and the coast, there was plenty of room for the wind to blow up four foot seas. They were rolling in from the port quarter (left rear corner of the boat), but the *Blue Moon* didn't seem bothered by them. She rose lightly and let them slip under her keel without fuss. The self-steering gear held us on a steady course. I was as relaxed as I'd been so far on the voyage. The *Blue Moon* was taking care of me for now—perhaps just paying me back for all the loving care Helena and I had lavished on her.

I cast a wary glance towards our only company: a large container ship several miles off the starboard beam, also heading south. I wasn't worried about her running us down. We were roughly following the three fathom line on the chart. The big ship and her sisters stayed in the shipping lanes and wouldn't venture into shallow water just to bother us. As long as we stayed out of their way, we'd be fine.

Someone once said that there are only two wildernesses left on earth: the tops of mountains, and the sea. That night, as we rolled along under reefed main and staysail, watching the tip of the mast draw figure-eight's in the star-filled sky, I understood what he meant. The sea hadn't changed since the pirate Jean Laffitte roamed these waters in his schooner *La Diligent* in the early 1800s, and the *Blue Moon* wasn't all that different from Laffitte's ship. We had the same amount of electrical power, for instance. That is to say, none, except for the small amount I managed to generate by solar power. Just like Laffitte, most of the lights we had on board were oil lamps. And like the furtive pirate, we weren't showing any running lights, except for a kerosene light hanging from the mizzen mast.

The Coast Guard, I knew, would take a very dim view of this arrangement. I hadn't seen a Coast Guard boat since arriving in Florida, but I wouldn't set sail again until I had a full set of running lights installed.

Wind, waves, stars, the gentle rolling of a good sea boat... what more could one ask for?

A cup of tea, of course. Must drink something to stay awake.

I soon had my gimbaled stove roaring. It was a delight to be out of the wind, down below, in my snug little cabin, while the *Blue Moon* steered us towards Tarpon Springs. Why were we the only boat out here on this beautiful spring night? Why didn't everyone want to do this? At that moment, I couldn't imagine.

Nevertheless, I didn't dawdle in the cabin. Swooping along at five-and-a-half knots, it wouldn't take long to come up on a fishing boat. I made my cup of tea, and hurried up the companionway to take a look. On the way up, the boat jogged unexpectedly, my foot slipped on the ladder, and I banged my shin.

"Dang!" I said. "I should have brought shin guards!"

In the past few days, I'd banged my shins more times than I could remember. There's something about the motion of a boat that makes this easy to do. Even the Amazons, in Arthur Ransome's *Great Northern?*, had the problem:

> *There was the noise of somebody slipping on the way up the companionway ladder. "Jibbooms and bob-stays! I wish shins were made of iron!" It must have been Nancy who slipped.*

I'd whacked my leg a good one this time, even drawing a few drops of blood, but I was in too much of a hurry to get back on deck to give it much thought. After taking a good look around, I forgot all about my poor, battered shins.

* * *

It was three am when I spotted the red flashing light I'd been looking for. I was really tired by then, so I had trouble counting the seconds between flashes, trying to confirm its identity.

"Two and a half seconds… Wait, is that right?"

My foggy brain had trouble keeping hold of simple facts for more than a few moments. I again studied the chart in my lap and confirmed that, yes, that must be the buoy marking the entrance to the harbor. At last.

I pointed the *Blue Moon*'s bowsprit towards the flashing light and tried to make a plan. We were ten miles from the anchorage. Two hours, if we kept up our rollicking pace. That meant we'd arrive at five am, a good two hours before sunrise. But perhaps there would be light enough to guide us into the anchorage, either from the pre-dawn sky, or from shore-lights. Perhaps.

I watched a large container ship, lit up like a frozen fireworks display, sail out of the harbor, heading for points west. It was traveling fast.

"We'll have to stay well outside the main channel," I reminded *Cabin Boy*.

The ship's clock said 4:10 am when we sailed past the buoy marking the tip of Anclote Key and the entrance to the harbor. To port was the mainland—a confusing mass of shore lights and dark shapes. To starboard was Anclote Key, looking like a black smudge against the black night. A lighthouse flashed on the island's southern tip, three miles away. According to the chart, if we made straight for the lighthouse, we'd sail right into the little anchorage.

I looked towards the east, hoping to see a sign of the approaching dawn, but there was nothing visible except black night. We were going to be too early.

A half-hour later, we approached the lighthouse through total darkness. The tall, bright light flashed over Anclote Key, but below it, the island was a formless, black mass. I could not make out the shoreline or any detail whatsoever. It was impossible to judge distances. I stood on towards the lighthouse as far as I dared, fearing every moment that we'd run aground, but before we actually entered the anchorage, I lost my nerve, turned tail, and headed back the way I'd come. It was just too risky.

I had two choices: stand off and on until I had some daylight to see with, or navigate into the anchorage in the dark using more precise navigation techniques.

At first, waiting seemed the easiest thing to do. With the east wind, I could easily tack up and down the harbor between lighted buoys for an hour when, surely, the dawn would come. The alternative meant taking some pretty precise bearings on various lights, calculating a course, and feeling my way into the anchorage. I was too tired for that. My brain wasn't up to the task. I was sure to make a mistake.

Then I remembered my primitive GPS. GPS was a new thing for me and—to be honest—seemed a bit of a cheat. Jean Laffitte didn't have no stinkin' GPS. If he'd wanted to anchor off Anclote Key, he would have waited until dawn to enter the harbor. Of course the pirate king had a fresh crew to do the work while he nipped down into his cabin for a nap. The captain of the *Blue Moon* had no such luxury. But he did have a GPS. Perhaps just this once…

I fetched it from the cabin, used my paper chart to find the latitude and longitude of the center of the anchorage, entered that waypoint into my GPS, and pressed the 'Go To' button. The little green screen showed the direction and distance. All I had to do was sail on the bearing until the distance counted down to 0.0 nautical miles. Easy-peasy.

But scary. As we got closer, I pulled down the mainsail, and continued to sail slowly with just the staysail.

The island was still a black smudge. I knew it was there, but I could not tell how far off it was. All I had to go on was the glowing screen in front of me. 1 mile. ½ mile. 1,000 feet.

The lighthouse now seemed very close. When it flashed, it blacked out my night vision, so I took to closing my eyes before it flashed to preserve it.

500 feet. I got the lead line working. Talk about feeling your way in. I glanced astern, wondering if we were really on the right bearing, but all the lit buoys were so far away, it was hard to tell.

100 feet.

Enough! My nerves were ready to snap. I pointed the *Blue Moon* into the wind, hurried forward, pulled down the staysail, and—as we lost way—dropped the anchor. It hit bottom with just six feet of chain out. We were definitely close enough to the island. As I let out more anchor rode and waited for the anchor to dig in, I held onto the samson post and felt the bow pitch up and down. The wind blowing across the bay kicked up a good chop. It was going to be another bumpy night, but I desperately needed a couple hour's sleep. By then, it would be dawn, and I'd find a way to get us into Tarpon Springs, to a quieter, safer anchorage.

I watched for a little longer, to make sure we didn't drag. Then I allowed myself a moment of relief. It had been a long sail, but we'd made it. Not bad for an inexperienced crew.

'We're okay for *now*,' I corrected myself. "But we *do* have a problem."

Brute strength and will-power were only going to carry us so far. The captain of the *Blue Moon* needed to get smarter, so his crew wouldn't have to work so hard, or so long. How was he going to do that? I didn't know. I'd have some ideas tomorrow, probably. Meanwhile, I needed to sleep.

I left the lamp in the rigging for an anchor light, and headed down into the dark cabin. Someone else must have taken off my clothes and unrolled my sleeping bag and fetched my pillow, because I swear it wasn't me.

CHAPTER 8

OTHER PEOPLE'S BRAINS

*No way of thinking or doing, however ancient, can be
trusted without proof. What everybody echoes or in silence
passes by as true to-day may turn out to be falsehood tomorrow, mere smoke of opinion, which some had trusted for a
cloud that would sprinkle fertilizing rain on their fields. What
old people say you cannot do, you try and find that you can.
Old deeds for old people, and new deeds for new.*
— *Henry David Thoreau, Walden*

"Apparently, I don't get sea sick."

This was the first thought that passed through my mind when I woke a couple hours later. I pulled a corner of my sleeping bag over my eyes, to block out the bright Florida sunshine that seemed to flood every corner of the cabin. I ignored the lurch that tugged at my innards every few seconds. I closed my ears to the thrumming of wind in the rigging. In short, I managed to sleep thirty seconds more until Duty shook me awake.

"Nag, nag nag…"

I sat up and looked out a port hole to see where we were, then consulted the GPS to see if we'd dragged our anchor.

I flopped back down. No, we hadn't.

"I'd kill for another thirty minutes sleep."

I closed my eyes and tried to pretend I was home in bed. Nothing to worry about. No waves tossing my bed around. No wind threatening to blow my home onto the beach. Just sleep, and maybe a hot shower. Mmm, a hot shower…

A particularly large lurch, followed by a shudder, caused every item in the boat, including my brain, to rattle. Obviously the *Blue Moon* had other plans.

"Okay, okay!" I said. "Demand, demand, demand. It's all about you, isn't it? Move me, reef me, replace my line, paint my deck... it goes on and on!"

By this time, I was out of my bunk and on my feet, peeking out of the hatch, looking around at the brilliant morning, and feeling every ache in my body.

Here is something the romantic cruising books don't tell you: *boats bite*. In the last couple days, I'd found every possible way to bang my shin. At least, I hoped I had. At last count, I had 414 black and blue marks. And by the way, I never exaggerate. Never.

I could see the line of buoys marking the dredged channel into the Anclote River. A mile or so up that river was Tarpon Springs, but more importantly, just inside the mouth of the river was a good anchorage where I hoped I could get some unbroken sleep.

Sleep... what an entrancing concept...

So entrancing that I skipped breakfast and was soon motoring towards the green buoy that marked the entrance to the channel—the same green flasher that I'd taken bearings from last night.

The east wind still blew, and of course it blew right down the channel, making it very difficult to sail into Tarpon Springs. No matter. I'd try the engine again. It was only two miles to the new anchorage, and the short harbor chop was nothing compared to the seas that had thwarted me near the Crystal River. I'd be there before the outboard overheated.

I started the engine, picked up my anchor, and headed out of the anchorage, which didn't look half as scary as it had in the dark.

I'd just rounded the first buoy and was motoring up the channel when the engine died. And for once, it stubbornly refused to start.

Having no trust in the outboard, I had the sails ready to go up in an instant, so before we drifted out of the channel, I hoisted the mainsail. The channel was too narrow to tack in, so I turned around and sailed back to the anchorage.

In the interest of good taste I will skip over the lecture I delivered that morning to my moody outboard motor. Suffice to say, it contained more than the usual number of short, Anglo-Saxon words. Whilst delivering this lecture, it occurred to me that every time the motor stalled, I'd been running at high power. Perhaps if I just kept the speed down…

I gave the engine a half-hour to cool off, then restarted it. I got my anchor up and motored at half-speed towards the channel. All seemed well. I proceeded up the channel, with my sails ready to go up again if the engine stalled, but it continued to run smoothly.

"Now *that* is a useful trick," I told *Cabin Boy*.

If I could keep my engine running simply by keeping the throttle down, that would be a big problem mitigated, if not eliminated. I wasn't entirely convinced of my diagnosis, but I was cautiously hopeful.

A half-hour later, we entered the river and were at last out of the wind. Trees and formerly expensive homes lined the river. On the left bank, a wide channel branched off and headed up to what

Anchor down in a snug harbor at last

looked like a low dam. There was room for several boats, and two were already anchored further up the channel. I chose a spot near the entrance, just in case we had to sail our way out. I soon had the anchor down. Safe in a snug harbor, at last.

Did I pitch into a well-deserved breakfast? Did I fall into my bunk for the sleep I craved? Not with Captain Bligh in charge.

"You, AB," he barked at me, as soon as the anchor dug in. "Get those sidelight boxes built and installed before you even think about hitting your rack. Never know when we might need to put to sea again."

Groans and teeth-gnashing from the crew of the *Blue Moon*, but the captain must be obeyed. The woodworking tools were hauled out of the fo'c's'le, as well as some lumber, and we were soon making sawdust and boring holes for screws. By late afternoon, the boxes with their brass oil lights were lashed in the shrouds and the captain was serving out a double ration of rum, with congratulations all around.

He wasn't such a bad captain, really.

* * *

The next morning I discovered a secret I probably shouldn't reveal: cruising in a wooden boat makes it really easy to meet people.

Yes, it's true. Imagine an anchorage with twenty shiny white plastic sailboats, and one classic wooden gaffer. Which one would you row over to see? The *Blue Moon* and *Cabin Boy* had helped me make friends in Steinhatchee, and in Cedar Key, and the same thing happened again in Tarpon Springs.

I was sitting on deck, enjoying the sun and my second cup of tea, after sleeping almost 'round the clock, from 4:00 pm to nearly 8:00 am. After waking, I'd rowed ashore to the Anclote River Park, on the edge of the anchorage, and found that luxury of cruising luxuries: a shower. Delicious. So I was rested, clean, and ready to row up the river to Tarpon Springs for some Greek food, when I noticed a guy in a dinghy slowly circling us.

He might have been shy, but I wasn't, and I was soon answering his questions about my boats, the trip ("You're sailing her back to New York?!"), and the state of my mental health, and before you could say 'boomkin', we were best friends. He and his wife, Louise, were cruising from Pensacola to the Keys. They were going to dinghy up to Tarpon Springs and did I want a ride? Their dinghy was twice the size of *Cabin Boy* and was equipped with a bigger, better engine than the *Blue Moon*. Which wasn't saying much, of course.

"Yes, please!" I said. After going back to fetch Louise, we headed up river.

* * *

The city of Tarpon Springs is strangely connected to woodworking and boats. It was founded in 1882 by Hamilton Disston, who's father, Henry Disston, manufactured the best handsaws in America, including the one I'd inherited from my grandfather. The skewback saw he invented in 1874 was so successful that his son was able to buy four million acres of Florida land in 1881. *"What is claimed to be the largest purchase of land ever made by a single person in the world,"* said the New York Times at the time.

Fourteen years later, the Greeks arrived. Soon the river was filled with colorful wooden sponge boats. By 1900, the city was the largest sponge port in the United States.

As Dave and Louise and I strolled through the tourist shops along the old docks, Greeks and sponges were still at the heart of the city.

"They say you can't visit Tarpon Springs without buying a sponge," Louise said.

"I don't see the attraction," I said, picking up one of large, tan-colored sponges, which looked like a creature that had evolved on Mars. The sponge was hard and rough and nothing like the perfectly rectangular, soft, florescent-pink ones they sell at the grocery store.

"Hello," said the large-eyed, blond saleswoman, in delicately accented syllables. "My name is Maria-Phaidra. Come here, please."

She lead us to a table which held a plastic dishpan half-filled with water.

"You see?" she said, taking the sponge out of my hand. "Very hard. Not nice." She made a face. "Now, you put in water…"

She put the sponge in the water, and it seemed to bloom, to come alive. She squeezed the water out of it, and placed it in my hand. It was cool and soft. Just the thing, I thought, for a sponge bath in the cockpit.

"You see?" she said. "Now nice."

"Sold!" I said.

They say you can't visit Tarpon Springs without buying a sponge. Not true. I bought four.

* * *

We ate lunch at a dock-side restaurant overlooking the river. A large-eyed brunette had just taken our order.

"It's funny," I said, after she'd gone to get our drinks. "They all have Greek accents. But the Greeks have been here for over a hundred years. She's probably fourth-generation American. You think it's just marketing?"

"How is your leg?" Dave asked. He'd noticed me limping earlier.

"Fine," I said. "Just banged my shin the other night. It's fine." Actually, it was a bit sore, but I was more interested in picking Dave and Louise's experienced brains. "So you are headed straight to Key West from here? No stops along the way?"

"That's right. We sailed here from Pensacola, cutting right across the Gulf. Took us three days and two nights. We'll head offshore again tomorrow. Should get to Key West in two or three days, depending on the wind."

"Ah, if I could only do that," I said. "It's going to take me two weeks to get down there, sailing port-to-port every night."

"That's the advantage of having the two of us on board."

"Maybe I could do it. It's only a few days…"

Dave looked skeptical. Louise was more direct. She shook her head. "It's too far. You can't sleep out there. There's too much shipping."

"She's right," said Dave. "Sailing offshore is a strategy that works for two, barely. Three is better. But you need a different strat-

On the dock in Tarpon Springs

egy. Something that will work for you."

"The problem is, just getting in and out of port each day takes a few hours," I said. "By the time you sail the five mile channel and up the river to an anchorage—an hour or two each way—it's time consuming."

"Have you thought about the ICW?" said Louise, meaning the Intracoastal Waterway, which started just south of Tarpon Springs, and lead almost all the way home to New York.

"Not really," I said. "It sounds even slower. There are all those bridges and twists and turns…"

"It's beautiful, though," said Louise. "I prefer it. Much more relaxing than sailing offshore. My macho-sailor husband won't agree, of course."

"I don't know," said Dave. "If I was sailing alone, I'd be tempted. There are loads of places to anchor along the ICW, and you can cut out the two-to-four hours wasted each day getting in and out of port, as you say. Lots of things to see, and you can anchor for lunch or a break whenever you need it. It's not a bad strategy for a single-hander."

"Particularly a single-hander in a small boat," said Louise.

"No, the *Blue Moon*'s a good little sea boat," Dave said. "But it's a case where the boat is tougher than her crew. She can do it, but you can't. You gotta be practical and not take risks in the shipping lanes."

"The ICW sounds like an interesting option," I said, still not convinced. "But I'll keep making tracks offshore as long as the wind stays in the east or north. I need to take advantage of the fair wind as long as it lasts."

"What about the Okeechobee?" Dave asked. The Okeechobee Waterway was a canal that cut straight across the state of Florida.

"Haven't really thought about it," I said. "The plan is to sail around Florida, through the Keys. The Keys sound amazing."

"They are. But you should seriously think about taking the Okeechobee. It would cut weeks off your schedule."

The thought of missing the Keys was even more distressing than trading the romance of off-shore sailing for the practicality of the ICW. I'd wanted to pick the brains of experienced cruisers, but I was getting more advice than I'd bargained for.

"Is the Okeechobee Waterway deep enough for the *Blue Moon*?" I asked. "Have you ever done it?"

"No, we haven't gone through it," said Dave. "Frankly, I don't know anyone who has, but it might be worth looking into. If it will save you some time…"

"It's a long way to New York," said Louise.

* * *

Early next morning, Dave and I hoisted our anchors at the same time. We were both headed south: he and Louise to the crystal blue waters of the Keys, and I for an anchorage on the Manatee River.

The Manatee was just inside Tampa Bay, about fifty miles south. Doable, I thought, if I could whistle up some wind. With two good nights sleep, I was rested and raring to go. The morning was beautiful, the sky clear blue, and the east wind just starting to ripple across the water. I felt incredibly lucky, happy, and optimistic. Even the *Blue Moon* and *Cabin Boy* seemed to be moving easier. It looked to be a good day.

As I followed in Dave's wake, I considered the advice I'd sought and received from him and Louise. Their recommendations were practical, even prudent, but I wasn't ready to give up on offshore sailing: under the right conditions, it was so much faster. Nor was I ready to pass up the Florida Keys just yet. They were the highlight of the whole trip. How could I skip them, just to save a few miles?

Besides, I knew from long experience that sailors love to say, "It can't be done," or "It's too dangerous," or "Why don't you do it my way?" So I owed it to myself, and to the voyage, to find out what I could do, or rather, what we could do, since much depended on the capabilities of the *Blue Moon*. Maybe we would surprise everyone.

Never mind. I put the question out of my head for the moment. I'd make a final decision when I reached Ft. Meyers, over 100 miles south, where the Okeechobee Waterway began.

Dave and I motored through the inlet south of Anclote Key, and onto the wide Gulf of Mexico. Once reaching the green buoy that marked the end of the channel, I turned south towards Tampa Bay, while Dave and Louise continued to head west, wanting to get further offshore before turning south for the Keys. With a final wave, they headed for the horizon, and I wondered for a final time if I should have followed them.

But I didn't. Even I was too sensible for that. I didn't have the food, water, or crew for a long leg offshore. Or, for that matter, wind.

I looked around at the clear blue sky, wondering if we'd get more than a light breeze that day. I hoisted all sail, set up my self-steering gear, selected a good book from my library, and got comfortable in the cockpit.

Tampa Bay seemed a long way away.

* * *

As the sun dipped towards the western horizon, we found ourselves exactly ten miles south of Tarpon Springs. The wind had remained frustratingly elusive all day. I studied the chart and grimly considered my choices.

We were off the Clearwater Inlet. The next inlet—John's Pass—was fifteen miles south and the forecast was for light winds the rest of the night. We could give up and head into Clearwater, or spend another night offshore and perhaps make John's Pass by morning.

It didn't seem worth a night's sleep to make fifteen miles, so I turned towards Clearwater Inlet.

My guidebook described a lovely anchorage not too far inside the inlet. With little wind or wave to hinder us, and with the engine running at half speed, we were soon motoring around the large cove, looking for a good place to drop the hook.

We had the whole anchorage to ourselves—too many choices, perhaps. I picked out a good, practical spot in eight feet of water, then noticed a large, old-fashioned house on shore, with a wide lawn and beautiful trees. The horizontal rays of the sun painted the house with rose-colored hues.

Perhaps I wanted the secondhand comfort it seemed to offer. Perhaps it called to me like a Siren, and I had no choice. Perhaps I just wanted something to look at while I sat in the cockpit and drank my daily rum ration. Whatever the impulse, it was rudely disrupted by a bump under the *Blue Moon*'s keel.

We bumped several more times before I could reverse the engine. Too late! Even full power could not budge her off the sandbar. And a sandbar it was. Through the clear water, I could see sand, shells, and the waving fronds of some aquatic plant. How could I have not seen a sandbar rearing up in front of us? Looking too longingly at that old pile of a house? Damn fool.

The tide was falling. While I fruitlessly tried to back us off the sandbar, the tide drained away another half-inch of water, and we settled even more firmly aground.

Well, there was nothing for it. Instead of sipping a cocktail and watching the dying sun paint someone else's house with hues of gold, I grunted the spare anchor (kedge) over *Cabin Boy*'s stern, rowed it out into deep water, and dropped it so I could pull us out whenever the tide floated us off the sandbar again.

Over the next few hours, as the tide ebbed and the *Blue Moon* settled further and further to starboard, I rearranged the plastic boxes in the fo'c's'le so they wouldn't spill open, and moved my bunk mattress onto the cabin floor so I'd have a place to lie down, and gradually adapted to life at a forty-five degree angle.

At low tide, I stood on wet sand under bright stars and reconsidered life, the universe, and my way home. Perhaps it wouldn't be such a bad idea to take a shortcut through the Okeechobee. Maybe I should be a bit more practical.

"Practicality has never really been my strong point," I confessed to *Cabin Boy*, who was as firmly aground as I was. I was still determined to get to the Keys and—if truth be told—was more than a little nervous about trying the ICW, with its narrow channels and numerous bridges and locks.

"I'll decide when I get to the Manatee River," I said.

Cabin Boy seemed to be sleeping whilst his master considered these weighty matters, but I could almost hear him mutter in his sleep.

"*Running aground... putting out anchor...*" he seemed to say. "*Best day of my life!*"

CHAPTER 9

JUMPING DOLPHINS, BATMAN

It is not the beginning but the continuing of the same
until it be thoroughly finished that yieldeth the true glory.
— Sir Francis Drake

The *Blue Moon* finally lifted off the sandbar at 2:00 am. Using the anchor I'd laid out, I hauled us out into deeper water. Then I restored the cabin to something like order and fell gratefully into my fabulously horizontal bunk.

The next day, we were again plagued by light winds, and again failed to reach the Manatee River. Twenty miles short of my goal, I'd been forced to drop the hook in the only anchorage we could reach—a suburban cul-de-sac, surrounded by posh, waterfront homes. I got to practice my friendly-skills when one of the home owners rowed out to say hello and ask about the *Blue Moon*.

The next morning, I awoke to a dead calm and finally resorted to my engine. I was determined to reach the Manatee River, even if we had to motor the rest of the way. Luckily, the wind picked up in the afternoon and we had a good sail across Tampa Bay, and into the lower reaches of the Manatee.

I was exhausted from the sun, discouraged by our slow progress, and on top of everything else, my leg ached. The place I'd been striving to reach for so long looked wild, lonely, and desolate. I'd chosen the anchorage because it was in a semi-secluded wildlife refuge that was home to alligators, manatees, and mangroves. Only one other boat was anchored there—a large derelict fishing boat that seemed to have been abandoned to rust and the elements. But it was company, of a sort, and I anchored a few hundred yards off its silent bow.

After furling the sails and snugging down the ship for the night, I poured myself a large rum and limped into the cockpit to watch the sun go down. I knew I should eat something, but I wasn't hungry. I was too depressed. How was I going to get home at this rate? Everyone had said it was a long way to New York, but the full meaning of that depressing platitude was just starting to hit me. I'd left Steinhatchee nine days ago, and had only managed 150 miles since then. At that rate, I'd prove Helena right, and arrive home just in time for Thanksgiving—if I was lucky.

But I couldn't give up. I had to keep pushing on in the hope that I would get better at it, and start making more daily progress. How? I didn't know, but determination and blind faith had never failed me before. Somehow, I'd find a way.

The sun went down over the lonely shore and, one by one, the stars peeked out. The dark water shimmered like glass and I wondered if I'd see a manatee in the Manatee River. I lit my kerosene riding light, hoisted it up the mizzen mast, and hobbled down the companionway steps, careful not to bang my already sore leg. I still wasn't hungry, but decided I needed to eat something anyway, so fetched an energy bar from my stores and took it to bed with me.

I picked up the book I was reading—Jerome K. Jerome's *Three Men In A Boat*—but after reading a page or two, I must have dozed off because the next thing I knew, Mr. Moon was looking down the companionway, into the cabin. I'd been woken by a splash. Not a delicate splash, like a fish flipping out of the water, but a Bronko Nagurski-sized cannonball splash, right outside the open starboard porthole.

I slowly climbed out of my bunk, stuck my head out the companionway, and looked around. No Bronko swimming around the boat, smiling and waving his helmet at me. Nothing.

"Strange," I thought. I looked back towards *Cabin Boy*. "You see anything?" But apparently he had been sleeping, too.

After a little while, I shrugged, climbed back into my bunk and rejoined the boys sculling up the Thames.

Moments later: another huge splash. I quickly looked out the companionway again, but all I could see were the stars twinkling, and a large ripple spreading across the water. Something was out there, but what?

The next moment, a moon-gray dolphin swooshed out of the river, took a good look at me with its huge left eye, and belly flopped back into the water.

Three more times the dolphin blasted out of the water and each time we seemed to make eye contact.

Then he was gone.

"Did you see that?" I asked *Cabin Boy*. He nodded on the waves thrown up by the dolphin.

My heart thumping, I stayed on deck for a long time, hoping he or she would return. Never had I had such a close personal encounter with a creature of the wild. Certainly not in such lonely circumstances. But apparently, the animal's curiosity had been satisfied. It did not return and eventually I climbed back into my sleeping bag, thrilled, and feeling more alive than I'd felt for days.

"And that," I thought, "is why this trip is worth the effort."

* * *

As soon as my right foot touched the cabin sole it began to throb, and the throbbing grew with every pulse of my heart to a crescendo that seemed likely to blow my leg apart like a burst balloon.

Gradually, the pain subsided and I was able to breath again, though I felt sick and feverish. I looked at my battered right calf. Though not blown up like a balloon, it was clearly thicker than my left calf. Swollen like a fat sausage.

Now that the throbbing had subsided, I thought I could put some weight on it, so I gingerly stood up, and poked my head out of the companionway for a look around.

Morning had long since dawned, and a lovely breeze was blowing from the north. It felt cool on my sweaty brow. The wind was stronger than any we'd seen for days, with the promise of more to come in the afternoon. With a breeze like that, we could be anchored off Sanibel Island by tomorrow morning, lopping another seventy-five miles off the voyage, and putting us at the mouth of the Okeechobee Waterway, where I'd have to choose between the practicality of a short cut, and the romance of tropical isles.

I climbed into the cockpit, then took a few turns around the deck, to see how my leg felt. It felt sore, but not considerably sorer than it had been for the last few days. It would probably be all right—probably my calf had been swollen yesterday, and I just hadn't noticed. It would be a shame to waste this beautiful wind.

"Of course we won't waste it!" I said, giving myself a pep talk. "The show must go on. When the going gets tough… and… and so on!"

Cabin Boy did not seem impressed by my brief soliloquy.

I cooked a hearty breakfast to get a good start on a long day and night of sailing. While fetching something from the fo'c's'le, I banged my right shin. This re-awoke the throbbing monster in my leg, which gave me a double dose of what-for, before returning to its lair. By that time, my forehead was wreathed in sweat and I was gasping for breath. I decided to call Helena.

"You need to get that looked at," she said, rather firmly.

"But I need to make some progress," I said, sounding petulant, even to myself.

"Don't worry so much about the schedule," she said. "Do what you need to do to take care of yourself. This trip is supposed to be fun."

She was obviously right, so I returned, briefly, to the world of marinas and cabs, credit cards and pale green waiting rooms.

"Staph infection," was the brisk diagnosis of a doctor at the Bradenton hospital.

"Antibiotic," was the prescribed remedy. "And keep that leg elevated for a few days."

"Ha-ha," I said, meaning to set sail that very afternoon to catch that north wind.

But by the time I hobbled back to the excellent Regatta Pointe Marina, where I'd docked the *Blue Moon* for the day, I was exhausted and sick. I wrestled with myself for a half-hour and then threw in the towel and admitted that maybe it wouldn't hurt to rest for just one night.

* * *

Three days later, at the crack of dawn, I was motoring up the Manatee River towards Tampa Bay.

The antibiotic and three days of rest had worked their magic. The swelling had gone down, the pain had disappeared, and the fever that had clouded my mood and judgement had lifted. I was back to my old self and ready to tackle a new challenge.

I hadn't spent all three days lounging in my bunk. The dock master at the marina had taken pity on me and given me free run of all the facilities. I'd taken a dozen hot showers and caught up on my laundry in the marina's self-service laundromat.

While I was folding a batch of warm, fluffy towels, I struck up a conversation with an obviously well-off cruising couple in the early stages of their early retirement. They had just come up the ICW, from Ft. Meyers, and as usual, I was hungry for 'local knowledge'.

"Of course you can do it!" said Jeanne, in response to my question about the feasibility of tackling the ICW in a small sailboat.

"There's nothing to it," said her husband, Mike. "It's like driving down the freeway. You just gotta stay between the buoys. Any idiot can do it."

"There are lots of bridges to deal with," said Jeanne, a bit more sympathetically.

"There's nothing to them," insisted Mike. "You call the bridge tender on Channel 9 and tell him to open the bridge for you. Easy."

"Some bridges only open on the hour or half-hour," said Jeanne.

"Of course you want to *time* them right," said Mike, as if this nuance should have been self-evident, even to a sailboater. "Pain in the ass to miss an opening by a few minutes."

"And there are some shoals you have to watch out for," said Jean.

"Just keep an eye on the depth sounder," said Mike.

"We almost went aground right in the middle of the channel, coming up."

"The depth sounder gives you plenty of warning. Only an idiot could run aground in the ICW."

"I don't actually have an electronic depth sounder," I said. "Just a lead line."

Mike didn't seem able to process that information. He screwed up his face for a moment, trying to absorb this 19th century fact, then shook his head and moved on.

"Just keep your depth sounder pinging and you'll do fine," he said.

Jeanne looked at us both doubtfully for a moment, as women do sometimes, when listening to men 'talk'. Then she looked me in the eye and said: "You can do it!"

During my three day convalescence, I'd had plenty of time to think about what lay ahead. If I was going to tackle the Okeechobee—a 154 mile canal with lots of bridges, lots of locks, and no escape—then I needed to make sure the *Blue Moon* and I were up to the challenge. The best way to test us, and gain some useful experience, was to try a stretch of the ICW.

Thus, at the mouth of the Manatee River, where it opened up into Tampa Bay, instead of heading out into the beaconing Gulf, I turned south into Anna Maria Sound, into the man-made channel that was the Intracoastal Waterway. The Anna Maria Island bascule bridge was about three miles downstream. Just the thought of that formidable obstacle set my butterflies fluttering, but I ignored them. If bridges and other challenges on the ICW proved too much, I could escape into the Gulf through any number of passes, but I was determined to give it a two-day trial, at least.

"Just take it one step at a time," I told *Cabin Boy*.

What is a bascule bridge, anyway? 'Bascule' is the French word for seesaw and balance, and bascule bridges work much like a seesaw. The weight of the span or 'leaf' is balanced by counterweights below the deck, allowing the leaf to swing up with minimal effort. The Anna Maria bridge was a double-leaf bridge, meaning that it had two lifting spans, but single-leaf bridges are also common.

All this I'd read on Wikipedia the night before. I made sure my hand-held VHF radio was charged, but I'd never used it before.

I'd never needed a VHF on Long Island Sound (who was there to talk to?), and hadn't needed it in Florida, yet, either. I assumed it worked, since it was practically brand new, but what if it didn't?

In that case, I had a fog horn standing by. Supposedly, a long blast followed by a short blast meant "open the bridge, please!" in bridge-tender lingo, but communicating by horn sounded positively Edwardian to me. It was hard to believe that a 21st century bridge tender would understand such low-tech signals.

We cruised around a wide bend in the ICW. The bridge hove into view. It looked like a steel and concrete machine specifically designed to dismast and sink wooden sailboats. We were still a mile away, but I figured it was better to call early, than late. I picked up the VHF, made sure it was on channel 9, and hesitantly thumbed the push-to-talk button.

"Ummm…. Anna Maria Bridge, this is the sailboat *Blue Moon* requesting an opening, please."

Squelch!

That, supposedly, was the correct way to ask for an opening. I'd practiced the phrase about 100 times in the last few hours.

No answer.

I waited.

Dead silence.

I took a deep breath and repeated my call.

"Anna Maria Bridge, this is the *Blue Moon* requesting an opening?"

Squelch!

Much to my delight, I heard an answer: "*Blue Moon* this is the Anna Maria Bridge… Ummm… where are you, *Blue Moon*? We don't have you in sight."

"Sorry… I'm north of you… just past the #59 buoy… first time I've ever done this… not quite sure…"

"*Blue Moon*, I'm still not seeing you… oh, wait… are you the small sailboat way up the channel?"

"Probably…" I looked around. "Yes, I'm the only one up here that I can see."

"*Blue Moon*, you're a bit far away," he said in a deadpan voice.

"Come on down and I'll open for you when you get a little closer."

"Roger, thanks."

So we motored down towards the bridge. As we got closer, I kept expecting the bridge to open, but it seemed the bridge tender had forgotten about us. When we were 300 yards off, I decided we were close enough. There was no wind, but the current was sweeping down the ICW towards the bridge. If my motor stalled, it would be a mad scramble to get the anchor down before we were swept under the span and dismasted.

There were two large sailboats on the other side of the bridge by now, obviously waiting for the bridge to open. I put my engine in neutral and we drifted down towards the bridge with. *Why didn't he open?*

The seconds ticked by as we drifted closer and closer to the bridge.

"We are getting too darn close," I said to *Cabin Boy*, as if he could do anything about it.

I was just about to put the tiller over and turn around, when the bridge tender let off a long, loud blast of his horn.

"That means the bridge is about to open!" I told *Cabin Boy*.

With bells ringing, the crossing gates on the bridge went down, stopping automobile traffic. Then two 'leafs' seemed to separate in the center, and slowly lift.

"Wow, we're about to go through our first bridge," I said. "Where's my camera?"

I grabbed the camera, flicked it on, and took a photo of the bridge with the first sailboat coming through from the other side.

"Wow, this is great!"

Then I noticed how close the other sailboats had been to the bridge when it opened. We were still much farther away. They would both be through soon, and I was fooling around taking pictures.

"*Blast!*"

I stowed the camera, threw the engine into gear, and gave it half throttle. We started moving towards the bridge as the second sailboat cleared it. The bridge was now waiting for us, and—as I eyed the long line of cars waiting on the bridge roadway—we still seemed an awfully long way away.

"*Blue Moon* this is the Anna Maria Bridge. Can you speed it up please?"

I nodded at the window high up on the bridge, and waved my hand, too busy to fool with the radio. I twisted the throttle and gave the engine full power.

"We just need to get under the bridge," I said to the engine. "Just behave for once. You can do it!"

And for a while, it looked like it might just 'do it', but at the critical moment, when we were about to pass between the massive concrete pillars of the bridge, where the current started to twist and boil, the engine stalled.

The bridge loomed over us. The *Blue Moon* turned slightly askew in the current. The bridge tender looked down at us from his little window, high above. His face was impassive. He obviously didn't care if we lived or died, as long as he could close his bridge. *Pass through, or get crushed and dismasted. It's all the same to me*, his face said.

I turned, prayed, and pulled the starter cord. The awful outboard started on the first pull. We had headway. I straightened out our course, and kept the throttle at quarter-speed.

"Let him wait," I said.

The buzz of my little engine echoed off the bridge spans. The current turned and twisted under us. Little gusts of wind blew at strange angles out of the interlaced ironwork. And then we were through.

I looked up towards the bridge tender and gave him a wave of thanks.

He looked down on us without expression and then shook his head, as if he'd never seen anything so pitiful. Five loud blasts sounded from overhead, and the bridge started to close.

"That was pretty bad, eh?" I asked *Cabin Boy*.

As usual, he didn't disagree.

CHAPTER 10

FOUL WIND, FAIR CITY

What fates impose, that men must needs abide;
It boots not to resist both wind and tide.
— Shakespeare (Henry VI)

With my heart back to normal operating speed, I proceeded down the Intracoastal Waterway. In my imagination, the ICW was a 2,000 mile long canal dug by supermen in the Age of Building, when no project seemed too large for our mighty nation. So I was surprised to find an ICW that looked like a wild, saltwater river. It was—when one wasn't threatened with immediate extinction by mechanical means—quite beautiful. We had finally reached the part of Florida where the water is that tropical combination of blue and green that frozen northerners are willing to pay cold cash to see. As if to welcome us to paradise, a pair of dolphins attached themselves to our bow wake for a time—diving and twisting and leaping out of the water, playing with each other and with the steady *Blue Moon*, who they must have regarded as a larger, less playful cousin.

Balmy weather, dolphins, boats stuffed with bikini-clad girls—what more could you ask for? It was the perfect day, and I was going to enjoy it to the full.

A little while later, we transited a second bascule bridge without quite as much drama as the first. This time, I motored close to the bridge before it opened, kept the throttle in the non-stalling range, and slowly but steadily motored between the spans without earning a baleful look from the bridge tender. I did not, however, get a photo of that bridge—or any other bridge for many a long mile.

Without headwinds or waves to slow us down, we made a steady four knots south. If we maintained that pace for eight hours a day we'd be home in, oh, two months. Hmmm. I wondered if I could do ten hours a day?

By and by, it got on towards lunch time and the sun—set in a metallic blue sky—was hot. Offshore, the *Blue Moon* could sail herself while I made lunch down below, but self-steering only worked while sailing. The ICW was so narrow, I couldn't even dive below for a drink. Without my hand on the tiller, the *Blue Moon* would have run aground outside the channel in seconds. We'd have to stop and anchor for lunch.

I studied the chart in my lap and soon found a likely looking lunch spot on the far side of Jewfish Key, just ahead. Out of the corner of my eye, I noticed a feathery tendril of smoke curling out of the engine. I listened to the engine noise, alert to any faltering, but it ran smooth and steady. I eyed the thin grey wisp hanging over our wake.

"Not enough to worry about," I assured *Cabin Boy*. "Just something to keep an eye on."

But by the time we reached the near side of Jewfish Key, the *Blue Moon* looked like she was powered by a coal-fired steam engine. Greasy black smoke trailed in our wake. Water skiers, zig-zagging behind us, coughed, wheezed, and tumbled head-over-heels. Blondes turned jet-black. Dolphins headed for deeper water. The engine cowling was hot to the touch, but there was no place to stop. On either side of the channel, the water quickly shoaled. We had to make it to the anchorage.

I cut the throttle to dead slow. *Keep going, baby!* This was optimism gone wild, but somehow we had to make it. Jewfish Key slid slowly by. Men in passing boats shook their fists at me. Children cried. But I ignored them all. We were almost there! I could see the south end of the island. A channel split off to the right. We were going to make it.

I turned into the anchorage, pointed the *Blue Moon's* bow towards an empty spot, cut the engine, and ran forward to drop the anchor.

As the anchor hit bottom and the smoke cleared, I sat on my heels. We'd made it—barely—but clearly the engine had failed the ICW's first test: it wasn't up to a whole day's run. Something had to be done.

* * *

After a cold drink, a light lunch, and a long think, I called my Uncle Marty.

If anyone was to blame for my building and sailing adventures, it was my Uncle Marty, so it seemed fair to drag him into it. He'd trained as a sailmaker in post-war Germany, emigrated to the US around 1960, married my mother's sister, and hooked my land-lubber father (and thus me) on sailing. Even in his seventies, he still sailed the Newport to Bermuda race every other year. He was a vast well of practical experience and had been following my misadventures through the Internet, so he was generally acquainted with my engine problems. I caught him up on the latest details.

"You need to get that engine fixed," he said. He still had a slight German accent. "I don't suppose you know anything about outboards?"

"Not a lot," I hedged.

"Just enough to start it, in other words," he said. "You need to find a good mechanic who works on that type of engine. What make is it?"

"I wish I knew. The cover is bleached white, with no name on it. The only name I can find is marked on the motor itself, under the cover: Bombardier."

"Never heard of them."

"I did a little research. They're a Canadian company that makes both Evinrude and Johnson outboards. I think this must be a Johnson because of the cream color. That's my best guess, anyway."

"So you need to find a Johnson mechanic. Certified. Someone who knows what they are doing."

"I hate to stop again," I said.

"If you are going to have an engine on a boat, it needs to be reliable. Something that won't stall just when you need it most."

"You sound like Helena."

"That's because she's right," he said. "Stop and get it fixed. By a professional."

Did I mention Marty is German?

So I pulled out my mobile phone and started calling around for a certified Bombardier (or Johnson?) outboard mechanic. The typical call drawled along these lines:

"Can I help you?"

"Hello, do you work on Bombardier engines? Or maybe Johnsons?"

"Yeah…"

Sound of person talking to someone else, or perhaps TV droning in background.

"Hello? Hello, are you there?"

"Can I help you?"

"Do you work on Bombardier outboards? Johnsons?"

"Yeah… we work on everything…"

More sounds in background…

"Hello?"

"Can you hold on a minute?"

Extensive discussions in background… something about outboards, but mainly about lunch…

"Hello?" I said.

"Yeah… can you bring it in next Thursday?"

"No, I need someone who can work on it tomorrow. Today would be even better."

"Might be able to look at it next Thursday… or maybe Friday… probably need to order parts… can you hold on a minute?"

Click. Arghhhh! Next call.

Six or seven phone calls later, I found a marina that sounded like they knew what they were doing, and might even be able to fix something before the turn of the next decade. Even better, they were right off Sarasota Bay, only seven or eight miles south.

I put my hand on the engine cover, to see if it was still hot. It was. *Cabin Boy*, tugging at the end of his painter, looked sooty and nervous.

"Don't worry," I said. "We'll make it. Probably."

* * *

After an hour's break, the engine was cool enough to try again. As usual, it started with the first pull. I got the anchor up, then slowly motored out of the anchorage and back onto the ICW. It was three miles to Sarasota Bay. With the engine barely ticking over, we covered the distance in about an hour. Then the ICW spread out into the wide bay. I cut the engine and hoisted my sails. The wind was on the port quarter again; soon we were skimming over aqua blue, sun-dappled water. Another small sailboat hove into view and—as often happens when two sailboats meet—a race broke out. It was a beautiful day. For once, I forgot the long way to New York and just enjoyed the sailing. But all too soon, I had to wave goodbye to my friendly competitor and head for the bay's eastern shore, where Bowlees Creek and the marina awaited.

Bowlees Creek was named after a Seminole Indian chief renowned for his elusiveness: Billy Bowlegs. Unfortunately, the entrance to his eponymous creek was almost as hard to find as Billy had been. I crept towards the inlet—or where the inlet was supposed to be—but all I could see was a line of private markers leading straight towards some millionaire's front lawn. There, the channel seemed to end. Was the millionaire actually a pirate? Was the line of buoys a lure to trap unsuspecting sailors? Would we run aground on his manicured lawn and be boarded by pirates in pinstriped suits?

I considered this threat carefully, and then thought, "probably not." The chart said the channel made a sharp turn to the left, but strain as I did through my binoculars, I couldn't see it.

I didn't like to venture so close to an unknown shore, particularly one guarded by shoals six inches deep, as the chart warned, but I had no choice. I triple-checked the chart one more time, then slowly motored up the narrow channel. It wasn't until we were close enough to read the golfballs on the millionaire's lawn that I finally spotted the sharp turn.

Having made the turn, it was clear sailing to the marina. A dock boy waited to help. The dock was a very long 'T' dock, which is exactly what it sounds like: a long dock with a cross-bar at its end. The dock boy stood on the very end of this crossbar, waving. He pointed to the slip right beside him. I was relieved. It was a straight run in. Easy-peasy.

I slowed the *Blue Moon* to a crawl. I hadn't maneuvered into a slip since Steinhatchee. The approach couldn't have been easier, but my butterflies took flight. Thanks to her long keel, the *Blue Moon* maneuvered like a tank. I gripped the tiller, determined not to scrape her beautiful paint. My steering was precise; we entered the slip without a touch. I was so proud I forgot to put the engine in reverse.

The dock boy gamely grabbed the shrouds to stop us, but the *Blue Moon's* 8,000 pounds of momentum was too much for him. The young man skidded down the dock, yelling something about cutting the engine. At the last moment, I threw the outboard into neutral, threw a line over a dock cleat, and held on tight. We came to an abrupt halt just before ramming the main dock.

Note to self: practice boat handling skills.

After tying up, I tipped the dock boy for his courage (and silence), and marched down to the service office to get the slow gears of Florida commerce turning.

* * *

Parts *did* need to be ordered. They would take several days to arrive. I rented a car and went to visit my dear old mum on the east coast of Florida. A few days rest did wonders for my still sore leg, and when I returned to Sarasota, I was healed, rested, and raring to go.

While tied up to the dock, *Cabin Boy's* bottom had grown a remarkable crop of slime and weed. Somehow I'd never gotten around to painting his bottom with anti-fouling paint. That hadn't been a problem as long as we were moving every day. But sitting in the warm water of Sarasota Bay had given tiny sea critters the op-

The Blue Moon in Saratoga Bay

portunity they'd been waiting for: the slime was a half-inch thick.

No matter. I hauled poor *Cabin Boy* onto the dock and gave his bottom a good scrubbing. It was soon as good as new.

I also gave the *Blue Moon*'s deck a coat of non-skid paint. Back in Steinhatchee, Helena and I had naively painted her deck with a hard, oil-based paint. We'd ooo-ed and ahh-ed over the shiny, smooth surface, but a shiny, smooth surface is not what you want when the deck is tilted at forty-five degrees and slick with sea-spray. Actually, it was a dangerous blunder caused by my profound lack of knowledge and experience. I was lucky to escape with a few dozen bruises.

To fix this mistake, I bought a small bag of ground pumice—a fine, glassy sand made from volcanic rock—and mixed it in with the paint. After rolling this mixture on and letting it dry, the deck was transformed into an incredibly grippy surface. My boat shoes felt like they were glued to the deck with every step. Like velcro.

"That's much better," I told *Cabin Boy*.

I also added stick-on non-skid strips to my companionway steps. Anything to cut down on slipping and shin-banging.

Meanwhile, the marina's service department identified the engine as a Johnson, rebuilt the carburetor, repaired the cooling system, and generally depleted my bank account. But when reinstalled on the *Blue Moon*'s transom, the engine purred like a contented cat.

And just in time. The weather had changed for the worse. The spring northerlies, which had pushed us south ever since leaving Steinhatchee, had been replaced by a strong southerly wind (that means the wind was blowing from the south.) The weather radio reported four-to-six foot seas on the Gulf. A small boat like the *Blue Moon* would make very slow progress beating into wind and seas like that, so the only realistic option was to motor south through the ICW. I'd fixed my engine just in time.

When I finally backed out of the slip one fine morning (*before* the dock boy came on duty), it was a great relief to hear the engine running smoothly. Out on Sarasota Bay, I ran it at full throttle for a quarter hour as a test, and all seemed well.

Nevertheless, I didn't want to push it. The *Blue Moon* was a heavy load for the old 6 hp motor. If it was to last all the way home, I'd have to baby it. So, testing complete, I killed the engine, hoisted sail, and spent the rest of the morning tacking down the bay. I would motor when I had to, and sail when I could. That was the best I could do for my poor old engine.

During the next couple days, we followed the ICW through a series of beautiful, but relatively narrow bays: Robert Bay, Little Sarasota Bay, Dryman Bay, and Blackburn Bay. When we finally anchored off Don Pedro Island, I rowed ashore and hiked across the island to the white sand beach, to have a look at the Gulf of Mexico. The wind still roared from the south and the waves marched north like ranks of huge, white-hatted soldiers, ready to crush anything in their path.

Sailing in sheltered ICW had been easy, but tomorrow we'd have to face twenty-five miles of open water as the ICW passed through Gasparilla Sound, Charlotte Harbor, and the famously treacherous Pine Island Sound. If the wind continued to blow from the south, it would be a rough passage. I intended to get an early start.

* * *

The next morning, we set off as soon as I could make out the buoys on the ICW. The relentless southerlies had departed during the night. The *Blue Moon* motored over glassy black water. A half-hour later, as coffee pots gurgled in the still-dark homes that lined the shore, we reached the swing bridge dividing Placida Harbor from Gasparilla Sound. At our first radio call, bells on the bridge rang. One or two cars, their headlights still on, slowed to a stop at the railroad-style gates. The bridge swung open and we motored through like old pros.

Grey mist hid the far end of the sound, four miles distant. There was room to sail, but no wind, so I kept the motor running at half speed. This was enough to keep us moving through the water at four knots. At that speed, we'd cover the twenty-four miles to the Sanibel Island anchorage in six hours. There, at the junction of the ICW and the Okeechobee Waterway, I'd have to choose between the shortcut and the Keys. I still felt torn between the two, but like the diner who can't choose until the waiter is standing at his elbow, I knew I had one more day to decide.

"I'll know the right thing to do when we get there," I assured a sleepy *Cabin Boy*, who was no help at all. He wanted to try *both* ways.

The sun peaked over the horizon, suddenly splashing color on the scene. A light southerly wind picked up, rippling the water ahead into patches of sapphire and tourmaline. Low green islands dotted the sound and a band of islands nearly closed off its southern end. This was prime fishing country, and small fishing boats crisscrossed our path: families heading out to their favorite spots. Two dolphins jumped in tandem alongside the *Blue Moon*. I grabbed my camera, hoping they'd jump again, but they swam off towards an anchored fishing boat with several kids in orange life jackets aboard.

By then, the sun was fully up and with the sun came the south wind again, soft at first, then stronger. For once, the chop stayed light—six inch waves that merely lapped at the *Blue Moon's* bow. Nothing to slow us down. The ICW had grown on me by then. Jeanne was right, on the ICW there was always something to look at, we always had company, and so far—knock on wood—we'd made faster progress than we would have made offshore. An hour later, we approached the pass between Jack Point and Devil Fish Key. I could see the deep and wide-open Charlotte Harbor beyond. The water looked rougher, but nothing the *Blue Moon* couldn't handle. Just four miles of open water, and then we'd be in amongst the many islands off Cayo Costa.

As soon as we passed into Charlotte Harbor, I knew it wouldn't be so easy, after all. The chop—just six to twelve inches—seemed to slow us down immediately. The wind felt heavier. I checked the GPS and watched our speed over the ground drop from four to three knots.

Should I use more power? I wondered. No. Even at three knots, we'd be across the harbor in a reasonable amount of time. I wasn't in a hurry. It was more important to baby the engine. Just sit back, relax, and enjoy the scenery.

I tried. I really did. In particular, I admired the trees on Gasparilla Island, a thousand yards off to starboard. I admired how the tops of the trees bent north at a jaunty forty-five degree angle. No doubt which way the wind was blowing today.

A little while later, I admired them again. And then again. The *same* trees. They crawled by so slowly. I glanced at my GPS. Inexplicably, we'd slowed to two knots. I looked at my engine. Listened to it. It seemed to be running as well as it had all morning. A quiet, steady buzz. No smoke, no heat. What was wrong?

I increased the throttle to ¾ speed. That helped a bit. We moved past the grove of bent trees, but soon slowed again.

By now, my eyes were glued to my GPS. There was a strange fascination in watching the speed drop from 2.5, to 2, to 1.5 knots. What was going on? I risked full throttle for a few moments, but it didn't seem to help. Our speed dropped to 1 knot. At that speed, it would take three hours to cross Charlotte Harbor, including an hour crossing the busy Boca Grande inlet, with monster fishing boats roaring in and out, and the possibility of meeting a container ship or two.

It didn't make sense. The wind wasn't blowing that hard. The waves were less than a foot. The engine was running great. So why weren't we moving?

I was stumped. I didn't have an answer. And that made me very nervous.

This was the moment my ignorance of inland waterways fully revealed itself. Weeks later, I would discover the answer to this mystery in an obscure children's book, but at the time I was mystified, baffled, and not a little scared. If my wits and confidence had not been so shaken, I might have thought to hoist my sails. There was plenty of room to sail in Charlotte Harbor. We would have had a merry time tacking to windward, but the thought never occurred to me. Instead, I fixated on that sinking GPS number, and looked for a way out.

A line of buoys lead off to starboard, towards the island. I hurriedly consulted my chart. The buoys led to Boca Grande Harbor. Inside, was a small anchorage. That line of buoys beckoned to me as the Sirens did to Ulysses. After a moment's hesitation, I gave up the fight, and followed them in. There was the usual half-mile long line of buoys leading up to the inlet, then we entered the tiny outer harbor. The wind dropped immediately. The relief I felt was palpable.

We continued to follow the channel around to the right. The channel narrowed sharply just ahead. Was there room to fit through? Was the channel deep enough for the *Blue Moon*? It didn't look like it, and the chart didn't give enough detail to know for sure. Would I have to turn around and head back out?

Just then, a forty foot sailboat emerged from the channel. If it was big enough for her, it was big enough for the *Blue Moon*. I motored ahead. The channel was so narrow, I could have pole-vaulted across it, but once through, we entered an idyllic tropical anchorage surrounded by palm trees and scented by flowers. The protected cove was flat as a millpond, and though the wind continued to blow overhead, there was just a gentle breeze in the anchorage.

Twenty or more yachts lined the east side of the anchorage. They were moored Mediterranean style—lined up, as if in assigned parking spaces, with their sterns tied to a mangrove tree and an anchor off the bow. I had no idea how to anchor that way, but I wasn't going to let that stop me.

I found an empty spot, and dropped my anchor in front of it. That left the *Blue Moon* anchored in the center of the cove. I tied one end of a long line to a stern cleat, and climbed into *Cabin Boy* with the other end. I rowed into the empty parking spot, tied the line to a mangrove root, and rowed back.

By easing out the anchor line, and hauling in the stern line, I gradually 'warped' the *Blue Moon* into position, alongside her bigger, plastic sisters.

A neighbor, sitting in his cockpit under a dark awning, must have been watching.

"Neatly done," he said.

"Thank you!" I said. "First time!"

He cracked open a beer and held it out across the six feet of water separating our boats. I grabbed my boat hook and pulled us close enough to grab the beer.

"Welcome to paradise," he said.

"Thanks!"

Fate had landed us in the little village of Boca Grande, which turned out to be one of the most beautiful towns we visited on the whole voyage. Over the next two days, while waiting for the miserable south wind to blow itself out, I roamed all over the old village, which seemed suspended in an earlier age. I walked its Main Street, which had that old Florida feel that is so hard to find now. I adopted a favorite bar, which in true tropical style was open to the air and cooled by fans. No one in the village was in a hurry. No annoying waiter bothered me while I sat for hours, reading over a single beer. I swam off a white-sand beach, watched a free movie in the town hall, and visited and was visited by many of the other cruisers. If I still didn't know how King Neptune had stopped me, I at least knew why—it would have been a shame to miss that wonderfully backwards, island village.

But finally, the wind stopped blowing. I said good-bye to my new friends, worked my way out of the narrow harbor, and set sail south. That evening, after a long day's work, we sailed into the Glover Bight, at the very mouth of the Okeechobee Waterway.

I'd made up my mind: we'd take the shortcut across Florida.

CHAPTER 11

ON THE OKEECHOBEE

*Sometimes, if you stand on the bottom rail of a bridge and
lean over to watch the river slipping slowly away beneath you,
you will suddenly know everything there is to be known.*
— *Winnie the Pooh, (A. A. Milne)*

For days, people had been telling me that marinas were rare on
the Okeechobee. I found that hard to believe, but I was taking no
chances. The thought of running out of gas in the middle of the
Florida 'jungle', with alligators and piranha circling *Cabin Boy* as I
rowed to the nearest filling station, was just too unnerving. So the
next morning, I rowed to the marina at Glover Bight and filled my
two five-gallon gas cans. With those and the five gallons in the
main tank, we had enough gas to motor half-way across Florida.
Surely we'd find at least one marina along the way.

After topping up, we set sail and headed up the Caloosahatchee
River. I hoped to cross Florida in five days: two days to reach Lake
Okeechobee, one day to cross the lake (seventh largest in the US),
and two more to reach the Atlantic coast. The guide books showed
that there were only a few anchorages on the Waterway. I'd have to
plan each day carefully to ensure we had our anchor down before
sundown. No one traveled on the Waterway after nightfall: it was
just too dark.

For the first day's run, I planned to anchor just beyond the major obstacle of the day: the cavernous Franklin Lock. This was the
first lock I'd ever encountered, and my butterflies rose in panic just
thinking about it. I had no idea what I was was getting into, but as-

suming we weren't crushed in the enormous lock gates, or sucked down a whirlpool, we should have enough time to 'lock through' and reach the anchorage before dark, as long as we could maintain a steady four knots for most of the day.

A light breeze blew on our port quarter, but the wind wasn't strong enough to maintain the needed four knots, so I kept the engine going, too. 'Motor sailing', as my Uncle Marty called it. For thirty years I'd sailed or motored, but for some reason I'd never thought of sailing with the engine running. He had urged me to give it a try, so I was. Any help the sails provided would be that much less strain on the engine. More importantly, the sails helped shade the cockpit—the sun was already hot and the shade cast by the sails made it bearable.

For the first fifteen miles, we wound our way through the cities of Cape Coral and Ft. Myers: beach front homes, high-rises, and white plastic motor boats. It was all neat and tidy, but I was tired of looking at beautiful coastal Florida. I was ready for a change of scenery; ready for *inland* Florida, with its swamps, alligators, and cowboys.

Yes, cowboys. A long time ago, Lake Okeechobee was the heart of the Everglades—a trackless swamp that covered most of south Florida—and was home to the Calusa Indians who gave their name to the river we were on. Then Hamilton Disston—handsaw baron, founder of Tarpon Springs—had his way with this part of Florida, too. In 1881, he sailed a dredge to Ft. Myers (which really *was* a fort, back then) and started digging a canal from the Caloosahatchee River to Lake Okeechobee.

Disston's plan was to drain the swamp and turn the reclaimed land into lucrative cattle farms. Eventually, this plan succeeded, and today much of the land on either side of the Waterway is not swamp at all, but hot, dusty land, with plenty of cowboys. Or so I'd read. How many cowboys I'd actually see from the deck of the *Blue Moon*, I did not know, but I was eager to find out.

After a few hours sailing, the leafy banks of the river—over a mile apart at Ft. Myers—drew closer together, and the signs of civilization petered away. People in Florida like to live within easy

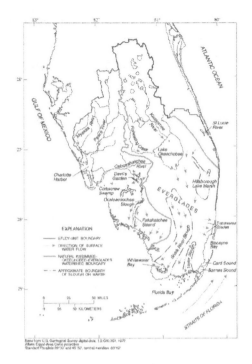

*Flow of water before development
of the Everglades.
U.S. Geological Survey*

driving distance of the coast, so the further inland you go, the fewer signs of people. We sailed past the aptly named Beautiful Island and then under a towering bridge. The bridge was like a gateway into a different world. Once through, we entered a smaller, more primeval world of silence, oppressive heat, brown water, tropical trees, and lots and lots of birds.

I didn't know much about birds, but I'd packed a bird book for the trip. So I whiled away the long, hot morning identifying ospreys, herons, and snowy egrets. At one point, something unusually large circled high overhead. Even with binoculars it was hard to see its markings, but I could see it was some sort of bird of prey. Could it be an eagle? My heart beat faster as it swooped down into the trees where I lost sight of it, but moments later it flew low over the waterway, clutching something small and writhing in its claws.

By midday, we'd lost the last trace of wind. The sun was a

bonfire, not 92 million miles away, but seemingly just overhead. It poured heat down on us, like flame from a bucket. I'd become pretty tolerant of the sun by then, but my wide-brimmed hat, long-sleeve white shirt, and sunblock just weren't cutting it. The sails weren't pulling, and the shade they provided was minimal, so I took them down and rigged an awning that Helena had sewn for just this purpose. It was small—small enough to use even while sailing—but the pool of shade it threw was lifesaving. Literally.

The day rolled slowly by. The banks of the river were overgrown with trees and sinuous vines. Some of the old trees were enormous, standing on bare roots that stepped out into the water. Great turtles sunned themselves on these roots, but they were shy. I couldn't get close enough for a good photo. One-by one, they dropped into the water as we approached.

Then I spotted my first alligator—his back a knobby ridge just above the surface of the water—and he spotted me too. Unlike the turtles, he did not dive as we passed, but silently stared back, as if he knew I didn't belong there.

"I was here when the dinosaurs ruled the great swamp," those eyes seemed to say. "And I'll be here when *your* kind is long gone."

There were no other boats. We had the whole silent, lonely river to ourselves. After a long while, we came to a bascule bridge, looking like a rusty remnant of a lost civilization. It had twenty-seven feet of vertical clearance, which might have been just high enough for the *Blue Moon* to pass under, but I was taking no chances and waited for the bridge tender to raise the leaves. He waved from his window, high above the muddy water, as if he was as happy to see another human being as I was. It was good to wave back, but once through the bridge, my thoughts turned to the next big challenge, a very concrete symbol of civilization: the Franklin Lock and Dam.

The Franklin Lock and Dam cost $3.8 million dollars when it was constructed in 1965. Its purpose was flood control, water control, and the prevention of salt-water intrusion into the Everglades. The lock chamber was 56 feet wide, 400 feet long, and 14 • feet high.

All this I got from Wikipedia, and none of it told me what I really wanted to know, which was, "How the heck do I get through it?"

I'd never gone through a lock before. I was not totally unprepared, of course: I'd picked other people's brains. I knew I must wait until the green light came on; I knew I must tie up on the starboard side, using long lines that could reach up to the lip of the lock; I knew that I must tend these lines, letting them out as we descended, and pulling them in as we rose, to stay close to the lock wall and out of the swirling vortex that could swallow a small boat whole.

Okay, I made that last part up, but the vortexes were real, as was my fear of them. All I really knew was that I didn't know what I was getting into. I wished I had another pair of hands.

An hour later, when we rounded the last bend and the enormous lock gates hove into view, my nerves turned to outright panic.

I called the lock tender on the radio and—keeping my voice steady—told him I wanted to 'lock through'. That's the nautical term for passing through the lock. He told me there was a westbound boat in the lock and I would have to wait for the lock gates to open and for the boat to pass out. The green light would illuminate when it was safe for me to enter.

Okay, I thought, that didn't sound too difficult. While I waited, I took down the awning. All day, it had provided a much needed patch of shade in the blazing tropical heat, but now I was afraid it would be in the way. By the time the lock gates opened ten minutes later, I was too nervous to worry about the heat. I was still not confident about handling the *Blue Moon* under power in confined spaces. When the green light finally came on, I slowly motored into the vast concrete and steel chamber, and edged towards the starboard wall, right under a leathery-looking lock tender who calmly took my lines and waited for me to put fenders between the rough concrete wall and the *Blue Moon*'s thin layer of paint.

Behind us, the heavy steel lock doors slowly closed, then the ones ahead began to open. The two doors opened about a foot. A six foot high waterfall began to pour through the gap between the doors. The cascade sent waves spilling through the lock, rocking the *Blue Moon*, and sending me scrambling from fore to aft, adjusting the lines.

But my eyes were drawn back to that waterfall.

"What is the water flowing over?" I asked myself. Was there a shelf of rock, right outside the lock? That didn't make sense.

Then it hit me. The water wasn't flowing over anything. The water outside the lock doors was just six feet higher than the water inside the lock. The brown wall of water I was looking at was the body of the river itself.

For some reason, I found this astonishing. I'd never seen anything like it. I left the lines for a moment, grabbed my camera, and took pictures, hoping that—for once—they would capture the wonder of the scene.

Soon, the lock was full of water. The level of the water inside the lock was the same as outside and the doors swung the rest of the way open. Since we were the only boat in the lock, I waited for the swirling vortexes to subside, then took in our lines, and slowly motored out of the lock, much relieved.

"That wasn't so bad," I told *Cabin Boy.*

He wasn't convinced. He hadn't been tied to the wall and had taken a few nasty bumps and scrapes. Next time, I'd tie him securely alongside the *Blue Moon* where he'd be out of danger.

The sun was low in the sky by then: blood red, steaming, and enormous. The Hickey Creek anchorage was only a mile upriver, to port, i.e., on the left side of the waterway. Motoring at four knots, we covered that mile in fifteen minutes, but I couldn't see anything that looked like a creek. I went a half-mile further, then decided I must have missed it. I turned the boat around and slowly motored back towards the dam. The creek wasn't small. It looped behind an island. According to the cruising guide, it was supposed to be big enough to hold a number of boats. How could it have just disappeared?

The sun was going down. It would soon be too dark to travel on the unlit waterway. I had to find the anchorage soon, but it just wasn't there. Exasperated, I turned around and headed back east. I'd look one more time, then give up and head for a marina

The 'waterfall' inside the Franklin Lock.

which the guide book said was another mile down the waterway. I expected to see the creek any minute, but it never materialized. No creek, not even a hint of an opening in the solid wall of trees. The Hickey Creek was just gone.

I called the marina on the VHF radio and asked if there was room in the inn. There was. I hated to spend money on marinas, but as we approached the nearly dark dock, I spotted an illuminated swimming pool through the trees that looked deliciously cool, and thought, "Oh, what the hell."

The pool was even better to swim in than it looked. As I floated on my back in that marvelously cool, blue water, with the stars blinking overhead, I was glad I hadn't found that blasted lost creek, where I would have spent a miserable night swatting mosquitoes. It wasn't until I was writing this chapter, studying my old water-stained chart, that I noticed Hickey Creek was still there, but on the *starboard* side of the waterway. I must have sailed past it three times, looking the wrong way.

And that's how easy it is to get lost.

* * *

Next morning, while the air was still cool and fresh, I checked out the rest of the marina. The place was unique. Whereas most marinas are forgettable collections of sun-bleached docks, with even more forgettable shoreside 'facilities', this was more like a campground for boats.

The 'harbor' was actually a loop cut into the southern bank of the Waterway. Individual wooden piers—one dock for each boat—lined the loop's southern shore. Each dock had its own flower garden, water, and electricity. There were acres of wooded grounds to stroll through and small rustic cabins that housed a laundry, showers, and bathrooms.

But the best part were the trees. They were tall enough to shade the *Blue Moon* on her dock, which was as close to bliss as I could imagine. I'd become a connoisseur of shade. We were almost never close enough to shore to catch any. We were always out there, in the direct sun, which was great for sun bathing, but I was way past sun bathing. 'Shade bathing' was what I was into now. Shade bathing was cool.

After stretching my legs with a walk through the trees, I made some breakfast and ate it on the bank-side picnic table, reading the newspaper I'd found on my dock. Another one of the Harbor's homey touches.

I lingered as long as possible over my breakfast and paper, but then it was time to go. I had to be in Moore Haven, on the western edge of Lake Okeechobee, by dark. It was a long way, and there were several bridges and the Ortona Lock to contend with along the way.

As soon as we motored out of the shady harbor and into the main channel of the Waterway, I felt the power of the sun again. I knew it must be an illusion, but it seemed like I could feel the pressure of millions of photon hitting me in the chest, like water from a fire hose. 'How do people live here in the summer?' I wondered. It was only May. What would it be like in July or August? I was glad I wouldn't be around to find out. I'd be far north by then. Maybe even home.

Home. I pulled out my phone and checked for a signal. Nothing. I sighed.

Cell phone coverage comes and goes when you're on a boat. It's hard to predict. Sometimes you can be anchored right off a fair-sized town and have no coverage at all. Another time, I had four bars several miles offshore. You never knew. But I usually had a good signal at least once a day so I could call Helena to check in and to pass the time. It could get boring, motoring hour after hour. Talking to Helena was never boring.

The sun rose higher and higher in the sky as we penetrated deeper and deeper into the Florida swamps. The river had a Huck Finn feel to it. The trees were close at hand on either side; the water was brown and thick with sediment. We didn't see another boat all morning, just birds standing on long legs in the water, watching us with unblinking eyes. And 'gators. There were lots of them to see if you kept your eyes open. It made me think of Huck and Jim on their river...

> *... it was so still, and sounds come so far; and by and by you could see a streak on the water which you know by the look of the streak that there's a snag there in a swift current which breaks on it and makes that streak look that way; and you see the mist curl up off of the water, and the east reddens up, and the river, and you make out a log-cabin in the edge of the woods, away on the bank on t'other side of the river ... then the nice breeze springs up, and comes fanning you from over there, so cool and fresh and sweet to smell on account of the woods and the flowers ... and next you've got the full day, and everything smiling in the sun, and the song-birds just going it! — Mark Twain, The Adventures of Huckleberry Finn*

The sun rolled through the sky slowly. We passed through several flat and dusty towns, including La Belle—"the belle of the Caloosahatchee"—which was another town that Hamilton Disston had a hand in founding. Back in the 1890s, it was a tiny settle-

On the Okeechobee Waterway with awning rigged over cockpit.

ment straddling the banks of the river, populated by cattle drovers and trappers. Today, its waterfront looks 'revitalized'. A hundred years ago, it was probably a wild and exciting place to visit. Today, not so much. I kept going.

Past La Belle, the meandering river seemed to straighten out. We'd entered Disston's Caloosahatchee Canal, which connected the river to Lake Okeechobee. We started to see other boats, including a few big ones. In the late afternoon, we locked through the Ortona Lock without any drama. I was an old hand at locks by then.

After the lock, there were a few long, straight sections of the canal which—being so old—looked wild and untamed. Then, suddenly, the first leg of the Okeechobee was over. We were in Moore Haven and I was trying to find the town dock.

Town docks—where transient vessels can tie up for free or a reasonable fee—were my new favorite thing in the world. All waterfront towns should have them. Surely, 100 years ago, they all *did*. That was the very purpose of building towns on the water. But today, they are rare. Either the town turns its back on the water altogether, or the docks are handed over to commercial marinas, which generally charge yachty prices. So I was excited to be in Moore Haven—not for the town itself (which, according to the guide book was a sleepy village of 1,000 people and exactly one restaurant), but for its rare and precious town dock.

The 300 foot dock ran along the north side of the waterway. Only one boat was tied up, but it was a big one—one of those enormous powerboats that looked like destroyers when they bore down on the poor, little *Blue Moon*.

This one was more elegant than usual, with enough varnished wood to soften the harsh look of white plastic, but I was slightly put off by its opulence. I have nothing against rich people, per se, but the ones I'd met so far in Florida tended to be jerks.

"Ah well," I told *Cabin Boy*. "We don't mind sharing a dock with the King of Freedonia, do we?"

Cabin Boy didn't seem to mind, so we headed in towards the dock. As we did so, a fit looking, middle-aged man in dark golf shirt, khaki shorts, and boat shoes, stepped off the stern of the big motorboat, and walked down the dock to take our line.

"Thanks," I said when we got there, handing him the bow line. I stepped onto the dock with the stern line and we tied up the *Blue Moon* with a couple fenders out to keep her off the wooden dock.

"Great boats," the man said, admiring both the *Blue Moon* and *Cabin Boy*, although the *Blue Moon* was a bit of a shambles, with the cockpit full of easy-to-reach food, drink, charts, and other gear. "You build them yourself?"

I told him my story. With practice, I'd gotten the elevator version down to one minute, which was all most people wanted to hear. But this guy knew enough about boats to be genuinely interested, so we stood on the dock and talked for a half-hour about wooden boats and my 2,000 mile voyage home.

I finally realized we'd been talking about my little boats for a long time, when all most sailors want to talk about is their own boat. So I politely said: "That's quite a nice boat you've got there, yourself!"

"Oh, that's not mine. I'm just the captain. The owner is on-board. We passed you this afternoon and we both enjoyed seeing your boats. Don't see many wooden boats down here."

Ah... I remembered. There was one power boat that slowed down to pass me that afternoon. I remembered two heads, looking down from the bridge far above...

"Thanks for slowing down," I said. "Not everyone does."

"The owner wanted me to ask you aboard for dinner."

I was a bit surprised by this, but long distance cruisers have to be light on their feet when it comes to accepting invitations.

"Sure, that sounds great!"

"We'll give you time to register with the office across the road and clean up. Say an hour or so?"

"I'll be there," I said. "Thanks for the offer."

An hour later, I was showered and dressed in my best shore-going clothes, which were much the same as my sea-going clothes, only not caked with salt. I presented myself at the stern of the big powerboat, which towered overhead, and then wondered how one "knocks" on a boat to gain entrance. There was no front door, no door bell, just a small gangway crossing over to large, smoke-black windows.

Luckily, the captain must have been watching for me. He opened the sliding glass doors and welcomed me aboard. He led me into the main cabin and I was shocked, first by the air conditioning—which was set to McMurdo Station levels—and then by the decor, which was dark wood, deep carpeting, high ceilings, and even more luxurious than I expected.

The owner was there, a tall, lean, older man with a cool hand-shake and a warm smile, who lived in Washington, DC, but preferred to cruise on his boat. I thought he might be a well-known Senator. While I gushed a bit about the air conditioning—which truly *was* luxurious to someone who'd been traveling for two days across central Florida in a small boat—they pressed a large Scotch with plenty of ice into my hands, and sat me down on a plush, comfortable chair in the main salon.

"I hope you don't mind if we eat in here," said the owner. "We're pretty informal when it's just the two of us. I save the dining room for when my wife is aboard."

While the owner made conversation and drew out my whole story again, the captain served appetizers and then a man's meal of thick steaks, red potatoes, and buttered peas. They were indeed informal, eating off a low, varnished coffee table, but the food was served on real plates, with real silver, and we swiftly went through two bottles of rather good wine.

Over brandy and cigars, the owner and captain got down to brass tacks. Neither one of them liked my plan of sailing off-shore up the east coast.

"It's too dangerous," said the owner, shaking his head.

"Not that your boat couldn't make it," said the captain. "If her rigging and hull are sound, you could sail a boat like that around the world."

"You're the problem," said the owner.

The captain nodded. "If you had another crew member to stand watch, it might be different. But the ports on the east coast are too far apart. One man, sailing on his own, has to sleep sometimes."

"And there's too much shipping for that," said the owner.

"Far too much. Ships move fast. You spot a big container ship on the horizon, and the next thing you know, she's right on top of you."

"We're fast enough to stay out of their way, but you'd be a sitting duck, even if you were awake."

"I've got a radar reflector," I said. "I used it on the west coast of Florida a few times."

"Not good enough," said the captain. "Ship's radar is set up to see ships, not small boats. Chances are, you won't even show up on their radar until they're a few miles away. If the watchstander isn't alert, they won't even know they've run you down."

"Now, if you had an AIS transponder..." the owner said.

I didn't even know what that was. They explained it was an electronic system that told big ships where you were, and rang an alarm if you were on a collision course. That sounded great, but the

Blue Moon didn't have enough electricity to run gear like that for more than a couple hours—assuming I could afford one, which I couldn't.

"You should use the ICW," said the owner.

"Only sensible thing," said the captain.

"I'm not sure my engine is up to motoring all the way home," I said, doubtfully.

They didn't have a lot to say about that. The owner looked off into the distance, as if trying to remember—or imagine—what it would be like to be so poor you couldn't afford a decent outboard motor.

The captain just said, "You need to figure something out."

We finished our cigars and drinks on the fantail, under the stars, looking down at the *Blue Moon*.

"She's a beautiful little boat," said the owner, somewhat wistfully.

"Good luck," said the captain.

I thanked them, and walked back down the dock to my beautiful little boat, wobbling slightly.

I climbed aboard and sat in the cockpit for a few minutes to clear my head. *Cabin Boy* was tied up to the dock, well out of stem-banging reach.

"We got a lot to think about," I told him. "Tomorrow. We'll have plenty of time tomorrow."

As I went below, I could almost hear *Cabin Boy* talking to himself...

"Almost crushed in lock today! Crossing Lake Okeechobee tomorrow. Best day of my life!"

* * *

It was still dark when I climbed up on deck the next morning, but the big power boat was already gone and probably half-way to Georgia. I meant to be away by dawn, myself. Sundown was at 8:00 pm. By then, we needed to be in Port Mayaca, on the other side of the lake.

That was thirty-nine miles by my reckoning. We needed to

leave ASAP.

A half-hour later, we steamed through the open gates of the Moore Haven Lock into the Okeechobee rim canal, which circled the lake.

There were two routes from Moore Haven to Port Mayaca. Both had their issues.

The Lake Route was the shortest and most direct. This route exited the rim canal at Clewiston and headed northeast, straight across the lake to Port Mayaca. According to the guide book, this route was for fair weather, only. Because of the shallowness of the lake, any breeze over fifteen knots kicked up a heavy chop. If the wind exceeded twenty knots, cruisers were advised to stay in port and play a few more card games.

The Rim Route was longer but safer. It followed the rim canal all the way around the lake. This 'canal' was actually open to the lake for much of its length, but got some protection from a string of islands near the town of Pohokee. It was supposed to be well sheltered from easterly, northeasterly, and southeasterly blows; but when the wind blew from the west or northwest, it was time to break out the cards again, since waves from the lake swept right across the channel, and the lee shore was scary close.

The Rim Route was ten miles longer than the Lake Route. Neither route was navigable after dark.

As long as the wind was fair, I planned to take the more direct Lake Route. I was not too worried about a little 'chop'. I mean, it was a *lake*. How bad could it get? Anyway, I wouldn't need to make the decision until we reached Clewiston, which was twelve miles away.

Twelve long miles. The canal lead through marsh grass and cypress swamps. The water was thick with alligators. I was careful not to fall overboard. Small, flat-bottom fishing boats zoomed around, just to keep things lively. I sipped my coffee, nursed a small scotch and wine induced headache, and tried to stay out of their way.

At 11:00 am, we reached Clewiston. The village itself was hidden off to the right, behind a high grassy dyke. A hurricane lock—looking like a castle gate—penetrated the wall, giving boats access to the village harbor. Both lock gates were open, but I didn't see much as we passed by. Clewiston would remain a mystery.

I turned left, away from the Clewiston lock, into a channel that wound between islands of marsh grass out onto the lake. We were hemmed in by tall grass for about a mile, but then the channel ended and we were on the open lake itself. It took my breath away. It was not a lake, it was a sea. To the north, to the south, to the east, no shore was visible. Just unbroken water stretching clear to the horizon.

To be honest, it was a bit intimidating.

"What are we getting into this time?" I warily asked *Cabin Boy*.

He seemed to be following the *Blue Moon* a bit more closely than he normally did. But there was no wind, we had plenty of gas, and the engine seemed to be running well.

"Just buck up," I said. "It's only a matter of time. In five hours, we should be across. All we need is nerve."

For the next ten miles, we followed the channel buoys on a jagged course through shallows and shoals. Eventually, we passed a large floating platform with lights and antennas that marked the end of the channel. We were finally clear of the shoals, and could head straight across the lake for Port Mayaca, fourteen miles away.

Just a few hours. Easy-peasy.

Nevertheless, I left the floating platform behind reluctantly. The next buoy, half-way across the lake, was well over the horizon. There was no land in sight. The lake was only twelve feet deep, but it might as well have been 100 fathoms.

A light wind blew by then, but it blew from the northwest, right on the nose, as always. I worried about the strain on the engine. There was plenty of sailing room, but it was already 2:00 pm. I did some quick calculations in my head and decided there was no way we could tack all the way to Port Mayaca by dark. Only the engine could take us directly upwind fast enough.

I took a deep breath and pushed my anxiety down. There was no reason to worry about the engine. It had been working well since Sarasota. The lake was just a few miles across. Chill. Relax.

But it was hard to relax while motoring. Without the wind

and sails to provide the corrective power, I couldn't use my self-steering gear, so I was glued to the tiller. The continual buzz of the engine wore on my nerves, and it was bloody hot. I set the mizzen, just to provide a bit more shade in the cockpit, but it was still hot. I had plenty of water with me in the cockpit, but I had no appetite for food.

I just kept going…

Two hours later, the red #6 buoy that marks the half-way point hove into view. The wind had increased to ten knots, still right on the nose. It had kicked up a one foot chop. Nothing the *Blue Moon* couldn't handle, but it slowed us down. My brain ran the calculations. Even at three knots, Port Mayaca was only a couple hours away. We were practically home free.

I smiled at that thought, and stood up to check the horizon in front of us for sight of land. Still too far away, of course, but it was good to see that solid-looking #6 buoy right there off the port bow. Other than that, nothing. We hadn't seen another boat since turning off the rim canal. It was pretty amazing to have the 6th largest lake in the United States to ourselves.

The tone of the engine changed slightly. A squirt of adrenaline put me on full alert. Engines didn't change tone for no reason, and the reason was usually bad.

"Keep going, baby," I said.

But then the engine died. Just stopped, as if it had run out of gas.

"Can't be."

I dropped the tiller and lifted the five gallon plastic gas tank. It seemed to be about a quarter full. I unscrewed the cap and thrust in my wooden dipstick to check the level. The stick came out showing a couple inches wet.

We were now lying beam to the wind, rolling in the one foot waves. Uncomfortable, but not unsafe. Not yet.

I pulled the starter cord on the engine and it roared to life, just as it always did.

"Must have been a glitch," I told *Cabin Boy*, reassuringly. But when I put the engine into gear, it seemed to have no power. After a few moments, it died again.

"Blast," I said, along with a few other salty phrases that only sailors know.

Again I pulled the cord, and again the engine started, only to stall again when I threw it into gear. I began to worry.

I wasted forty-five minutes trying this and trying that: removing the cowling, checking the oil, looking for something—I didn't know what—that could be fixed by someone who didn't know beans about outboard motors.

Finally, with the engine running, but out of gear, I noticed a fine spray of fluid shooting out the side of the engine, onto the water. I smelled it. It was gasoline. Gasoline. Spraying out of my engine. My *hot* engine.

"Double-blast!"

I lunged for the kill switch...

CHAPTER 12

OKEECHOBEE ANGELS

Never give in, never give in, never, never, never, never—
in nothing great or small, large or petty—never give in except
to convictions of honor and good sense. — Winston Churchill,
May 1940

No, we didn't blow up in one of those dramatic TV cop show fireballs. The engine stalled again before I could even hit the kill button.

I sat on my heels in the heaving cockpit for a moment, slowly and thoroughly cursing the infernal machine fastened to the back of my boat. Then I put the cowling back on, pretty sure the engine would never start again. In fact, I was sorely tempted to pull it off its bracket and drop it to the bottom of the lake, but I had more important things to do.

"Revenge is a dish best served cold, anyway," I said in my most chilling voice.

We were out of sight of all land, and the wind was now blowing fifteen knots, gusting up to twenty A nasty sea was rising quickly. It looked as though the weather would get worse before it got better, but there was nothing I could do about that. I turned my attention to the decision at hand: sail on to Port Mayaca, or back to Clewiston?

While I considered those options, I set the main and staysail, and heaved-to. That steadied the *Blue Moon* remarkably, and helped her ride more comfortably over the growing waves. I felt safer immediately. Time to think.

I climbed down into the cabin to make a cup of tea and to fill a bowl with bread, cheese, and fruit. Whatever decision I made, I had a long afternoon ahead of me. I needed fuel to keep me going. It felt good to get out of the wind and sun for a moment.

I sat on my bunk and studied the chart.

It was roughly fifteen miles back to Clewiston. With the wind blowing from astern, that would be less than three hours away. I glance up at the ship's clock: 4:45 p.m. Time enough to get back to Clewiston before dark.

It was only seven miles to Port Mayaca, but it was dead upwind. Tacking, we'd have to cover more like eighteen miles. Possible, but that would cut it awfully close, and when we reached the port, there would be the lock to contend with. I'd have to wait for the lock to open, and then somehow sail upwind into the lock.

"Is it even legal to sail into a lock?" I wondered.

I shook my head. I wasn't sure. Anyway, it hardly mattered. The lock might block the wind, or generate fluky turbulence. If there had been no wind at all, I could have towed the *Blue Moon* into the lock behind *Cabin Boy*, but against a fifteen or twenty knot wind? No way.

With the rising sea, there was a good chance I'd arrive after dark, after the lock closed down for the night. Then what? Beat back and forth until dawn? Anchor?

I hated to give up all the ground we'd covered, but heading to Port Mayaca just didn't feel right. If I knew the port well, it might have been different. But sailing into a complicated, unfamiliar situation… There were too many things that could go wrong. Finally, I remembered there was no marina in Port Mayaca. Even if we could get there, there would be no help. That made the decision easy.

I climbed back into the cockpit.

"It's back to Clewiston," I told *Cabin Boy*, but he was too busy bouncing up and down on the already peaky waves to take much notice.

We bore off the way we'd come. I was ready to pile on the sail if necessary, but we were soon flying downwind under the main and staysail, so I left the jib and mizzen down.

I cast a wary eye at the sun, which seemed to be speeding west as fast as we were.

"As long as we get there before dark," I muttered.

* * *

Two hours later, we approached the large floating platform again. Beyond that was the winding channel through shallows and grassy islands, leading to the Clewiston Lock. The wind blew from astern at twenty knots, kicking up a nasty, following sea, but the wind was fair to Clewiston and we should, I thought, be able to sail right through the lock, into the town harbor.

Unlike the Port Mayaca lock, which is part of the Okeechobee Waterway, the Clewiston Lock is a hurricane lock, designed mainly to protect the town from storm surges. In normal weather, both doors are left open, so the *Blue Moon* could sail straight through.

But straight through into what? *What* was on the other side of that gate?

When we passed by that morning, I had a brief look through the lock. All I saw was a sea wall and what looked like the side of a house. Not much to go on.

I studied the chart, but it covered the entire Okeechobee Waterway. Clewiston Harbor was just a blue dot with practically no detail. I could see a small harbor behind the lock, but that was all. I couldn't tell where the marinas were, or where we could anchor, of if there were any obstructions.

We passed through the gap in the 'Rocky Reef', and turned to starboard, following the channel. With the wind on our beam, it was clear we had too much sail up, but now that we were in narrow waters, it was too late to pull down a reef. The *Blue Moon* heeled over until water surged into her scuppers. It was terrific sailing, but all I could think of was the far side of that lock. Was the tiny harbor jammed full of moored boats? Was there room to maneuver? To anchor?

They say what a sailor most fears is closing with an unknown shore, and once again I felt that particular kind of fear. It was crazy to shoot through a lock into an unseen harbor, with half a gale behind us, but that was what I had to do, apparently. Did I have any other choice?

As I made the turn into the Approach Channel, with less than five miles to go, I had an idea. I grabbed my iPhone from the cabin and checked for a signal. Not good. Only one bar. I tried to bring up Google Maps, but it refused to load. Blast... if I could just get a better view of the inner harbor. Maybe I had enough signal to call Helena. It rang and she picked up.

"Hello my darling. How are you?" she said with her slight Brazilian accent.

"Oh, pretty good," I said, carefully choosing my words so I didn't freak her out.

"Did you make it across the lake?"

"Not quite..." I said, trying to sound casual. This failed, of course. She came to full alert.

"What's wrong?"

"Well, the motor died..."

"Oh, no."

"...right in the middle of the lake."

"You are kidding," she said, reflecting my disgust.

"I'm not, unfortunately," I said. "Listen, I need you to do something..."

I explained that I need her to look at the satellite view of Clewiston on Google Maps. I held on while she brought it up on her computer.

"Okay, I see it," she said, all business now. "What do you need to know?"

"There is a lock that leads from the lake, through a dike, into the town harbor."

"Yes, I can see that."

"What's on the other side of the lock?"

"Just a little bit of water, and then what looks like a dock."

"How much water?"

"Hmmm... It's hard to say. Not much."

"Is it bigger or smaller than the channel outside the lock?"

"Smaller. Much smaller. About half the width of the channel and maybe two or three times as long as the lock itself."

"Oh," I said. "That is small."

"What are you trying to do?"

"I'm trying to reach the marina in Clewiston. But I'm worried about sailing blind through the lock and into the harbor. Are there any boats anchored in the harbor?"

"No. It doesn't look wide enough to anchor. There are no boats, not even on the dock."

That was worrying. "Maybe the photo was taken off season, if there is such a thing."

"You're being careful, right?"

"Always," I said. "Okay, I'm getting close. I need to decide what to do pretty quickly. I'll call you once I'm anchored, to let you know I'm okay."

After the exchange of a few hurried endearments, I put my phone away and focused. I could see the lock by then. It was per-haps a quarter mile away—just a few minutes. We were flying down the channel with too much sail up. Would there be room to take down the sail, after I went through the lock?

If I went through the lock. Did I dare? Did I have any choice?

Wait, yes. I did have one other choice: to turn into the south-bound leg of the rim canal and anchor close to the grassy island on the lake side of the canal. The anchorage would be protected from waves, if not the wind and—as it was nearly dark—there wouldn't be much traffic to worry about. We'd be right outside the lock. In the morning, I could row in and check out the harbor with my own two eyes before deciding what to do next.

"The marina will be closed tonight, anyway," I said. There was no need to rush.

I felt a great sense of relief. The new plan just felt right.

"And when in doubt," I told *Cabin Boy*, "go with your gut."

We blasted down the final hundred yards of the approach ca-nal, with the lock gate looming ever larger. I could see the rim canal crossing ahead. I'd have to time my turn perfectly. I hoped we wouldn't come face to face with a speeding powerboat.

We reached the rim canal and I gibed the *Blue Moon* sharply to port. I trimmed the main and we sailed close-hauled for another 300 yards, to get well away from the lock traffic. Then I shot us up into the now howling wind. As we approached the grassy island, the *Blue Moon* slowed quickly and I went forward to drop the anchor. The anchor dug into the muddy bottom, and just like that, we were safe.

With my supply of adrenaline cut off, I suddenly felt exhausted. I pulled down the thundering sails and quieted them with sail ties. The silence almost rang in my ears.

I sat wearily in the cockpit and pulled out my phone. The sun was just going down and the sunset was gorgeous. There wasn't a cloud in the sky.

"I made it," I told Helena.

"Oh, good." She sounded relieved.

"I decided to anchor outside the lock. It was safer."

"You always make the right decision."

Even I wasn't buying that one, but I didn't argue. "I'll row through tomorrow to talk to the marina guys."

"Excellent."

"There's just one thing," I said, looking at the edge of the grassy island, not too far away, where a dozen large, unblinking eyes stared at me from just above the water.

"What's that?"

"I think I'm surrounded by alligators."

* * *

Three days later, I rowed triumphantly out of the now-familiar Clewiston lock. Three days in which Lake Nemesis and the forces of Good fought over the future of my voyage.

Nemesis, of course, was the Greek goddess who took particular pleasure in punishing those who succumbed to the sin of Hubris, or "being out of touch with reality and overestimating one's own competence or capabilities." Nemesis was my new name for Lake Okeechobee.

The battle was a closely fought one in which the tides of Hope and Despair, Hard Work and Frustration alternately swept over the field, but now the angels of Good seemed to be winning. The final battle, set to take place tomorrow afternoon, would tell all…

Three days ago, after repelling my first attempt to cross the lake, Nemesis had strengthened her attack that night. She'd blown hard and loud until morning, forcing me to keep a good anchor watch. The lee shore was just across the channel, perhaps 200 feet away. If the anchor dragged, we'd have been wrecked against the wooden posts (called 'dolphins') that lined the bank.

The anchor held, but I didn't get much sleep.

The next morning, I rowed through the hurricane lock, down the narrow channel to the marina. The marina dock was a long one, and ran right alongside the channel. I could see that I might indeed have been able to sail the *Blue Moon* up to it, but it would have been dicey.

I tied *Cabin Boy* to the dock and found my way to the marina store. It was a big one, with a pair of fishing boats in the showroom, and lots of outboards on display. They had a long service counter, with loads of parts hanging on the wall behind it. If you had to break down, this looked like a good place to do it.

I explained the urgency of my situation to the service manager. I needed help today. Right now, in fact. Absolutely no time to lose.

The service department was backed up, of course. Could not possibly look at my engine for at least three days. There was a local guy they could recommend, though. Someone who had worked for the marina and was now working independently. A first class mechanic named Billy who could probably jump on my problem right away.

A phone call brought Billy to the marina with all the speed and efficiency one could hope for in a mechanic. We borrowed a boat from the marina and zoomed out to the *Blue Moon*. He diagnosed the problem in the time it took to take the cover off: broken fuel pump. One of the plastic ports that the fuel lines attach to had developed a crack and thus a leak. Enough gas still got through the line to keep the engine running badly, but not enough to keep it from stalling when I put it into gear.

"It's an easy fix," Billy told me. "Just need to order a new pump."

But which one? He studied the engine. There was no model or serial number anywhere. The cover was pure Johnson cream, but had no markings on it. The only readable label on the engine said, "Bombardier". The engine's lower half seemed to be made by Suzuki.

"Strange," was all Billy said.

He pulled the engine off the back of the *Blue Moon*, lowered it into the tender, and we hauled it back to the marina. Then the other mechanics puzzled over it. One thought it was a Johnson. Others thought it might be a Mercury. And then there was that Suzuki lower unit…

After listening to the debate for an hour, I remembered the marina in Sarasota had already ordered a carburetor repair kit. Surely they knew what the engine was. So I called the Sarasota service manager. She confidently gave me a part number for the fuel pump.

"That's the one you need," she said.

Argument sorted, part ordered with overnight delivery. There was nothing left to do but while away the rest of the afternoon at the marina's tiki-bar.

Next day, the part arrived by FedEx.

"I am home free," I thought, elated that the problem would be solved so easily and quickly.

Just one problem: the part didn't fit. It was the wrong pump. Billy and the other mechanics scratched their heads. Now they had no idea what model engine I had. Or even the make.

"It's an odd ball," said Billy, shaking his head. "That's for sure."

That's the moment I broke. I gave up. I just could not deal with that engine a single day longer.

After a quick consult with Helena by phone, we agreed I needed to buy a new outboard. Much relief on my part. I walked into the marina show room and talked to the sales guy.

"Sailboat, right?" he asked. "How big? Hmmm… a Yamaha T9.9 hp long-shaft would be perfect for you. Enough power… high-thrust gearing… good long shaft. Yup, that's the engine you need."

"Great. How much?"

He mentioned a figure that made me slightly dizzy, but I figured I could always build another website to pay for it. As Helena was fond of saying, it was only money.

"Just one problem," he said. "We don't have one. No demand for them around here. Have to order it. Take a few weeks to get here."

"A few weeks?!?!" I questioned his estimate, then his sanity, but he insisted. I told him that was too long for me, and he shrugged. I walked away overwhelmed with frustration, but sure I could find a Yamaha T9.9 hp long-shaft outboard somewhere in vast boating state of Florida.

I spent the rest of the afternoon calling every Yamaha dealer in the state of Florida. I do not exaggerate: every single one.

"Have to order it," was the universal refrain. "No call for them down here."

Really? No small sailboats in Florida?

They all shrugged. "Two weeks. Minimum."

I kept dialing.

That night, I rowed back to the *Blue Moon* in despair. Was Nemesis going to defeat me? It sure looked that way, but that very night, the first of the Okeechobee Angels flew to my side.

I'd been blogging about my voyage, mainly to keep in touch with family while I was away, but slowly my exploits had attracted an audience. People who, I assumed, read my blog for the same reason that people watch auto races—for the crashes. But, whatever the reason, my little band of readers were a great comfort to me. Whether I was beset by wind off Tarpon Springs, aground in Clearwater, or anchored in an alligator infested canal in the middle of nowhere, I was never really alone. There was always a cloud of readers, hovering over my shoulder, watching me.

And watching out *for* me, too.

As I read my email that night, I was astounded to find one from Steve D., one of my readers.

"I've been following your adventures with interest," he wrote.

"Would you like to borrow my outboard, to get you to Stuart?"

Stuart, Florida, he meant, at the eastern end of the Okeechobee Waterway, where he had a home.

"All you have to do is pick it up," he wrote.

I normally like to solve my own problems, but Steve's offer was obviously a gift from heaven, and no sailor should spurn angels bearing gifts. But how could I pick it up?

That is when the second Angel sprang into action. My brother, Bruce—the one who looks good holding tools—lived in nearby Jupiter, FL. He offered to pick up the engine, drive the seventy-five miles to Clewiston, and deliver it to me tomorrow morning. Tomorrow morning!

I sent 'thank you!' emails to both, and then climbed up into the cockpit to enjoy what I hoped would be my last night in Clewiston. I was practically giddy with happiness. What luck!

I looked out over Lake Nemesis and sneered.

"Thought you could defeat me, eh?" I said. "Ha-ha-ha!"

* * *

My eyes opened. The wind howled in the rigging as it did every night on the Okeechobee. Tonight it was stronger, louder, but that wasn't what woke me. Something else had alerted the animal part of my brain that refused to sleep at night—the watchman who frets through the dark hours, listening for saber toothed tigers, waiting to ring the alarm bell. Something had changed.

I swung out of my bunk and looked out the companionway hatch.

"Blast!"

By now I was so used to the Clewiston view—the grassy island, the high dike, the lock with its harsh halogen lights, the black water of the channel—that I knew instantly we'd changed position. We were dragging our anchor across the channel, right towards the massive dolphins on the other side.

I climbed on deck and stumbled forward to the anchor, but before I could grab the line, we were more than halfway across the channel. The *Blue Moon*'s stern was less than 100 feet from the first dolphin. I pulled the anchor line off the Sampson post and quickly played out more line. That was the classic way to stop an anchor from dragging, but if I let out too much, we'd hit the massive post.

Holding the line in my hands, I could feel the anchor dragging across the bottom of the canal, like a fish nibbling. All of a sudden, the anchor caught and the full weight of the boat came on the line. Luckily, I was ready for it: I had a turn around the Sampson post which kept the line from slipping through my hands.

I glanced over the stern. The first dolphin was twenty, maybe twenty-five feet behind us. Backlit by the shore lights, it looked menacing, but we weren't getting any closer. The anchor was holding, at least temporarily.

The wind gusted and the anchor line groaned as it stretched. Nemesis hadn't given up yet. I had to get us out of there, but how? I had no engine!

The storm anchor.

I looked for *Cabin Boy*. He was tied alongside, of course. I tied him there every night so he wouldn't keep me awake with his incessant bumping.

"Time for you to earn your keep, buddy."

I ran back down to the cabin and threw my bunk cushion, sleeping bag, and pillow aside so I could get into the locker under the bunk. This was where I kept my 50 lb. storm anchor. It was heavy and awkward, and hard to get out.

"Stupid place to store an emergency anchor," I growled as I manhandled the steel hook out of the locker, up through the companionway, and into the cockpit. Ordinarily, this would have been a heavy job, but I seemed to have super-human strength.

"Adrenaline," I thought. "I'm going to pay for this tomorrow."

I fetched the spare anchor line from the fo'c's'le, and threw that into the cockpit too, then climbed up the companionway steps.

The anchor line must be laid out just right, I knew, but someone else seemed in control of the situation. I seemed to be floating above the deck, watching myself lead the end of the line outside the shrouds to the Sampson post, tying it off, running back to shackle the other end to the anchor chain.

I couldn't put the heavy anchor directly into *Cabin Boy*. That would have been too dangerous. Standing in the back of a dinghy and throwing an anchor overboard in a storm whilst surrounded by alligators is one of the most sure-fire ways to kill a sailor. There was a better way.

I tied a light rope to the anchor, patted the knife in my pocket, then climbed over the side into *Cabin Boy*. He bobbed around under my feet like a nervous pony.

"This is the tricky bit."

I lifted the heavy anchor out of the cockpit, and hung it off *Cabin Boy*'s stern with the light rope. I tied the other end of the rope to the center seat. Now all I had to do was cut the light rope and the anchor would drop to the bottom, with no drama at all. I hoped.

I put the coil of anchor line on *Cabin Boy*'s floor, making sure the turns were right-side up so the line would run free when the anchor fell.

I double-checked the set up, but it all looked good.

"Right, now *this* is the tricky bit."

I put the oars into the oarlocks, and cast off *Cabin Boy*'s painter. Instantly, we were blown downwind towards the dolphins. I dug in with the oars, and started rowing hard directly up wind, towards the grassy island.

It wasn't easy, but slowly we battled across the channel as the anchor line played out behind us. People always laughed at my extra-long oars, but that night, they were the magic blades I used to fight Nemesis. She hit me with everything she had. The wind was blowing thirty knots, with higher gusts. Weeks of rowing and pulling on ropes with my bare hands were paying off. I could feel the muscles in my back and arms straining, but we were winning. The dolphin slowly fell behind us. We were at least half-way across the channel. The gap continued to widen. I kept my strokes long and the recovery short and clean.

"We must be getting close, now."

I felt *Cabin Boy*'s stem push into the marsh grass. I decided to drop the anchor right there, right next to the grassy island. I shipped my oars and instantly Nemesis tried to blow us away from the island, but I was too fast for her. In a moment, I had my knife out, and cut the rope.

The anchor plunged three feet to the bottom. I hung on to the anchor line as the angry wind tried to push us down channel. I caught my breath. The other end of the line was tied to the *Blue Moon*'s Samson post. When my heart returned to normal operating speed, I pulled us along the line, across the channel, to the *Blue Moon*'s side, and climbed aboard. The battle wasn't over, yet.

I went forward and took up the slack on the anchor line. It ran right across the channel to my storm anchor. But could I pull us across against the wind? Against Nemesis? I had no winches aboard the *Blue Moon*, so I had to do it by hand.

I stood up and braced my feet in the anchor well.

"Only one way to find out."

I started to pull on the anchor line, hoping the heavy storm anchor would dig in and hold. It did, and we started to move away from the massive dolphins and across the channel.

When we were directly over the old anchor—the one that had dragged—I tied us off temporarily, and hauled it aboard. Then I picked up the new anchor line again. The grassy island still looked a long way away.

"You can do anything," I told myself. "As long as you do it slowly enough."

This was the mantra that had served me well while building *Cabin Boy*. I found myself chanting it as I slowly hauled us across the channel. When we were half way across, and a world of danger from those ugly piles, I even allowed myself a short rest. There was no hurry now. No hurry at all.

When we were fifty feet from the grassy island, I decide we were close enough. Even with a 50 lb. anchor in three feet of water, I wanted plenty of scope out. I didn't want a repeat performance.

I was exhausted, but we still weren't done. I tied the original anchor off *Cabin Boy*'s stern, and rowed it out at a thirty degree angle to the storm anchor. Back aboard, I hauled in the anchor rode until we were swinging to both anchors.

"That should be enough for a hurricane," I told *Cabin Boy*. "And maybe even for Nemesis."

The battle was won. I sat on the cabin top, in the fierce wind, with four fingers of medicinal rum in a glass. I swallowed two aspirins, and chased them down with half the rum. The adrenaline had worn off. My legs and arms felt like rubber. My hand shook as I lifted the glass. The knots in my shoulders gradually loosened as I watched the marsh grass whip in the wind. Nemesis howled in frustration, but the anchors held. We weren't dragging. I was alive. My boats were floating. Nothing had been broken.

"That was pretty darn exciting, eh?" I asked *Cabin Boy*.

"*Carrying storm anchor… Saving Blue Moon… best day of my life!*"

I took my time and finished the rum. All except for a sip, which I tipped over the side as a kind of peace offering. Then I stood up, turned my back on the wind, and quietly went below. We'd defeated Nemesis again, but I wasn't stupid: I wouldn't laugh at her again.

* * *

I slept through the alarm and woke, groggily, at 8 a.m. As I made my first cup of coffee, I surveyed the world from the companionway hatch. Was last night just a bad dream? Seemed like it, somehow, but the two anchor lines, streaming off the bow, told me it wasn't.

My sore muscles confirmed it.

I puttered around the boat, putting the cabin back together and washing an unlikely amount of mud off the deck. At 10 a.m., I rowed to the marina and tied up just as Bruce arrived with Steve's engine. We borrowed a large tender from the marina and installed the engine on the back of the *Blue Moon*. It was the first time Bruce had seen the boat, so we spent some time admiring her, before returning to the marina. We pitched the old Johnson/Bombardier/Suzuki/Whatever into the back of Bruce's pickup, and celebrated with a good old BBQ lunch at the tiki-bar restaurant.

Then it was time for Bruce to head back to Jupiter, and for me to resume my voyage.

I rowed back out through the lock to the *Blue Moon*. The first order of business was to get the 50 lb. storm anchor up. How had I manhandled it the night before? It weighed a ton and I could barely lift it over the bow.

The power of adrenaline.

After stowing the storm anchor down below and tidying up a bit, I was finally ready to go. The wind still blew five-to-ten knots, but I figured we could handle that, as long as it didn't blow any harder. Surely, Nemesis must have given up by now. She must have realized she'd met her match.

I squatted in the stern to look at my new engine. It was a Yamaha two-stroke. The old engine—whatever it was—had been a four-stroke, but other than putting oil in the gas, the new engine should operate the same way.

I squeezed the fuel bulb to prime the engine, pulled the choke out, adjusted the throttle to the 'start' position, took a deep breath, and pulled the starter cord.

Nothing.

"Okay, probably hasn't been started for awhile. Just needs a few good pulls," I told *Cabin Boy*, who looked worried.

I pulled the cord a few more times. Still nothing.

Dang. What was I doing wrong? I double-checked everything. Fuel line primed? Check. Choke out? Check. Throttle setting? Check.

I was out of things to check, so I tried a few more pulls on the starter cord. Again, nothing. Not even a sputter. What was I doing wrong?

"Oh, blast." The kill cord. The safety thingy that must be installed for the engine to start. I'd forgotten to clip it on. What an idiot.

I fetched the cord from the cabin and clipped it under the kill switch.

"Okay, here we go…" This time it would work, for sure.

I pulled the starter cord again, but still, nothing!

I will spare you—dear reader—the dialog I held for several

minutes with my wonderful new outboard. Just withdraw, and imagine yourself standing high atop the dike, looking out over Lake Nemesis, averting your eyes from the spectacle of the grown man yelling on the little yacht below... begging... crying... rending his garments...

Is that Nemesis, herself, standing astride the lake? Is she laughing? Pray, do not tell the poor, insignificant mortal who, we know, has been as patient and as faithful to his voyage as Job. Give him a moment to collect himself. It won't take long.

A few minutes later, I stopped flogging myself, sat back on my heels and thought objectively about the problem. I'd probably flooded the engine, whatever that meant. I'd flooded my two-stroke lawn mower engine plenty of times. All it ever needed was a bit of time. I had time.

I made myself a cup of tea, picked a few choice biscuits out of the tin, and looked up the engine's Owner's Manual on the Internet. I read the section on "Starting Your New Engine!"

Pull out the choke, give it a bit of gas, make sure the kill cord is in...

I stared at the ship's clock and forced myself to wait thirty minutes. Then I tried again.

Again, nothing. I gave it two more pulls, then sat back on my heels. No sense flooding it again. I needed a plan.

I pulled out my phone and called an expert; the only expert I knew on the subject of outboards; my third Okeechobee Angel, Billy.

"Oh," he said, after I described what had happened. "You've flooded it."

"Yes, but I waited thirty minutes."

"Here's what you have to do. Ready?"

"Yes."

"Push the choke in all the way," he said.

"Okay," I said, warily, pushing in the choke.

"Now turn the throttle all the way up."

"What?! That's exactly the opposite of what the Yamaha manual says!"

"Just try it," he said, in his quiet, southern voice.

"Okay," I said, in my skeptical, New York voice. "Hold on."

I put the phone down, took a deep breath, and gave the starter cord a good yank.

The engine roared to life.

I picked up the phone and yelled into it, "What?!?"

"It's an old trick," he said.

"But the manual…"

"Just ignore it. They don't know everything."

"I owe you one, buddy."

"Don't mention it," he said. "Have a good trip."

And I did. I tried the direct route across the lake, but the waves were still mountainous and I didn't want to stress Steve's engine or give Nemesis another chance at me. So I turned back and took the longer but surer Rim route, all the way round to Port Mayaca. The Yamaha seemed twice as powerful as my old Bombardier, so we were able to cruise at the breath-taking speed of five knots.

"So this is what a decent outboard is like," I said to *Cabin Boy*.

We arrived about an hour before dark, passed through the lock without incident, and puttered past the small town of Port Mayaca to an anchorage at the foot of an old railroad bridge. I anchored there and turned off the engine, which had run without a hiccup all day.

I patted its cover fondly, then sat in the cockpit with a drink and watched the sun set in glorious colors over the lake.

We were on the other side. We'd defeated Lake Nemesis.

* * *

Next morning, the outboard started with the first pull and we were soon puttering down the St. Lucie Canal towards Stuart, civilization, and the north-bound ICW. It was only about thirty miles, an easy day's voyage at five knots. Wow! I couldn't wait to get to Stuart to order a new engine of my own. Even if it took two weeks to arrive, no problem! I was willing to wait.

Besides, I had a plan.

If I had to wait two weeks for delivery, why wait in Florida? Why not fly home for a two week holiday with Helena? Just the idea had me buzzing with excitement.

All I needed to do was find a marina in which to leave the *Blue Moon*, order an engine, and hitch a ride to the airport.

With a bit of luck, I could actually be home by tomorrow night.

Home… Although it was blazing hot down on the Waterway, it was only May 15. Springtime in New York. Cool breezes, daffodils, delicate new leaves on the trees, shade…

Not to mention hot water, showers, shade, and a real bed.

I could really use a break. And some shade.

The more I thought about it, the more it seemed like destiny and a huge stroke of good luck. Bring it on, spring break!

But in the meantime, I needed some gas. The two-stroke engine burned a lot more fuel (mixed with oil) than my old four-stroke and there was only one marina between the lake and Stuart, at the old Seminole trading post at Indiantown. I'd stop for gas, and maybe even some lunch. At five knots, I had time to spare!

I passed another hour in good humor, and then spotted the entrance to the marina, which was just a narrow gap in the trees. I circled past a few times to get a feel for what I was getting into, then headed in. The practically land-locked marina was amazingly well protected and the fuel dock was easy to get to. I was a little more confident in my handling of the *Blue Moon* near docks by then. I just ignored the sailors standing on the dock, watched my approach, and repeated my mantra:

"If you're not bored when approaching a dock, you're going too fast. If you're not bored…"

I coasted up to the dock and smoothly handed the bow line to one of the waiting sailors, then calmly stepped off with the stern line. In a few seconds, the *Blue Moon* was tied up, with nary a bump.

"Nice," said my helper.

"Oh, it's nothing," I said demurely. I'd practically forgotten about dragging the dock boy half-way down the dock back in Sarasota. That was *soooo* last week.

A small crowd of admirers gathered alongside the *Blue Moon* as I filled my three gas tanks. We chatted about the usual things.

Then I remembered about picking other people's brains for local knowledge, and started to quiz them about marinas in Stuart.

"You're thinking about leaving this boat for two weeks on a mooring in Stuart?" a salty old character asked. He sucked in a breath through his teeth and shook his head. "Wouldn't do it. Too many break-ins down there. Strip you clean in three minutes flat."

"Break-ins?" I asked, a bit incredulous. So far, I hadn't spent a single moment on this trip worrying about crime or criminals. "Really?"

"And storms," said a tall, lean man with a Texas or maybe Oklahoma accent. "Get some nasty thunderstorms there. Drag your mooring half-way across the harbor. That is, if one of them super-yachts don't run you down, first."

"But, surely, a mooring would be safe," I said, thinking of the hundreds of boats that were swinging on moorings in Stuart at that very moment. Were these guys overly paranoid, or just indulging in the usual sailorman doom-and-gloom tall tales?

I quizzed them some more, trying to decide if I should take such talk seriously, but frankly, I couldn't read them. They seemed sincere in their loathing for Stuart, and its crime-ridden, storm-wracked moorings, but it seemed a bit crazy to me.

Besides, Steve lived in Stuart and I had to return his engine. I had all figured out. It was going to be so easy.

"Nothing is ever easy when it comes to boats," I reminded myself.

I suddenly realized I hadn't eaten a thing all day. I was ravenous. I talked to the dock master about a place to eat and she recommended a local Mexican place in town. An easy walk, she said. No problem leaving the *Blue Moon* on the dock for an hour or two, she said.

"Wow, what a great place," I thought, and headed down the road towards the village of Indiantown.

The 'Mexican' place was in a strip mall on the main drag. One of those little restaurants that made good, inexpensive food for the hardworking Hispanic guys who worked on the farms. Homey atmosphere and good, simple Central American cooking. Breathtakingly delicious, compared to what I'd been eating lately. I left happy and full, but still uncertain about Stuart.

As I walked back to the marina, I decided to call my number one Angel. I explained my plan and the 'local knowledge' about break-ins and storms that had me nervous.

"If I can find a good, safe place to leave the boat for a while, I was thinking of flying home while I wait for the motor to be delivered."

"Oh, now that's a good idea," Helena said.

"But these guys have me nervous about Stuart. They're probably crazy, but…"

"How's the marina you're in now?"

"Seems real nice. It's mainly for people who lay up their boats here during hurricane season. We're thirty miles from the coast, so it's pretty protected."

"Why don't you just leave the boat there?"

"Here? They only have docks. No moorings. It would cost a fortune."

"Do you know how much the moorings are in Stuart?"

"Yes, I've been calling around. Got a pretty good idea of the range."

"Maybe you can get a dock for the same price, or a little more."

"Oh, I don't think so."

"You said it was in the middle of nowhere. It won't hurt to ask."

"Yeah, maybe," I said. "You're right. Won't hurt to ask."

A few minutes later, I emerged from the dock master's office, kicking my heels. I called Helena back.

"You were right!" I said. "It's the same price as a mooring in Stuart, but so much better!"

"That's great!"

I stopped and looked out over the peaceful little marina that would be the *Blue Moon*'s home for the next couple weeks. It was the perfect spot to leave her and *Cabin Boy*.

"I'm here," I said. "I've made it to the east coast. My shake-down cruise is officially over."

"You did it," Helena said. "How do you feel?"

How did I feel? The change in plans was so unexpected, and so brilliant, it was hard to know how I felt. I'd been so geared up to deal with the hassles and inconveniences of busy Stuart, but now, I didn't have to. I was done. Though I still had a long way to go, somehow, I felt like I was half-way home. And maybe I was.

"Relieved," I said. "Happy. I don't know. It's weird thinking about not being on the *Blue Moon*, fighting our way home."

"You miss her already."

"I'll tell you who I miss," I said, warmly. "Get ready. I'm coming home!"

CHAPTER 13

TURNING NORTH

To reach a port we must set sail—Sail, not tie at anchor.
Sail, not drift. — Franklin D. Roosevelt

Two weeks later, I was back on the *Blue Moon* feeling fresh and rested, and looking forward to resuming my voyage in a more 'professional' and 'efficient' manner, by 'leveraging' my new experience and capital equipment...

And that's what two weeks in New York will do for you.

However, I did feel my voyage transitioning into a new phase. I had accumulated lots of experience in the month it had taken me to sail from Steinhatchee to Indiantown. To some extent, I'd had to learn by doing (i.e., winging it) on my shakedown cruise, simply because I couldn't anticipate all the problems I'd encounter. Now it was time to apply those hard won lessons to make the rest of the voyage less arduous, and a bit more fun.

Florida's boating-industrial complex didn't help much. You'd think it would be easy to order an outboard motor in the "Boating Capital of the World," but, no. Not a long-shaft 'sailboat' motor. Not something as small and 'inexpensive' as a 9.9 hp outboard. Even the dealers who said they'd have to order one, refused to actually do so.

"Just isn't worth our time," one dealer told me, frankly.

"Not enough profit margin in them," said another.

I was glad to hear the boating industry in Florida was doing so well in the midst of the Great Recession that they didn't need to bother with small fry like me, but I needed that motor.

Finally, I found one salesman, at one dealership, who seemed interested in selling me a $2,500 outboard. The dealer was in Jacksonville, FL, over 250 miles from the *Blue Moon*, but by the time I tracked him down on the phone, I didn't care. What was a 500 mile round-trip drive in the big scheme of things? Nothing!

Besides, new engines need to be serviced after the first twenty hours of use, and I would be sailing right through Jacksonville in a couple weeks. I could stop there overnight, and the dealer could pull the engine, service it, and get me back on my voyage with the absolute minimum down-time.

Now that's efficiency for you.

So, I had a plan. I'd also ordered two small luxury items to take advantage of the abundant electricity I'd soon have available from the outboard's generator: an electric light for over my bunk, and the biggest, quietest fan I thought would fit on the boat.

By now, I was more than aware of Florida's heat. Even in May the heat was no joke, but at least the cabin cooled down at night, so sleeping wasn't too bad. But in June, or July, or August, when the night time temperatures would be over 90° F, a fan could make the difference between life and death. Or at least between misery and a good night's sleep.

The electric light was another no-brainer. I had started my voyage with a kerosene lamp in the cabin. This had been a mistake. A kerosene lamp might cast a cozy glow if you are anchored somewhere in the Gulf of Maine, but in Florida it was just too darn hot. I'd long since reassigned the kerosene lamp to anchor duty, and switched to a battery-powered lantern in the cabin, but the lantern went through batteries at an alarming rate. The new cabin light would work off the main batteries, which would be recharged daily by the engine. Most sailors take electric lighting for granted, but for me, a bright, electric bunk light would be a luxury. I could just imagine: reading in a pool of light, a river of cool air flowing over me...

Ah! True bliss!

Now all I had to do was pick up the new motor and install it on the *Blue Moon*'s stern.

I packed a duffle bag, bade a fond farewell to Helena, and flew back to Florida. My mother was kind enough to lend me her SUV for the long trip up to Jacksonville and back, and before too long, Bruce and I were standing on the dock in Indiantown, looking at the *Blue Moon*'s bow, and mentally preparing ourselves for some hard work.

"I should have backed her into the slip," I said. If I had, the *Blue Moon*'s stern would have been snuggled up against the dock, and it would have been a simple matter to install the outboard on its bracket. But I hadn't, and now we had two choices: turn her around in the slip with no engine; or carry the outboard onto the boat and lower it over the stern—which seemed impossible.

"Backing in would have been smart," said Bruce.

"I think I will turn her around," I said, after a bit more thought.

"How are you going to do that?"

"Use *Cabin Boy* to put out a stern anchor, warp her out of the slip, turn her around where there's a bit more room, and warp her back in." 'Warp' means to move a boat by pulling on ropes.

"Sounds like a lot of work."

"Yes, well, as crew of the *Blue Moon*…" I was going to explain how a ship's crew was often ordered by their captain to perform miracles of seamanship that most landlubbers could hardly imagine. That sometimes these maneuvers took hours, but the crew just had to do what they were told and…

"I think we can just lower it off the stern," Bruce said, with a Floridian's aversion to long hours working in the sun.

"I don't know…"

Steve's 15 hp two-stroke had been a relatively light 80 lb. Bruce had shooed me aside and lifted the engine off the bracket himself. But the Yamaha 9.9 hp four-stroke was a beefier engine. It weighed more than 120 lb. The two of us could easily carry it into the *Blue Moon*'s cockpit, but lowering over the stern onto the bracket was another matter. There wasn't enough room for two people to work back there. It almost had to be a one-man job. And Hercules wasn't available.

"Let me feel how heavy it is," said Bruce.

We pulled the Yamaha out of the back of the SUV and Bruce tried to lift the awkwardly long and heavy engine.

"Ooof!" he said, lifting it a few inches off the ground. "I can lift it, but I don't know about leaning out over the stern, and lowering it onto the bracket. I might be able to do it, or…"

Or, he might just fall head-first into ten feet of muddy water.

"I think I'll turn the boat around," I said.

"Let me give it a try," he said.

So we did. I rigged a safety line to the motor, so it wouldn't actually plunge to the bottom if Bruce dropped it, but after lifting the motor over the stern, and trying to lower it, Bruce aborted the attempt.

"It's just too heavy," he said.

We sat in the cockpit while Bruce recovered his breath and I recovered my wits—of which I'd nearly been scared out of, seeing my precious motor dangling over the inky depths.

"I've got an idea," I said.

I fetched a pair of blocks from my bo'sun's locker, and quickly reeved some line through them, creating a power block and tackle with a three-to-one power advantage.

"We can hoist one end of the tackle to the top of the mizzen mast, attach the other end to the outboard, and use the tackle to lower the engine onto the bracket. The tackle will support all the weight. All you'll have to do is maneuver the engine into place."

"That might work."

"It *will* work," I said.

And it did, and in a seaman-like style. The small crowd of elderly dock-watchers applauded as the engine slid into place.

"There," I said, standing up to admire the gleaming gray engine. "That's beautiful."

I was ready to fire it up and give it a test drive.

"Great," said Bruce, sweating profusely in the mid-day sun. Maneuvering the engine onto the bracket hadn't been as easy for him as it had been for me. "I need a beer."

Well, that's what he gets for being the younger, stronger brother.

* * *

"Eighteen hours," I told *Cabin Boy.* "That's all we've got, more or less."

We were sailing down the St. Lucie River. Yes, *sailing*. After two hours motoring down the final reaches of the Okeechobee Waterway, we'd passed through the last lock and were back on a real river. Brown canal muck had been replaced by clear blue water, tall green trees lined the banks, and a cheery breeze sped us down river.

My new outboard motor had a twenty hour break-in period, just like a new car. After running for twenty hours, the oil would need to be changed. I hoped to have this done in Jacksonville, but if time ran out, I had the tools, oil, and filter required to do it myself.

Only eighteen hours of motoring left, and 250 miles to go. According to my calculations, we'd have to sail at least 150 of those miles.

"If this wind just holds up for a few days..."

I knew that was unlikely, but I was thinking positive. It felt like we'd turned a corner. We finally had a reliable engine *and* a fair wind. With luck, we'd anchor tonight within hailing distance of the ICW. And tomorrow morning, we should be sailing north for the very first time.

North. Even the word sounded marvelous: a cool breeze wafting through tall pines; ice cold water trilling down a mountain stream; warm kisses on a cold night...

"Get a grip, dude," I told myself.

I mopped my brow and leaned a bit to the left to stay in the patch of shade cast by my tarp. Not for the last time, I wished the trees were tall enough to shade the river.

We ran down stream all morning with the wind nearly at our back. At Pendaris Cove, the river opened up and was nearly a half-mile wide. A fleet of small sailboats tacked back and forth, racing in the lively breeze. I stayed out of their way, and the *Blue Moon* creamed steadily downwind, making up for all those days of motoring.

A mile later, we passed under several large bridges, then followed the channel around to the right. The river was even wider there—a couple miles, perhaps—but the wind was still on the beam and we ran on without tacking.

As always, the *Blue Moon* attracted curious boaters of all stripes. Sailboaters tacked over and shouted things like, "she's a real beauty!" and powerboaters zoomed out of their way to check out the oddity.

"Looks like a lot of work!" was the powerboater's favorite comment, as we rolled in their wake.

For once, I didn't mind.

Again the river bent around to the right, into the final leg before meeting up with the ICW. This put us straight into the wind, but as long as it kept blowing, we had plenty of time to beat up to the fabled Manatee Pocket.

I'd been hearing about the Manatee Pocket for 200 miles. It was supposed to offer great protection from all winds and was lined with marinas and restaurants.

As always, the wind seemed stronger as soon as we turned into it, but the *Blue Moon* seemed to love the sailing after her long time motoring. She drove eagerly into the wind, and the spray that blew over her bow was deliciously cool.

But an hour later, the wind faded, leaving us a few miles short of the Pocket. We could have motored the rest of the way, but I didn't want to waste precious engine hours. I used the last of the wind to sail into a well protected anchorage, just north of the Pocket.

As we ghosted into Hooker Cove, I dropped the anchor in eight feet of water and we slowly swung into the dying breeze. It's amazing how fast the energy drains out of you, once the anchor goes down. I used my final wisps of strength to tie up the sails. That did me in. It was all I could do to fetch a warm beer, but somehow I managed it.

I sat in the cockpit with a couple cushions behind my back. What a day it had been—we'd only motored two hours. If this southerly breeze held up, I'd be able to make it to Jacksonville within the break-in period.

Eating seemed too much trouble. When the sun went down, I lit my trusty kerosene anchor light and hoisted it to the mizzen top. A piece of cheese, a few crackers, and another beer did for dinner.

I lay in the cockpit and waited for the sharp white stars to appear in the deep blue blanket overhead, but the boat's gentle rolling must have put me to sleep…

The roar of a fast motor boat woke me. A stern light flashed past, and then a bow wake threw the *Blue Moon* onto her side.

"Get a brighter anchor light, you jerk!"

Gripping the gunnels, I sat up and peered after the motor boat racing away through the pitch-dark anchorage. It was a typical local fishing boat, with a small steering cabin, open in the back. The driver was silhouetted against two bright monitors mounted in the dash. Probably a big GPS chart plotter, and maybe a radar screen.

He'd sounded scared and angry, but not as angry as I was. He'd probably been driving through the dark, staring at his GPS screen, instead of preserving his night vision and watching where he was going. He could have killed both of us and I was glad we'd scared the bejeezus out of him.

But as far as I could see, the close call hadn't slowed him down. He was out of sight in a minute.

"What a jerk!" I said.

But then I looked up at the cheery anchor light that had stood guard over us all night, every night, for the past month. Compared to the wash of bright background lights on shore—halogen street lights, restaurant signs, car headlights—it looked dim, indeed. Its kerosene flame was just as bright as it had always been, but the places we'd been so far—the west coast of Florida, and the Okeechobee Waterway—had been much darker. Here, with the bright lights of Florida's Gold Coast all around us, the little flame just wasn't bright enough.

Sadly, I took down the old brass light and hoisted the much brighter battery-operated lantern I'd been using in the cabin. Not as homey, I thought, but probably safer.

We really *had* turned a corner…

* * *

Our luck held, and for the next week the wind blew strong and steady from the south or east. The ICW ran north for mile after mile, up the so-called Indian River. The width of this saltwater 'river' varied. Sometimes it was two miles wide and sometimes it was pinched between palmy islands, but usually it stretched a mile from shore to shore.

It was quite beautiful: aqua-blue water, dotted by islands rimmed, like Margarita glasses, with a fringe of white sand. Here and there, a lone fisherman stood in a small boat, angling under the bright, hot sun.

And always there was room to sail. The wind blew like a southerly trade wind, and every day we ticked off mile after mile, only starting the engine to motor in or out of anchorages.

'Happy families are all alike,' and so are happy sailing days. But lest the sailor become bored or jaded, King Neptune always provides excitement: in this case, in the form of violent thunderstorms. Every afternoon, black clouds gathered over the mainland. Slowly they piled up, up, up into angry, roiling mountains with white peaks and purple underbellies. They marched up and down the coast, unpredictably, while bolts of yellow lightning jagged down, skewering unlucky souls on golf courses.

Because the land and sea were so flat, you could see the storms approaching from miles away. But their movements were capricious. You never knew if they were going to stomp right over you, or slip past without leaving a drop on deck. The gates of Hades could open up on a fishing boat a quarter-mile away, while over the *Blue Moon*, blue skies reigned.

So every afternoon, these storms provided the entertainment. Usually they missed us by miles, but once a storm veered ominously in our direction and I scurried into the lee of an island to drop anchor, just in case it struck.

And strike it did. I hid in the cabin while lightening flashed all around us and rain gushed in through hastily-closed portlights. I dogged them down tight to turn off the drips, but that didn't keep the wind from tossing us around like a toy ship in a very small bottle.

It was marvelous.

At the end of each day, whenever I had the chance, I dropped anchor off a town or city, and rowed ashore to find a bar where I could drink a cold beer and watch a soccer game. The World Cup was in progress, and if I didn't catch at least one game each night, I felt cheated. But towns didn't always appear when I needed them, and when they did, they all looked pretty much the same.

Except for St. Augustine, which was Helena's favorite city in Florida. I anchored off the Municipal Marina just in time to sit out the daily thunderstorm, and when it blew over, I rowed to the marina dock and paid my ten-dollar landing fee. This granted me the luxuries of tying up *Cabin Boy* for the evening, and using the marina's showers and other facilities. By now I was a connoisseur of showers, and St. Augustine's were the best I'd seen so far. Clean, new, and with lots of hot water.

After showering, I took a long stroll around the city, looking for a good beer. St. Augustine's Spanish architecture is striking and unlike anything else in Florida. It's old, of course. The city is the oldest in North America, and looks more European than American. Also like a European city in the summer, it's crowded. Its main drag, St. George Street, is a tourist trap. But off St. George, the tourists thin out quickly and there are great restaurants, shops, and especially homes. I walked and explored, and for some reason decided I wanted an English beer. Nothing too exotic (this was Florida, after all). I didn't expect to find a bottle of Thomas Hardy's Dorchester Ale, for example. The beer he described as *"of the most beautiful colour that the eye of an artist in beer could desire; full in body, yet brisk as a volcano; piquant, yet without a twang; luminous as an autumn sunset; free from streakiness of taste; but, finally rather heady."*

No, that would be expecting too much. Perhaps just a Newcastle Brown Ale. The kind of beer you can find in any New York supermarket.

I should have known better.

Just before expiring from thirst, I found an olde English pub. Or so the sign said. 'Faux English Pub' would have been more accurate. The signs on the wall said, *Samuel Smith* and *Fuller's*, but the beer taps said, *Budweiser* and *Miller*.

"An English pub with no English beer?" I asked the bartender. She didn't seem to understand the question.

So I kept walking, and eventually found a Japanese restaurant run by a young English guy. I was happy to find a tap with *Boddington's Bitter* written on it, and he was happy to find someone interested in the World Cup. By the time I rowed back to the *Blue Moon*, a silver moon was rising over St. Augustine.

The next day, the Indian River narrowed into a channel that was too twisty to sail in. I cashed in the remainder of my engine break-in hours, and motored the rest of the way. Eight days after leaving Indiantown, we tied up at a marina in Jacksonville and celebrated.

Next morning, the Yamaha dealer showed up at the dock to pull my engine. We chatted for a few minutes while he admired the *Blue Moon*. It was the first time he'd actually seen her.

"So how did the engine run?" he finally asked.

"Like a clock," I said. "Started up easily. Plenty of power."

"Great, I'm glad to hear it."

"And the long shaft keeps the prop down in the water, where it should be. I love it."

"It's a great engine," he agreed. "I'm not crazy about your bracket, though."

I looked at the thin aluminum bracket that held the engine on the back of the *Blue Moon*. "What's wrong with it?"

"It's a little flimsy for a four-stroke engine," he said, frowning. "Four-strokes are heavier and more powerful than the old two-strokes," he said. "Probably won't happen, but under the right conditions, you could shear that bracket right off."

Great. I'd just about erased the image of my engine plunging to the bottom of the Indiantown Marina. Now I had a new, even worse image in my head.

"I do have a safety line rigged..." I said.

"The real problem is the angle. Your transom is raked at... what? Thirty-five degrees?" He eyed the shapely *Blue Moon*'s transom. "Yeah, about that. But most engines can only be adjusted about fifteen degrees. That's why the engine is tilted so much."

"Ah... I'd wondered about that."

"The problem is the oil."

"The engine oil?"

He nodded. "The engine needs to be vertical so the oil can circulate easily. With it tilted back like that, you're not getting the best lubrication."

"That doesn't sound good."

"You really should mount the bracket on a wedge, so the motor can sit upright."

"So I need a much heavier bracket, and I need to mount it on a wedge..."

"That's what I'd do," he said.

"Blast," I said, "I wonder if I should do that right now... while you've got the engine off the boat? Be a heck of a lot easier than taking the engine off again in North Carolina, or wherever."

"That would make sense."

"Double blast," I said, realizing—belatedly—that I'd just uttered the magic words '*I wonder if I should...*', which meant I must do it—whatever 'it' was—and do it immediately. I groaned. "That's sounds like a big job."

He nodded, then chuckled, as if I'd just said something funny.

"That's boats for you."

CHAPTER 14

YE OLDE DOG

The more efficient you are at doing the wrong thing, the wronger you become. It is much better to do the right thing wronger than the wrong thing righter. If you do the right thing wrong and correct it, you get better. — *Russell L. Ackoff*

Friction, I thought, drinking a cold beer at the marina bar that night. That was the problem: too much friction. No matter what I tried to do, a swarm of problems slowed me down. In an ideal world, a certain effort applied to wheel A, would turn axle B, and move the project ahead C. In the real world, a portion (sometimes a large portion) of effort was always wasted overcoming friction— the forty-five unexpected gremlins that drained time, cash, and energy—so it always seemed to take a massive effort to move the project forward.

"That's life, I guess," I said to the fellow on the next bar stool. I'd been explaining my theory of friction to him in some detail. Probably more detail than he actually wanted to hear, but it's the nature of marina bars to encourage both complaining and com- miseration: we'd all been there.

"Without friction, there'd be no sex," he said, shrugging his shoulders. "You gotta take the good with the bad."

For some reason, that insight struck me as exceptionally deep, as well as a classic example of *reductio ad absurdum*. While I dimly considered the proposition through a beery haze, the joke was bat- ted back and forth amongst the four or five other guys at the bar, while the female bartender rolled her eyes, until finally the joke ground to a halt.

Friction, again.

"I wouldn't mind so much," I said, returning to my topic—the impossible job of laminating a massive wedge on a dock, without any tools, clamps, or workbench—"but it's so hot!"

It was now July, and the prospect of trying to do real work under the brutal, unrelenting sun was daunting. I wasn't sure I could do it. 10:30 at night and it was still 95 degrees outside. I could hardly bear the idea of trading the chill of the air conditioned bar for my hot and stuffy cabin.

"How do people stand it down here?" I said.

"You think it's hot now?" one of the guys said. "Wait until you get to the Georgia swamps."

He looked around the bar, looking for and getting grunts and nods of agreement from the others. Then he turned his glazed eyes on me, and said, "You ain't seen nothing, yet."

That did it for me. Next morning, I called Helena.

"Why don't you come home for the summer?" she said. "You can build or buy whatever it is you need, do it properly, and install it when you go back."

"That *would* be easier than trying to build it on the dock," I said, warming to the idea. "And it is bloody hot."

"Come home. I don't want you dying of heat stroke down there."

I didn't need a second invitation. The next day I flew back to the relative cool of New York. I'd arranged to leave the *Blue Moon* and *Cabin Boy* in the Jacksonville marina for the remainder of July and August, and to have the Yamaha dealer hang onto my engine until I got back.

Two months later—in mid-September—I was back in Jacksonville with a sturdy new bracket, a beautifully laminated wedge to mount it on, and a few new tricks up my sleeve.

I'll skip past the miserable details and just say: four days later, I'd removed the old bracket (with the help of an angle grinder that created a spectacular fountain of sparks as I ground off the old bolts) and installed the new heavy-duty bracket on a beautifully laminated wedge. When the Yamaha dealer finally lowered the engine onto the bracket, the outboard hung straight up and down, just as it was supposed to.

"That's better," he said. "You could hang a small car off that bracket."

"Worth the time and money?" I asked.

"Definitely. It's one less thing to worry about," he said, mopping his brow after muscling the engine onto my boat. "And if you're lucky, the weather will start to cool soon, too."

It was still plenty hot, but not as hot as it had been in August, according to the locals. And it would quickly cool off as we moved north.

With the engine back on the boat, it was time to resume my voyage. In the past, I would have left the marina whenever I was ready. But not now. Now, I wanted to wait and 'catch my tide'.

This was an idea I'd picked up back in New York, where I'd been reading Arthur Ransome's *Swallows and Amazons* series of eye-opening children's books set in 1930s England. Ransome was an avid sailor and packed his books with practical sailing tips: from building a new mast, to using range markers, to not allowing monkeys to run around the deck of a schooner with a lit cigar (hint: don't leave the cap off your gas tank).

But it was an episode in Ransome's *Coot Club* that opened my eyes to a problem that had been plaguing me for most of my journey.

In this adventure, Tom Dudgeon and his fellow Coots sail the *Teasle*—a engineless Norfolk Broads sailboat—on an epic voyage down the River Bure, through Great Yarmouth, and up the River Waveney. The lower parts of these rivers are estuaries, meaning that twice a day, the North Sea floods in through the inlet at Great Yarmouth. The sea then overpowers the rivers and they flow *backwards*—upstream. And they flow fast—so fast that an engineless boat like the *Teasle* could not sail against them. To get through Great Yarmouth, Tom and the Coots had to sail with the currents, so the currents worked for them, rather than against them.

In short, they had to 'catch their tide'.

Tom's problem struck a loud chord with me. Many times on my own voyage, I'd been mystified by the *Blue Moon*'s speed (or lack of it) over the ground, even when we'd been fairly churning through the water.

The worst experience had been on the west coast of Florida, as we coasted down the side of Gasparilla Island. Our progress had *"mysteriously slowed to a crawl. Yes, the wind was blowing hard on our nose; yes the wind had kicked up a short chop; but the little engine on our transom was running gamely at nearly full throttle. We seemed to be fairly whizzing through the water, yet as I watched the trees on the shore, we were just inching forward. If the wind blew any harder, we'd start moving backwards! How could this be?"* — *The log of the Blue Moon.*

It was now obvious to me that the answer to this question was: 'current'.

I was embarrassed by my own ignorance. It hadn't been the wind or waves that forced me into Boca Grande. Clearly, the Gulf of Mexico had been flooding into Charlotte Harbor and up into the ICW. The current had probably been running 3 or 3.5 knots against me, reducing my speed over the ground to a crawl.

It seemed so obvious now. How had I sailed my whole life without taking any notice of currents? There were eight foot tides in my home waters of Huntington, NY, and everyone knew about strong currents in Plum Island Gut, but in the broad reaches of Long Island Sound, they were easily ignored.

But ignore them I could not in the long, restricted estuaries of the ICW, where the current frequently ran fast and furious for miles at a stretch—sometimes as fast as my new engine could push the *Blue Moon*.

If I sailed with the current, rather than against it, I could save both time and gasoline. That would clearly be an enormous improvement, but could I do it? Was it practical?

* * *

Even Tom Dudgeon found it difficult to time the currents. To transit through Great Yarmouth, he had to time the *Teasel's* passage so they could ride the *ebb* current down the Bure, arrive in Great Yarmouth when the current stopped flowing out to the sea (called *slack water*), and then ride the *flood* current up the Waveney.

He and his mates, the twins Port and Starboard, tried to calculate when slack water would arrive in Great Yarmouth, but the problem was too difficult for them. You might think slack water would coincide with low tide, but curiously, you would be wrong. Near the mouth of large estuaries, slack water always lags behind high and low tide. And not by minutes, but by hours.

How many hours? That is the difficult question. You can't calculate it—the problem is too complicated. You have to discover the lag from observation, from experience. Tom and the Coots leaned on 'local knowledge'—the experience of old timers who knew the movements of their home waters as well as they knew the movement of the sun in the sky. Those old salts knew when it would be slack water in Great Yarmouth, and how long it would take to get there, taking into account the varying speed of the current, the wind, and their boat. All without a calculator or iPhone app.

I had exactly the same problem ahead of me. Only the names of the rivers were different.

I had to sail down Pablo Creek instead of the River Bure; cross the St. Johns River, instead of Great Yarmouth; and sail up Sisters Creek, instead of the Waveney. The St. Johns was the largest river in Florida—an estuary with powerful currents that flooded into both Pablo and Sisters Creeks. The two creeks were estuaries that flowed fast in both directions, depending on the tide.

When I left this time, I meant to do it the Coot Club way: ride the ebb current down Pablo Creek, cross the St. Johns at slack water, and then ride the flood current up Sisters Creek. That was the goal. But I faced the same problem that had stumped Tom: when would it be slack water on the St. Johns?

Clearly, it was time to seek some local knowledge. I would start with the dock master. Surely he would know.

"We have a tide table you can use. Posted right over there," said the kid in the dock master's office.

"This is the tide table for Jacksonville Beach," I said, after in-

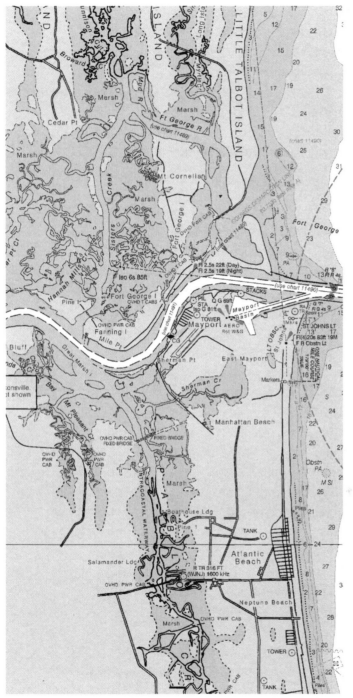

Pablo Creek, St. Johns River, Sisters Creek

specting the table—one of those cards printed with a real estate advertisement on the top. "That's nowhere near here."

"That's what everyone uses," the kid shrugged. "High tide here is about two hours later."

"I'm actually looking for a current table for the St. Johns."

"Huh?" he said. "What for?"

"I'm trying to figure out when slack water is on the river."

"Never seen a current table, just tide tables," he said. "Wouldn't slack water be at low tide?"

If only it was that easy.

I didn't have much better luck chatting with guys on the dock, or in the marina bar. They knew about the current (mostly) but didn't give it much thought.

"My boat does twenty knots," one guy said. "What do I care if the current is making me do twenty-two knots, or eighteen knots? Don't waste your time with that crap. Just get a bigger engine."

So much for local knowledge. I had better luck on the Internet, where I eventually found the current table I needed on the NOAA website. Tomorrow, it said, slack water would follow an ebb tide on the St. Johns at both 5:00 in the morning, and 5:30 in the afternoon. About 2½ hours after low tide. That sounded about right to me.

The St. John's was about seven miles down stream, so I'd need to leave the marina about 1½ hours before slack tide. I didn't want to travel in the dark, so that ruled out a 3:30 a.m. departure.

A 4 p.m. departure would give me enough time to stock my larder for the trip, and run a few last minute chores.

I sat back on my bunk, and laid aside my laptop.

"Right," I said. "4 p.m. it is then."

I went to dinner, feeling like a real Coot.

* * *

I had another new idea I wanted to try. When I started my journey, back in Steinhatchee, I had some odd ideas (in retrospect) about food and cooking: I figured it would be a hassle to constantly worry about ice, so I didn't bring a cooler; I thought I would enjoy whipping up tasty meals from basic ingredients, as I did at home—the one difference being that I'd limit myself to ingredients that didn't require refrigeration; I thought my crude one-burner stove would be adequate for my simple needs.

Wrong, wrong, and oh, so wrong.

Breakfast wasn't so bad. In the spring, when it was still chilly in the morning, my standard breakfast of tea, oatmeal, and fruit was simple and fast to make. I varied the oatmeal with honey or maple syrup, dried or chopped fruit, nuts and other grains, and never got bored with it.

Until it got hot. Firing up my one-burner stove in the morning, after sweltering all night, was not appealing.

As the weather warmed, my breakfasts evolved into hunks of baguette torn off and smeared with jelly, fruit, and tea. Not as nutritious, but easier to stomach.

Lunch was always a challenge. I never wanted to anchor for long, so there was no time for cooking. Without refrigeration, I couldn't depend on leftovers from the previous night. I needed something fast and simple, and more often than not, that meant sandwiches with fillings that didn't need refrigeration.

In other words, I ate a lot of peanut butter and jelly sandwiches. I mixed them up with sandwiches made with those small cans of corned beef or ham spread, with lots of hot English mustard. Add some cookies (oatmeal and raisin were my favorites), fruit, a warm Coke…

Not fine dining, but it worked.

The real problem was dinner. By the time I dropped anchor, I was usually too hot and tired to have much appetite. I'd think about cooking—digging ingredients out of my cupboard or storage boxes, chopping onions on a cutting board on my bunk, heating up the cabin with my one burner stove—and I'd quickly lose what little interest I had in food. So I rarely ate dinner. I'd have a glass of warm whiskey to unwind, tear off a piece of baguette, perhaps. Later on, have a cookie…

Between Steinhatchee and Indiantown, I lost twenty pounds. That was the real measure of my original meal plan: great as a diet, not so great for keeping sailors happy and energetic. My big mistake was thinking it would be hard to keep a cooler stocked with ice. That might be true for off-shore sailors, but not if you have to stop at a marina for gas every other day. Marinas cater to fishermen, and fishermen need ice for their fish and—more importantly—their cold beer. Case closed. Ice is *not* hard to find on the water. Not even a little bit.

By the time I got to Jacksonville, this fact had penetrated my sun-addled brain, so I purchased one of those large, six day super-coolers. The cooler was big enough to hold a large block of ice. Two plastic baskets hung on a lip inside the cooler, to keep food off the ice and out of the water that collected at the bottom. There was room at one end of the cooler to stand up a quart of milk, a pitcher of iced tea, and a few cans of beer. The thought of an ice cold beer at the end of the day made my mouth water.

I stocked the rest of cooler with proteins and luxuries: yogurts, several types of cheese and salamis, milk, eggs, butter, and that essential food of the gods: mayonnaise. I ditched most of my basic ingredients but kept a few meals-in-a-can that could be 'hotted up', as they say in the old books, and eaten.

In old yachting tales, hearty sailors often cooked their meals by boiling a pot of sea water and throwing in two or three unopened cans of food. After heating up, the cans were opened, and dished out. On less elegant boats, the food was eaten right out of the can. The pot of hot salty water was then used to wash up. Quite an efficient system, but I mainly intended to eat cool, fresh foods, like bread, cheese, salads, and fruit. These were the only foods that appealed to me when I was hot and tired. Nothing to cook, little to clean up. Lunch and dinner, sorted.

That was the theory, anyway. Only time would tell if it would work. But with my larder stocked with fresh food and ice, there was nothing to do but wait for my tide.

4 p.m. was a late start, but with a favorable tide, I hoped to do six or seven knots over the ground and make my anchorage in Alligator Creek, just off the Amelia River, some twenty-two miles north, before dark. Just before 4 p.m., I said goodbye to a few

new friends on the dock, backed carefully out of my slip, double-checked to make sure *Cabin Boy* was securely tied, and headed back onto the ICW. I'd promised Helena I wouldn't quit until I sailed past the Huntington lighthouse. This time, it was Long Island Sound or bust. Yeah!

The wind was light out of the east, so there'd be no sailing unless the wind picked up. The temperature was 87 degrees and there wasn't a cloud in the sky.

As soon as we turned onto Pablo Creek, I checked the first buoy to see which way the current was running, and how fast. I had an excellent set of pictures that showed what buoys look like when the current flows at different speeds:

At 0.3 knots, a small wake can be seen on one side of the buoy. The buoy inclines slightly.

At 0.6 knots, the wake deepens and the water is disturbed on both sides of the buoy.

At 1.0 knot, the buoy leans over and a whirlpool-like eddy forms.

At 2.2 knots, the buoy's 'wake' whitens.

With these simple photos to guide me, it was clear that the current was running towards the St. Johns River, at between one and two knots. Just as I'd hoped. The fastest part of the tide was over, but still ebbing us along. I didn't want to arrive at the St. Johns before slack water, so I throttled down until we were doing just six knots over the ground, according to my GPS. Perfect.

The engine was running like a top; the *Blue Moon* looked great. I had a new, larger tarp rigged over the boom and sat in blessed shade. We were headed north, it was a beautiful day, and all was right with the world.

I kept my eyes on the buoys as we passed them, one by one. It was easy to see that the current was slowing down. When we crossed the wide St. Johns around 5:15 p.m., it was hard to tell which way the current was flowing. It was slack water.

On the other side, in Sisters Creek, the current started out slack, as expected, but when we were half-way up the creek, it was unexpectedly running *against* us!

JOHN ALMBERG | 179

This confused me until I looked at the chart again. We were almost to Ft. George River, which is another inlet, just north of the St. Johns inlet. Clearly, the flood currents from both rivers had been fighting it out on Sisters Creek, but now we were far enough north that the Ft. George current was winning. When we crossed the Ft. George, we again rode the flood and had the current with us. Gradually it strengthened, and the GPS finally showed we were making 6 and even 6.5 knots.

After a couple miles, we came within the influence of the Nassau River—another estuary—and had the current against us for a while, but once we'd crossed that, and headed up the Amelia, we again had the flood with us.

When I dropped anchor in the Alligator Creek, it was a real pleasure to crack open a cold beer, and review our progress on the chart. The currents had been more complicated and varied than those Tom Dudgeon had to contend with, but they'd behaved reasonably and we'd minimized their bad effects, as much as possible. We'd run twenty-two miles in under four hours, which was something of a record for us. All in all, the experiment had been a success.

I ate a deliciously cool yogurt for dinner, along with a small handful of cookies.

Who says you can't teach an old Coot new tricks?

CHAPTER 15

HELMO

Fortune brings in some boats that are not steered
– William Shakespeare

The next day, I sailed across the wide blue Cumberland Sound, with a good breeze blowing off the ocean to our right. I was trying to find the imaginary line that ran down the center of the Sound.

"Do you think we've crossed it, yet?" I asked *Cabin Boy*. He was non-committal, so I gave it a few more minutes, and then decided that, yes, Cumberland Island was now closer than Amelia Island. We'd crossed the Florida-Georgia state line, which ran right down the middle of Cumberland Sound.

"We're in Georgia!" I said.

Cabin Boy was a bit blasé about reaching this important milestone, but I was not. Since leaving Steinhatchee in April, we'd sailed entirely within the state of Florida. The enormous state of Florida. The far-too-big state of Florida.

It was roughly 680 nautical miles from Steinhatchee to Cumberland Sound, via the Okeechobee. Cumberland Sound to Huntington, NY was only 1,138 miles. I'd sailed nearly 40% of the distance home while remaining within the state of Florida. So, yes, crossing into a new state—Georgia—was a big deal. A very big deal, indeed.

I celebrated with an ice cold beer.

The easterly breeze that had been pushing us north for so long was still with us. I took full advantage of it to sail up the western shore of Cumberland Island, up to the Sea Camp Ranger Station at the National Seashore. The National Park Service maintains a small dock there for visiting cruisers. As soon as I tied up to the empty dock, a frail old lady toddled down the ramp to pay me a visit. She told me her name was Jane. She wanted to know if I was sailing a West Wight Potter. I said, sorry, no, but she didn't seem disappointed.

"A Potter looks a lot like yours," she said. "My late husband, Harold, bought one thirty years ago, and he and I sailed that boat all over the East Coast for years."

Jane examined the *Blue Moon* knowingly as she told me of sailing into this very bay, way back before there was a dock or "so many people".

"I'm here with my grandchildren this time," she said. "Showing them some of my favorite places in the world." She laughed. "I'm not sure that they're interested in my old stories, but I'm making them listen, anyway."

"Good for you," I said, finding it quite easy to imagine her as a much younger woman, adventuring with her dashing husband.

"Buying that sailboat was the best thing we ever did," she said, mistily.

A while later, I walked up the beach to the ranger station. Hiking trails led all over the island. I decided to walk across the island to the ocean. The trail led through a grove of live oaks—those stately trees dripping with moss that say, "You're in the South," as soon as you see them. Live oak is a kind of white oak that is harder and heavier than normal white oak. It has a squirrely grain that makes it tough enough to stop cannon balls. That's why Revolutionary War hero Nathaniel Greene came to harvest the island's original old growth forest for shipbuilding lumber. The famous ship, *Old Ironsides*, was built from Cumberland Island live oak.

About half-way across the island, the path ran through a camp ground. The camp was mostly empty, except for a few wild horses that wandered fearlessly across the path. I knew the island was famous for these horses, but seeing them roaming free in the middle of a campground was startling.

On the other side of the island, the path emerged onto the

eastern dunes. These wild, barren hills stretched to the horizon, north and south, unbroken by human habitation. They looked like something you'd find on the coast of Cornwall. There were ten people on this massive stretch of beach, all clustered by the foot of the path, as if they were afraid to wander too far up or down that lonely beach. No one was swimming. Ever the rebel, I made a small pile of my clothes at the water's edge and dove in. The water was amazingly warm. People watched, as if waiting to see what would happen. Days later, someone told me that Cumberland Island had the largest population of man-eating sharks on the eastern seaboard.

I spent the night anchored about one-half mile north of the dock. For the first time on the east coast, it was dark. I mean, really dark.

"Welcome to Georgia," I whispered to *Cabin Boy*, while checking my anchor light, but he was already asleep.

* * *

It was midmorning before the current turned in our favor, but the minute it did, we headed up the relatively wide Cumberland Sound. I'd spent the morning studying the chart. We'd soon be winding our way through the Georgia swamps, which would require plenty of motoring. But for now, we could still sail. I was determined to leave the engine off for as long as I could.

The wide, nearly empty Sound seemed the perfect place to try out my new auto-tiller. Way back in April, at the very beginning of my voyage, I complained in my log about being relegated to 'crew member':

"I had been looking forward to Captaining my boat on a carefree cruise along a balmy palm-fringed shore. Instead, I seem to be nothing more than the Crew who is expected to do this and do that all day and all night long.

I resent it!

But after a few days, the Blue Moon and I have come to terms. I give it what it needs, and she is giving me at least as much back. I am happy to be 90% crew, and 10% captain. We are reconciled to this rela-

tionship. It fits us."

There were many reasons why I felt like an overworked galley slave, but the main problem was the tiller: I was a slave to it. My sheet-to-tiller steering system worked fine when sailing off-shore, but it didn't work at all when motoring, and was too hard to adjust while sailing in twisty, narrow channels. So I'd been glued to the tiller for hundreds of miles and was thoroughly sick of it.

The *Blue Moon* came with an auto-tiller—an old Navico Tillerpilot. Bob, the previous owner, told me it didn't work, and indeed it did not when I tried it. Didn't even power up. I'd never owned an auto-tiller before, so didn't appreciate how useful one could be. Auto-tiller? We tough sailors don't need no stinkin' auto-tillers! So I'd just sent it home with Helena and forgotten all about it.

But while I was home for the summer, I'd suddenly remembered it. It took me a while to find it, stuck in with the cans of paint and tools and supplies I'd sent home, but when I lifted the long, slender Tillerpilot out of a box, and held it up to the light, such was my longing for steering-salvation that it looked to me like Narsil—the sword that was broken:

> *"...on its blade was traced a device of seven stars set between the crescent Moon and the rayed Sun, and about them was written many runes... Very bright was that sword when it was made whole again; the light of the sun shone redly in it, and the light of the moon shone cold, and its edge was hard and keen."*
> *-- J.R.R. Tolkien,*

I put it on my workbench and carefully took it apart. If I could build a wooden boat, perhaps I could fix an auto-tiller... Such is the logic of hope.

Using small alligator clips, I hooked the auto-tiller up to a 12 volt power supply and threw the switch. Nothing happened. I took it apart and probed around its innards with a voltmeter, but couldn't find a hint of voltage anywhere. Obviously power wasn't reaching the main unit. Could it be as simple as a bad power cord or connector? There did seem to be a bit of corrosion on the contacts.

I cleaned the metal contacts with a pen knife and a bit of sandpaper and—crossing my fingers—hooked up the power again.

With a strangled beep and a single flashing light, the Tillerpilot came back to life after who knew how many years. I did a little dance, put it back together, and added it to my growing pile of equipment to be brought back to Jacksonville.

I'd been too busy to try the auto-tiller until now. With the wind on the beam and a wide channel to sail in, it seemed the perfect time. I tied off the tiller and dove down into the cabin to fetch the Tillerpilot out of the bottom of a storage box. Dumb place to put it. In the thirty seconds it took to find it, the *Blue Moon* veered forty-five degrees off course and headed straight for the shallows. Just in time, I climbed back into the cockpit and put her back on course.

"And that," I told *Cabin Boy*, "is why we need an auto-tiller."

Steering with one hand, and fiddling with the other, I plugged the Tillerpilot into the power socket that the *Blue Moon*'s Builder had installed in the cockpit for just that purpose. The auto-tiller warbled to life, its 'standby' light flashing.

The blessed Builder had also installed the two needed attachment points: one on the deck, and one on the tiller. I snapped the auto-tiller into place on both ends and then realized I could not steer anymore—the tiller was immobilized in the Tillerpilot's iron grip. Panicking a bit, I pressed its 'Auto' button. With a bleat, the auto-tiller began working: its push-rod pulsing in and out and the tiller waggling back and forth in response. Magically, the *Blue Moon* steadied on her course.

We were heading a bit too far to starboard, though. I pressed the 'Port' button several times. Each time the auto-tiller beeped and turned us one degree to port. We were soon headed straight down the channel, the auto-tiller quickly making the continuous course adjustments needed to keep the sailboat on track. All without me touching the tiller.

"Look!" I said to *Cabin Boy*. "No hands!"

I watched the auto-tiller work for a good half-hour, occasionally pressing the 'Port' or 'Starboard' buttons to make the course corrections needed to stay in the channel. It seemed slightly miraculous, but it worked! Worked so well that—after taking a good look around to make sure we weren't about to get run down by a Hullabaloo—I went down into the cabin and made myself a second cup of coffee. What luxury!

Of course, I popped my head out of the companionway every fifteen seconds or so to take a quick look around, but the auto-tiller steered a steady course.

I brought my coffee up into the cockpit, propped myself on some comfy cushions, and sat back to enjoy the ride.

"Let the crew steer, eh?" I asked *Cabin Boy*. "I'm the captain, after all. Five degrees to port, helmsman!"

I reached over and clicked the 'Port' button five times, and the *Blue Moon* settled on her new course.

"Very good," I said. "Steady as she goes."

Now that was sailing. Even better than having a magic sword.

"I should give you a name," I said, thinking for a moment. Then I held my right hand out over my new crew member. "I name you... what?" Wait, wait, I had it!

"I name you, *Helmo!*"

I looked back at *Cabin Boy*, splashing along behind on the end of his tether.

"*Cabin Boy*, meet *Helmo. Helmo, Cabin Boy.*"

Helmo was far too good a steersman to be distracted by this silliness; he just kept his eye on the compass and steered as straight a line as he could.

Cabin Boy was finally impressed: "*New crew member. Even better steersman than the captain. Best day of my life!*"

* * *

At the northern end of Cumberland Sound, we crept past the Naval Submarine Base at Kings Bay. I'd been hoping that one of their Ohio-class submarines would surface next to the *Blue Moon* during the night, to check us out, as the dolphin had back on the Manatee River. But then I imagined red laser dots swimming on my chest as I squinted into a spotlight, and a bit of the romance went out of the fantasy.

Anyway, from what I'd heard, the Navy closes Cumberland Sound to pleasure boats when a modern-day leviathans sails out of Kings Bay, whether to resume its patrol along the chilly shores of the Barents Sea, or to peep through periscopes at bikinis along the French Riviera. So it was probably a good thing I didn't run into one along the way. But I did hope to get a glimpse of one as we cruised past the entrance to Kings Bay. Maybe even snap a photo.

Not a chance. Two unfriendly looking gunboats cruised the entrance, making me feel guilty just by being there.

"That's ridiculous," I told *Cabin Boy*. "We haven't done anything wrong."

I gave the sailors a friendly wave, but their icy stares made me keep my camera in my lap.

"You don't need to see our identification," I said under my breath. "These aren't the boats you're looking for... We can move along."

We sailed past the glowering gray gunboats, and headed up into the northern reaches of Cumberland Sound, where the water is too shallow for nuclear submarines.

Still, I'd liked to have seen one.

I had just enough time to get my sails down before the ICW turned into a narrow channel bordered on either side by green and gold grass. This was my first taste of the vast marsh that protects the coast of Georgia, from the north end of Cumberland Island, all the way to Savannah.

The gloom-and-doomsters in Florida had called it the Georgia Swamp, but it's really a marsh. A marsh is dominated by grasses, rushes, or reeds, whereas a swamp is dominated by trees and bogs, but that fine distinction was beside the point for the gloomsters: 'Georgia Swamp' sounds so much more miserable than 'Georgia Marsh'.

As we motored into the first narrow channel, a sun shower swept over us, dappling the flat surface of the water with fat cool drops. The sun rayed through rifts in the clouds, and a rainbow arced across the golden marshes. I had a good feeling about the next leg of our trip.

I then had a decision to make. In a couple hours, the ICW would cross the wide, and apparently dangerous, St. Andrews Sound. Here's what I read in Claiborne S. Young's excellent, *Cruising Guide to Coastal South Carolina and Georgia*:

> *The ICW passage through St. Andrews Sound is one of the most dreadful sections of the entire Atlantic Intracoastal Waterway from Norfolk to Miami. What is the reason for all this worry? Simply this: The channel does not just cross the sound. Rather, in order to avoid extensive shallows that guard the sound's midwidth, the ICW cuts east for a short distance on the sound's inlet channel. Waterway cruisers are all but out to sea before turning into more sheltered waters to the (northwest). When winds and tide oppose one another in the inlet, this passage can be truly daunting.*

Dreadful. Daunting. That did not sound good, particularly since the east wind had been blowing onshore for many days, and the National Weather Service was reporting nine foot waves on the ocean, just on the other side of Cumberland Island.

Mr. Young continued:

> *St. Andrews Sound's inlet is not particularly recommended. Many of the markers are not charted, as they are frequently shifted to follow the ever-moving sands. While it is possible for strangers to run the channel, it can sometimes be a white-knuckle experience.*

Gulp. Luckily, the guide had an alternative:

> *In recognition of the often rough conditions on St. Andrew Sound, the Army Corps of Engineers has provided a marked alternate passage by way of Little Satilla River, Umbrella Cut, Dover Creek, Satilla River, and Floyd Creek. Unfortunately, the corps has not been too concerned about maintenance of this passage for some time. Currently, navigators can expect low-water soundings of as little as 4 ½ to 5 feet, with numerous unmarked shoals cutting out from the various points of land*

along the way. The passage is also quite narrow in places... If you can time your arrival to coincide with a rising tide, so much the better.

I weighed the two routes. The passage through the Sound was shorter but riskier; the alternate passage longer but safer. We might be able to handle rough conditions in the Sound, but I didn't like the idea of those 'ever-moving sands'. It just didn't feel right to me, and I'd come to trust my gut.

I always figured my confidence would grow as I spent more time on the *Blue Moon*. Indeed it had, but the experience had not expressed itself in the way I'd expected. Instead of making me more confident in my *abilities*, it had made me more confident in my *judgement*. And that judgement often came in the guise of a gut feeling. Today my gut was saying, *take the safer passage*.

Besides, I wanted to get a closer look at those marshes. They stretched for miles on either side of the main ICW channel, but sailing the ICW was like driving down a highway: it felt like we were cruising past the scenery, rather than through it. The alternate passage plunged into the thick of it.

So when the buoy marking the entrance to Floyd Creek hove into view, I made up my mind: We'd take the alternate passage.

I turned into the narrower channel, and reduced our speed to four knots. I'd only run aground two times since leaving Stein-hatchee, but I feared we might increase our batting average on this passage. If we ran aground on one of those 'unmarked shoals cutting out from the various points of land along the way', I wanted to run aground slowly.

I settled the *Blue Moon* on her new course, letting *Helmo* steer. He needed close watching in these narrow channels, but it was still better than hand-steering. With *Helmo* in charge, I had more time for looking around, for seeking out the marsh's secrets.

The first thing I saw was the largest alligator I'd seen so far, sunning himself on one of those famous shoals. I was surprised to see him, since I thought we were in salt water. He was a real monster with evil green eyes and teeth that glistened yellow in the sunlight. As we cruised by, he slid into the water behind us.

"Watch out," I told *Cabin Boy*. "He could eat you with one bite."

The marsh was a birder's paradise. More than once, I wished Dick Callum, of Arthur Ransome's *Great Northern?*, was aboard as we passed a strange bird roosting in the reeds, or spotted a hawk or eagle hunting far overhead. He could have told me a thing or two about those birds. But even a duffer like me could identify the pair of pink flamingos that stood ankle deep in the shallows beside the channel, fishing.

"Wow," I said to *Cabin Boy* as we passed them. "They really are pink."

Dick would have loved them.

* * *

Late in the afternoon, a particularly menacing thunderstorm gathered on the horizon. I'd grown used to these daily storms, but this one was bigger and blacker than usual. We were out of the alternate passage by then, sailing across the relatively open waters of Jekyll Sound. We raced the storm to the marina in Jekyll Creek, and tied up to their gas dock just before it hit. As lightning flashed and the rain fell hard, I ducked down into the cabin and pulled the hatch shut. It looked like we'd be spending the night on the dock. After eating a light dinner, listening to the rat-a-tat-tat of rain on the cabin top, I settled into my bunk for a good read.

A few hours later, I awoke. Most of the storm had passed over. The tail end of it still drizzled on deck. I cracked the hatch open to get a breath of fresh air and to look at the sky. Lightning played silently on the northern horizon, but it was peaceful in the marina.

When the lightning flashed again, I saw two green eyes staring at me from the far side of the channel. I caught my breath. Could it be the same enormous alligator I'd spotted on Floyd Creek?

"Careful," I told *Cabin Boy*. "He's still after you."

Cabin Boy huddled close under the *Blue Moon*'s stern and shivered. I laughed. Obviously it couldn't be the same 'gator, but it was fun to think it was. *Following us.* Ha! I slid the hatch closed.

After tidying up the dinner things, I turned off the light, and snuggled into my bunk. I was using a light blanket for the first time since Cedar Creek. It wasn't really cold, but with the damp, the blanket felt good.

While I waited for sleep, I planned the day to come. We needed to put some miles behind us. Autumn would be on us before we knew it. I wanted to be home before it got really cold, but how could we increase our daily distance? It was a puzzle.

As I pondered this weighty question, I noticed a faint ticking sound. My wind-up alarm clock? No, I'd ditched that long ago: it was too noisy. This ticking seemed to be coming from outside the ship. *Tick-tock. Tick-tock.*

It was eerie. The harder I listened, the harder it was to hear.

"Just my imagination," I decided. In another moment, I was asleep.

CHAPTER 16

ANGRY ALLIGATOR

If you're going to live by the river, make friends with the crocodile. — Indian proverb

I needn't have worried about seeing the marsh 'up close'. The next day, we were in the thick of it again. We sailed through a sea of grass cut by narrow twisting channels. The small, flat-bottom powerboats favored by locals could often use these cuts, but the *Blue Moon* had to stick to dredged channels—either the main ICW channel, or the occasional side channel that wandered off to a lonely marina or town. These became fewer and fewer as we motored into the heart of the great marsh.

Most of the ICW is adequately marked by red and green buoys. This is not true in the midst of the marsh. Five times the number of buoys would not be enough to mark all the twists and turns, shoals and shallows one finds there. Rather than relying on buoys to mark the trail, ICW sailors must rely on a number of conventions.

The first convention is, *stay in the middle of the channel*. Even for a boat that draws four feet, it's hard to get into trouble if you stick to the center line, although you will hear sailors complain "we ran aground right in the middle of the channel!"

Probably not. It's often difficult to know where the channel is, exactly. Buoys are often a mile or more apart. In most such places, if you stick to the centerline, you won't be far off. But in other places, the main channel is *not* midway between the two shores. It might hug one of the shores, or cross from one shore to the other, or a shoal might stick out into the channel like a thumb, or the grass might be under water at high tide, hiding the edge of the channel, or any of a hundred other complications. In those cases, a buoy can provide the essential clue needed to keep you off the mud. But often, the buoy does not exist. The Army Corps of Engineers apparently expects sailors to keep an eye on their chart and use other clues to stay in the channel.

A depth sounder would have helped. Unfortunately, the one I'd bought over the summer wasn't working yet. The box said it would work 'through the hull', but that didn't include wooden hulls, apparently. I couldn't figure out where else to install it.

Another rule you'll hear ICW sailors talk about is, *don't cut corners*. This sounds so obvious it hardly deserved mentioning. However, while the theory is simple, its practice is not. I'll cite an example that almost left me high and dry. I was headed down a straight cut, sticking to the center of the channel. Up ahead, the channel turned sharply to the right, almost at a ninety degree angle. There was a red buoy straight ahead, almost in the grass beyond the turn. The inside corner of the turn was clear of grass for almost 100 yards. Since my brain had been programmed to 'stay in the middle of the channel', the natural thing to do was to cut the corner—to steer halfway between the grass on both sides. But the red buoy tucked up against the grass on the outside of the turn was a subtle visual cue that said, "Hey, stupid, the channel is over here. Don't cut the corner!"

This leads to another rule, *study your charts*. The chart clearly showed that the channel swept along the outside of the turn—as indeed channels tend to do. So the chart plus the visual cue of the buoy should have been enough for an alert mariner.

Oh, if only it was possible to stay alert for eight or ten hours a day.

I must admit I did not study my charts closely enough. Every night I meant to pull out the charts and study the next day's route to pick out any difficult passages. And I often did pull them out, only to wake several hours later with the cabin light still burning. There is nothing more soporific, I found, than studying charts.

If I'd been a better student, I might even have noticed ranges, sooner.

Range markers are striped, rectangular signs arranged one behind the other at the end of a long channel. When the markers are lined up, one over the other, you are in the center of the channel. If you steer out of the center, the markers move apart. When you steer back again, they realign. We don't have range markers on Long Island Sound, so I wasn't used to watching for them. In the Georgia marshes they were everywhere, so I began to wonder exactly what those odd, stripped signs were.

Of course, I knew about ranges in principle. Arthur Ransome must have loved ranges, because he used several of them in his books. For instance, the Swallows set up a pair of lanterns as a range to guide them into their secret anchorage in the dead of night, and Captain Flint used a range to guide Swallow into dangerous Duckhaven on Crab Island. So as soon as I looked them up in Chapman, I wanted to slap my forehead for being such a duffer. Range markers. Of course!

Ranges are incredibly accurate—even more accurate than a GPS—so obviously they are useful for keeping to the center of narrow channels or piloting safely between dangerous rocks. In the marshes, a pair of range markers replaces many buoys, which is why it's important to watch out for them. If you ignore them, you're sailing blind!

With these low-tech techniques, I managed to keep the *Blue Moon's* keel in deep water through a hundred miles of twisting channel, with one curious lapse.

We were in an exceptionally narrow channel, hemmed in on both sides. The air smelt of grass and baking mud. The sun was so hot, I could feel the weight of hot photons pouring down upon my head. The engine was so quiet I could hear the sounds of insects tick-tick-ticking in the grass. Otherwise, the world was silent.

There was a mudbank on the right side of the channel. As we approached, I noticed an enormous alligator lying upon it. As we reached the bank, the gator stood on its four short legs and watched us with dead-green eyes, as we motored slowly by.

"It's almost as if he's waiting for us," I whispered to *Cabin Boy*.

As we passed, the gator slid into the water behind us. With a flick of his tail, he darted towards us. He snapped at *Cabin Boy*'s transom, then dove under the *Blue Moon*'s keel.

"Geez, did you see that?" I said. "I didn't realize how fast they could move."

I looked everywhere trying to spot him surfacing. Everywhere except where I was going, of course. I felt a hard bump under my feet.

"Is he biting the keel?" I asked. It was all too easy to imagine those yellow teeth sinking into the *Blue Moon*'s fir planking.

A second bump brought me to my senses. The alligator wasn't biting us, we were hitting bottom! I'd been so distracted by the gator that I'd forgotten to watch where we were going. We were dangerously close to the weeds.

I put the tiller down and guided the *Blue Moon* back to the center of the channel.

"Bloody alligator," I said to *Cabin Boy* after my heart had stopped racing. "You don't think its the same one, do you?"

Cabin Boy seemed to whimper. I shortened his painter so he rode a little closer to the *Blue Moon*'s stern. It wouldn't help if the monster returned, but it made him feel a little safer.

* * *

That afternoon, I started worrying about ice. It had been days since I'd been able to buy any. Just a few small cubes floated in cold water at the bottom of my cooler. I'd been studying the cruising guide. The next marina was still twenty-seven miles away. We couldn't make it that far before dark. My fresh food would not last long in the heat without ice. I needed to find some, and soon.

If only we were sailing off Greenland, I mused. I'd just throw my anchor onto a nearby iceberg, climb aboard, and chip off a bucket full of delicious vintage ice. Unfortunately, there aren't many icebergs in Georgia.

It looked hopeless. I'd just have to cook up a grand banquet and throw the leftovers to the gators. Maybe that would appease them. But just then, I spotted a fishing boat. I hadn't seen another boat since morning. I motored towards them.

"Ahoy there!" I shouted across the water.

This being the South, I couldn't just ask for directions without a bit of socializing. Pretty soon, we were gunnel to gunnel, yacking with the two fishermen: thirty-something Todd and his ancient grandfather.

"Don't see many wooden boats in these parts," Todd said.

I told them the short version of the *Blue Moon's* story. By that time, I had several versions memorized. It was too hot for the long version.

"Nice rig," piped in Grandpa in a high, reedy voice. I noticed his faded eyes scanned the *Blue Moon* eagerly.

"He don't say much," said Todd, tapping the side of his head. "A bit deaf."

"Thanks!" I said loudly to Grandpa.

I asked Todd, "Do you know of any marinas around here?"

"No," he answered slowly. "Next marina is twenty-five, maybe thirty miles north of here."

I must have looked a bit discouraged. "That's what my cruising guide says, too."

"Need gas?" he asked. "I could lend you a gallon or two."

"I have plenty of gas, but I'm running low on ice. The last marina didn't have any."

Todd stooped and took a look in his cooler.

"We need most of this for the fish, but I could lend you half a bag if that would help."

"Gosh, you sure?"

Todd just grabbed the bag of ice, dumped half of it into his cooler, and handed me the rest.

"I really appreciate this," I said, taking it. "If you are ever in New York, I owe you one."

"No problem, man. Gotta stick together out here."

"Tell me about it. Between the storms and the enormous alligators… In fact, I think there's one following us."

"A storm, or an alligator?"

"Both!"

"Tick-tock, tick-tock," said grandpa, mysteriously.

Todd glanced up at the lowering sun. "Well, it's getting late. Better get a move on."

"What did he mean?" I asked.

"Time to get him home for his supper," said Todd. "Have a great trip."

"Thanks," I said. "But what did he mean by 'tick-tock'?"

Todd waved, tapped the side of his head, and gunned his engine. The boat roared away, leaving a deep, straight wake down the middle of the channel. The receding sound of their engine was soon no louder than the insects in the marsh grass. They turned a bend, and were gone.

We were all alone again. I looked around, warily.

* * *

That evening, we anchored in a narrow creek just off the main channel. It looked like a thousand other creeks—a narrow thumb of tepid water surrounded by grass—with one difference: it was 6½ feet deep instead of the usual 2, and thus rated a brief recommendation in my cruising guide as 'an adequate anchorage for one small boat'.

One small boat was all I had, and I was glad to reach the creek before dark.

We were a long way from nowhere. I stood on the cabin top— the highest point for miles around—and scanned the horizon for signs of other humans. There weren't any. Just miles of grass and water, with a low hummock of dark trees far to the west, showing where the mainland was.

I flicked on my phone. The screen said, "No signal." I shut it off and stuck it back in my pocket.

"We're in a great spot tonight," I said to *Cabin Boy*. He didn't share my enthusiasm for lonely wildernesses, but it was thrilling for me to be in such an isolated anchorage. It's not easy to feel you are in the wild on the crowded east coast of the United States, but that night, I thought we'd found a bit of it.

JOHN ALMBERG | 197

It was half-dark before I finished tidying up on deck, and full-dark by the time I brought my dinner and a cold beer back up into the cockpit. I toasted Todd and his bag of ice. He'd given us enough to last until morning.

A hot wind blew from the southwest, and the dry marsh grass hissed and writhed like a hundred million snakes in the silver moonlight. Though I always welcomed a breeze at night—there being nothing worse than tossing all night in a hot, airless berth—I didn't like this wind. It was an uncomfortable wind, somehow, and I was glad to finish my meal and retire into the cabin with its cheery light. I closed the hatch and shut out the wind.

"Ah, that's better," I thought.

I found a baseball game on the radio and—lying on my bunk—read and half-listened to the scratchy, friendly voices that sounded so far away.

* * *

Have you ever been woken by water splashed on your face? I have, and I don't recommend it. But Zeus will have his fun.

When I awoke, Zeus himself might have been standing astride the creek, pouring buckets of water down on the *Blue Moon*, the way he did on the night of the Great Flood. Her decks thrummed under the weight of the downpour; she tossed and tugged at her anchor, as if wanting to get away; water poured in through the open portlights, right onto my face.

Instantly, I was out of my bunk. I slammed shut all eight portholes and dogged them down, but still the unnatural rain worked its way in under the heavy bronze and glass covers. How?

Eventually, I discovered the trick: each porthole had two dogs—hand-tightened screws that clamp the cover down—and both needed to be tightened evenly and just so to make the porthole tight enough to resist the deluge. It is not easy to make a major technical discovery like this, with Zeus standing over you, trying to sink your ship with a flood, as I'm sure Deucalion discovered. But I managed it. I shut off the flood. Mostly.

I sat on my damp bunk and listened not to the rain, but to the sound of the *Blue Moon*. It was like being inside a drum. When you are inside a drum, you don't hear the sticks beating on it. No, you hear the drum itself. Its tone; its voice. I liked the *Blue Moon*'s humming voice. I'd heard it before, but not so loud. That night, she sang to me, full-throated.

But after a while, when song began to fade away, I began to worry about poor *Cabin Boy*. He must have been half-drowned in this downpour.

I cracked open the hatch to take a peak at him. By the anchor light, I could see he had a good two inches of water in him, but was in no danger of sinking.

Then I noticed *Cabin Boy* had a companion, and not a friendly one.

A few yards away, mostly submerged, floated an alligator. He was twice as long as *Cabin Boy*, with black, leathery scales—black as the water—black on black. The rain made the water jump around him. His eyes were closed. He looked dead, until I noticed one eye open a slit. He was watching me with an eye that was blacker than black, as black as death itself.

"Get away from here," I hissed at him.

He did not move.

Cold rain dripped down my neck, but I continued to stare back. It was an experience much like my encounter with the dolphin on the Manatee River—wild and supremely primitive—and yet it was profoundly not the same. The gator was no threat to me (as long as I stayed on the boat, I reminded myself), so why should my soul sink instead of fly, as it had at the sight of the dolphin?

Dolphins, being mammals, were much closer relatives, of course. And being intelligent, they felt much closer relations than they actually were. Was my dread of the alligator just the dread of the 'other'? An 'other' that had forked off from mammals on the evolutionary tree so long ago that the memory of the event was lost in dinosaury times? That didn't seem fair of me. I tried to look at the gator in a more companionable light. Mustn't judge by appearances, after all. He didn't ask to be big and scary. It wasn't his fault his teeth were too large to fit in his mouth. Perhaps he was lonely, or afraid of thunder, and just wanted a bit of company.

Right, and maybe he just wanted a cup of tea.

"Go away," I told him. I pulled my wet head in, and slammed the hatch shut.

I listened for a ticking sound, but heard nothing.

There's a good reason why no one wants to "Swim with the Alligators." It's not fair, but that's the way the world is.

CHAPTER 17

BOWSPRIT

Life is for learning. -- Joni Mitchell

I lounged on my bunk with a cup of coffee, writing up my log, feeling lazy. The morning was deliciously cool. The rain had passed, leaving behind one of those gray days that are so easy on a sailor's eyes.

We had a big day ahead of us, the *Blue Moon*, *Cabin Boy*, and I. As soon as we left Cattle Pen Creek, we'd have to tackle St. Catherine's Sound: a wide inlet that would expose us to whatever weather was rolling in from the Atlantic. The wind was still in the east, but it was just a light breeze. The National Weather Service reported a one-to-two foot sea on the ocean, which was surprisingly low, considering the night we'd had, but a sailor should never question good luck.

I flipped through the pages of my log. The further back I went, the less recognizable the fellow who had written them. Was that really my handwriting, scrawled across those water-wrinkled pages? Perhaps, but Tarpon Springs and Cedar Key and Steinhatchee now seemed far, far away.

"Not as far as New York," I reminded myself.

I drank the last of my tea and swung my legs out of the bunk. Time to get going.

Was it cool enough for foul weather gear? I stuck my head out the companionway to feel the breeze.

The jacket, I decided. It would feel good over my shorts and t-shirt until the sun broke through the clouds. And the rain might not be done with us, yet.

I pulled on the new, red, waterproof jacket. My mom had bought it—along with matching overalls—for me over the summer, 'to keep you dry', as she said. It was soft and breathable, unlike the yellow plastic jacket it replaced. It felt good just to put it on.

I climbed into the cockpit to model my new fashion for *Cabin Boy*.

"It's the little luxuries, eh?" I asked him. He did not seem impressed.

I soon had the engine running and the anchor up, and before you could say 'fog' we were motoring down Johnson Creek, toward St. Catherine Sound.

I say 'fog' because there were patches of it hovering here and there over the marsh. I liked a bit of fog in the morning. It softened the air and added romance to the scenery. I wished Helena was there to share it.

We motored slowly out of Cattle Pen Creek, and when we merged onto the broader North Newport River, the breeze seemed to strengthen. I soon had the sails up, and then we were gurgling downstream, with a half knot current helping us along.

A half-hour later, the river began to widen as it approached St. Catherine Sound. The morning was still grey. All I could see around us were the misty banks of the river and—when it wasn't hidden by a patch of fog—the next marker, a red one, about a mile away. Beyond the marker, everything was hidden by a dark gray curtain that hung across the sound, as straight as a wall and as high as the low flying clouds.

I'd never seen anything like that curtain. Was it fog? I didn't think so. An approaching fog bank looked more like a wedge. This was something different. Something interesting.

Anyone with half-an-ounce of sense would have turned tail and fled, but I was curious about this new phenomena and held my course straight towards the advancing wall. By the process of elimination, I decided it must be either rain or a sandstorm. I had heard of sandstorms being blown far out to sea from Africa, but not so far out as Georgia. Perhaps a new volcano had erupted off the coast, and this was dust, boiling out of its mouth. I hadn't listened to the news that morning, but surely the National Weather Service would have mentioned a volcano.

No, it must be rain, I thought. Just rain. I felt oddly relieved, as if a solid wall of rain wasn't bad enough. It was only a quarter-mile off, now. I had to get ready for it.

Helmo was steering, so I was free to batten down the hatches. The chart was already wrapped in a waterproof envelope, so I placed it on my bunk: an easy reach from the cockpit. I lit my running lights, overhauled the lines in the cockpit, making sure the sheets would run free if I had to cast them off in a hurry, and flipped the jacket hood over my wide-brimmed sun hat. Finally, I slid the companionway hatch shut. I looked around, satisfied; we were as ready as we could be.

We were now closing rapidly with the dark curtain wall. It had a solidity to it, like a forest seen from the field. A forest is not actually solid, but a deer that runs into a forest is nevertheless soon hidden by the trees. As I watched, something emerged from this rain-forest: a forty-five foot ketch, all sails set, rocketing through the rain wall, into the open air. Three men in foul weather gear, at first hunkered down in her cockpit, raised their arms in triumph, as if glad to have survived the storm. The ketch flew past without any of her crew even looking towards me. I wondered—just for a moment—if I should have put on my waterproof overalls.

The next moment, we were in it. The *Blue Moon* heeled into a gust of wind, and a few seconds later, the rain hit us. I'd been looking forward, of course, to see what was coming; almost instantly, I was blinded by the rain on my glasses.

"Argh!"

You will allow my small vent of frustration. Rain-on-glasses was a problem that occurred frequently on my voyage. Bob, the previous owner and fellow wearer-of-glasses, had warned me of this problem and had recommended a pair of ski goggles that could be worn over regular glasses. The large, smoked-plastic goggles got just as rain-spattered, but were easier to wipe dry than glasses.

I reached into the cabin and grabbed the goggles off the hook

JOHN ALMBERG | 203

where they swung in easy reach. Sheltering behind the cabin, I wiped my glasses as best I could with a paper towel I kept in my pocket for just that purpose, and put the goggles on over the glasses. I took a quick peek over the cabin top: nothing coming, but the goggles were instantly be-spattered and I was just as blind. I ducked down behind the cabin again, and swiped the goggles dry without taking them off. Better.

I checked the compass: we were still on course. The wind was stiff and gusty, but nothing the *Blue Moon* couldn't handle. We probably had too much sail flying. I considered putting in a reef, but the time to take down sail is before a storm hits. Once you're in it, it's safer to stay in the cockpit and luff through any bad gusts. A squall like this would pass over before I could get the sail down, anyway. The main thing was too keep a good watch forward, despite the blinding rain. There might be another ketch charging through the rain-forest.

I took another peek. Visibility was probably a quarter mile all around. Good. At least nothing would pop out of a cloud and run us down without warning. I just needed to take a look every thirty seconds or so, and make sure we stayed on course. We were following a line of buoys, each about a mile apart, down the Sound. They were numbered: 116, 114a, and 114. I'd been able to see the #116 before the curtain had covered it. It should be visible again, just about now...

I took another look and spotted it off the port bow. Great. I ducked back down and wiped the goggles clean. So far, so good.

The rain was chilly, but my new jacket was thoroughly waterproof. Under it, I was warm and dry. My bare legs were streaming, but it wasn't uncomfortable. Rather exciting, in fact. I gave the thumbs-up signal to *Cabin Boy*, who seemed to be enjoying the rain as much as I.

The red #116 slid by on the port side and then it was time to take another look. This time, there was nothing but grey rain and grey waves in front of us, but I was sure the next buoy would appear soon.

Sitting with my back against the cabin top was the driest and most comfortable position. My hood and wide-brimmed hat kept the rain off my face and goggles. The cabin top blocked most of the wind and rain. The view aft was dramatic: *Helmo* steered a ruler-straight course and our wake was deep, broad, and white. We were making at least five knots. Terrific sailing.

Every thirty seconds, I repeated the cycle of peeking over the cabin, looking around until the rain obscured my vision (about five seconds), ducking back down, and wiping my goggles. In this way, I spotted and then passed the 114a buoy. One more to go.

We were now in the center of the inlet. The open Atlantic was just a mile to the east. Two-to-four foot waves rolled in from the ocean, but the *Blue Moon* climbed over each one in turn, her easy motion softening their blows. We were hard on the wind, but able to point our course. The wind blew fiercely—whipping the rain into my face when I took my peeks, but the *Blue Moon* was in a groove and we just drove forward.

"Not far now," I told *Cabin Boy*.

When we reached the red #114, we'd be as far out into the Atlantic as we'd need to go. We'd round the buoy, and then turn north into the Bear River, on an easy beam reach. The #114 was the hump, and we'd soon be over it.

On the other hand, if we missed the buoy, we'd be headed out of the inlet, into the open ocean. That would not be good. I took more frequent looks over the cabin top, eager to raise the big red buoy on our port bow. It would be hard to miss, but…

As the minutes ticked by, I fought the urge to adjust our course. This urge was irrational, but familiar. When a buoy didn't appear when I expected it, my mind instantly concocted logical explanations: the current was driving us too far to starboard; we were making too much leeway to port; the compass was wrong; the buoy must have dragged.

The current was, in fact, setting us to starboard, and no doubt we were making some leeway to port. I guessed these two actions roughly canceled each other out. That we'd raised the two previous buoys confirmed my reasoning, but fear is not reasonable, and so it thrashes about, looking for a lifeline. This is where the captain must stay cool and trust his navigation. A few rash course changes, and we would indeed be lost, with shoals all around us. But *Helmo* didn't panic. He steered a steady course. As long as I kept my fingers off his buttons, we'd stay headed in the right direction. I focused on keeping a good lookout.

A few minutes later, I really *was* expecting to see the #114. I took another look over the cabin top and was surprised to see the visibility reduced to almost nothing. A thicker, grayer curtain wall seemed nearly upon us. Instinctively, I gripped the cabin top with both hand and held on. A moment later, the *Blue Moon* heeled violently into a forty knot wind. The jib luffed for a moment, the thwack, thwack, thwack of the sail sounding like gunshots. Her rail briefly dipped under the water and blue water flowed into the cockpit. But then her heavy keel and firm lines took control. She righted herself and the water streamed out of her big scuppers as *Helmo* put her back on course.

There seemed more wind than rain now, and I stayed in my lookout position, holding on, and watching for the #114. The wind was fierce and came in great gusts. The end of my bowsprit caught my eye: was it bent slightly at the end where the powerful jib was fastened? Adrenaline flooded into my bloodstream—if the end of the bowsprit broke off, all hell would break loose. But it held and a moment later, the #114 emerged from the rain, right where I'd expected it.

I took the tiller from *Helmo* and made the turn to the north, around the buoy. The wind and waves now came from behind and instantly the world seemed a calmer place. The wind dropped by ten knots, the waves rolled slowly in from behind, and the *Blue Moon* sailed almost upright. I put us on our course to the next buoy, and gave the tiller back to *Helmo*. We were over the hump. The grim Atlantic disappeared behind us faster than we'd approached it.

With the wind aft, it was much easier to keep my glasses dry. I removed the goggles and wiped the fog from my glasses. The world emerged from a sepia-tinted fog into crystal clarity. What a difference.

What I most wanted to see was my bowsprit tip. I crawled

forward to the anchor well. The end of the bowsprit was just eight feet away and I could see it clearly.

Yes, it was bent. Just a bit, but definitely cocked upwards. That first gust must have exerted a terrible force on the end of the bowsprit. Its three stays had supported it, but something had given. Just what, I didn't know, but now wasn't the time to climb out for a look.

I took the jib down. That took all the pressure off the bowsprit. Whatever the problem was, it could wait until I had a chance to inspect it.

I crawled back to the cockpit. The wind was subsiding, the clouds were thinning overhead. Visibility slowly opened up. Two buoys in a line clearly showed our course. We'd made it across St. Catherine's Sound, despite my rashness.

"That was fun, eh?" I asked *Cabin Boy*.

"Almost dismasted in squall; blue water in cockpit; best day of my life!"

* * *

An hour later, I tied up at a marina in Kilkenny Creek. It was on the western shore of the marsh, on the very edge of dry land. An old manor house, reminiscent of "Gone with the Wind," overlooked the water. Live oak trees, dripping with moss, overhung the dock. The tiny, old-fashioned marina had ice, gas, a dock from which I could inspect my bowsprit, and not much more, but I was glad to be off the Sound.

I adjusted the dock lines so I could easily reach the end of the bowsprit from the dock. I opened my pocket knife and gently probed the spar's end. The knife-tip sank into the wood all too easily.

"That's not good."

I continued to probe from the tip of the bowsprit, back. The first six inches were soft. Beyond that, the wood seemed sound.

"Blast..."

Clearly I'd need to do something before flying my jib again. Exactly what and exactly how, I didn't know. I was on the outer edge of my expertise. I had no idea what to do.

"Double-blast…"

Some of the best sailing areas on the voyage were coming up: Pamlico Sound in North Carolina, and of course the Chesapeake. I needed my jib, but I couldn't replace my bowsprit. Not now, and certainly not here.

I looked up the dock towards the small marina store. They had Coke and ice cream and fuel conditioner, but nothing in the way of sailboat hardware. Whatever I needed to fix this bowsprit, I wouldn't find it here. I needed to find a bigger, better-stocked marina.

I climbed aboard the *Blue Moon* and consulted my cruising guide. The next major marine center seemed to be twenty or thirty miles north, in Thunderbolt. Claiborne S. Young's, *Cruising Guide to Sourth Carolina and Georgia* fairly gushed about it:

> *"One of the most impressive collection of pleasure-craft facilities to be found anywhere… With one of the best independent marine supply stores that we have ever visited."*

That sounded promising.

I looked up at the sun. I might just be able to make it before dark.

Decision made, I fired up the engine, threw the dock-lines aboard, and motored down the creek towards Thunderbolt. For the rest of that afternoon, I stared at the bent end of my bowsprit, and asked myself how a real boatbuilder would fix it.

* * *

By the time I reached Thunderbolt, I had a plan. All I needed were a length of chain, some shackles, a pair of blocks, some black paint, and—most problematical—a new cranse iron.

A traditional cranse iron is a metal ring (or cap) driven onto the forward end of a bowsprit. It typically has four attachment points to which are affixed the bobstay, shrouds, and—in the case of a cutter, like the *Blue Moon*—a block for the jib's tack line.

The *Blue Moon*'s cranse iron was a simpler affair, fashioned from what looked like heavy-duty pipe clamps, bolted together around the end of the 'sprit. The bobstay and shrouds were shackled to a ring that hung under the 'sprit. The tack line block was shackled directly to the upper bolt.

Unlike traditional cranse irons, mine was somewhat adjustable, but not adjustable enough if I had to cut six or seven inches off the end of the 'sprit. Because of the bowsprit's taper, the cut-off end would be too fat for the old cranse iron to fit around.

The solution was to find larger clamps and longer bolts—humble hardware that should be easy to find in a port *with the most impressive collection of pleasure-craft facilities to be found anywhere.*

With a shorter bowsprit, my wire bobstay and shrouds would be too long, but I had a plan to replace those, too.

The cranse iron was the critical bit. Did I need a new one? Or would the old one do? I couldn't tell just by looking. So the next morning, after fortifying myself with a good breakfast and two cups of strong tea, I carried my toolbox out onto the dock to find out.

First, I removed the old cranse iron from the end of the bowsprit—being careful not to drop it into the water. I probed the end of the sprit again with my knife: The wood was weak and soggy. I probed further and further back. It was all soft. Clearly, water had gotten into the end grain of the wood, and rot had worked its way up the sprit. I'd start by sawing off that bit. I picked up my razor-sharp Japanese pull-saw, eyed a spot on the sprit about an inch back from the bend, and started sawing.

Sawdust drifted down into the water, and before I could chant, 'dry rot begone!', the deed was done. I inspected the new wood and tapped it with a small hammer. It looked and sounded solid.

"Well, that wasn't so bad," I told *Cabin Boy*.

I tried fitting the old cranse iron over the new end of the bowsprit, but as I feared, it was too small to fit around the now larger end. I needed a new one.

I spent the rest of the morning walking around town, visiting each of the *impressive collection of pleasure-craft facilities* in turn. The chain, paint, etc., were easy to find, but not a new cranse iron.

Of course, I wasn't looking for a real one. Even in Maine or Newport or the Pacific Northwest a real cranse iron would be hard to find. In the powerboat capital of Georgia, it was impossible. Fishing gear, yes. Boat bling, yes. Traditional sailing hardware, no. But I did think I'd find some bit of bent metal that I could press into service, either at one of the chandleries or at a simple hardware store. But hunt as I did, I could not find anything that seemed suitable.

I returned to the *Blue Moon* with a growing sense of urgency and despair. There was no bloody way I was going to hang out on the dock for a week, waiting for a cranse iron to be mailed from Seattle or wherever. Winter was coming on too fast. I needed to make miles. Somehow, I needed to make do with what I had. That's what the old timers always did in the books. It was time for me to think like an old timer.

So I sat on the edge of the dock, with my feet dangling over the ICW flowing by, studying the end of my bowsprit and hunting for ideas in one of my favorite boat books, Tom Cunliffe's *Hand, Reef and Steer: Traditional Sailing Skills for Classic Boats*. A cranse iron, I read, was just "A hoop of iron driven onto a shoulder at the outboard end of the bowsprit."

A *shoulder*. That was it!

A shoulder is just a flat area surrounding a projection. Like the shoulders around your head. A metal hoop that just fits over your head would be stopped from going any further down by your shoulders. Your shoulders would hold the hoop up.

I could cut a shoulder in the end of my bowsprit, leaving a projection just the right size for my old cranse iron. The iron would bear on the wider shoulder, making the arrangement even stronger than the original.

I grabbed my all-purpose Japanese pull saw and got to work, shaping the end of the bowsprit. I made a stopping cut all round the bowsprit for the shoulder, about an inch and a half back from the end. Then I shaped the end using the old trick of making the end four-sided, then eight-sided, then sixteen-sided, then used a rasp and sandpaper to make it round again. When I was done, the cranse iron fit over the projection and against the shoulder perfectly.

I gave the whole bowsprit two coats of black oil paint by flashlight, finishing the last coat at 2 a.m. A long day.

The next morning, I set about rigging the bobstay and whisker stays. The originals were made from wire rope and were now too long. Shortening them was out of the question—the closest tools and parts were probably in Annapolis. I needed to make new ones from the materials I had on board.

Again, *Hand, Reef and Steer* provided the answer. Tom's book showed a bobstay made from chain, rope tackle, and tricing line. The chain provided strength and stiffness. The tackle and tricing line allowed you to either hoist the bobstay out of the way for anchoring, or haul it tight for sailing. *(Trice: to haul and tie up by means of a rope.)* It was an ingenious system and, again, an improvement over the fixed bobstay.

I set about cutting and splicing the rope for the bobstay and for the whisker stays. Rope stays would not be as strong as wire ones, but they would be plenty strong enough.

By early afternoon, the job was done. The bowsprit was a bit shorter than it had been, but with the rot removed it was much stronger than before, and the new rigging gave it a salty look it hadn't had.

I stood back to admire my work.

"She looks beautiful, eh?" I asked *Cabin Boy*.

Ever loyal, he seemed to agree.

CHAPTER 18

MAKING TIME

Attitude is a little thing that makes a big difference
— Winston Churchill

To avoid paying another night's dock fee, I set sail that afternoon at 4 p.m., just in time to make the last afternoon opening of the Causton Bluff bascule bridge at 4:30.

Restricted bridges are a pain. To keep automobile traffic flowing during the morning and afternoon rush hours, many bridges are simply kept shut for two or three hours at a time. No exceptions allowed. The restricted hours are well documented in cruising guides, on the Internet, and on huge signs posted on the bridges themselves. But unless you are one of those hyper-organized types, it's easy to find yourself stuck on the wrong side of a bridge for several frustrating hours. This is particularly annoying when you finally make an effort to get an early start, and find your good intentions stymied by a flowing river of harried office workers.

This time, however, I could see the bridge from the dock in Thunderbolt and remembered to check for restrictions. I left the dock in time to make the last opening with whole minutes to spare.

For hundreds of miles I'd been looking forward to seeing Savannah, but now I had no interest in stopping. All I wanted to do was put watery miles behind me. The feeling that time was running out was gnawing at me, and all my thoughts ran to how I could make more miles per day and—most importantly—how I could avoid long and costly delays.

Friction: that's what I called it. The forces that resist motion;

forces that sometimes seemed guided by a malevolent hand.

I wasn't the first to feel this, of course. Ancient man must have felt it often, looking over his shoulder, wondering if the troubles raining down on his head were accidental, or sent on purpose by a supernatural daemon—an evil spirit motivated by ill will, or jealousy, or just a misguided sense of humor.

There are only two ways to face friction or angry gods: give up, or fight. I wasn't giving up. So I turned my back on Savannah's fabled charms and headed down the Wilmington River. It was an easy run downstream. I used the Elba Island Cut to cross the Savannah River and, just like that, I was in South Carolina.

I was sorry to leave beautiful and friendly Georgia behind, but glad to tick off another state. By nightfall, I had my anchor down in the New River, with my bobstay neatly hauled up under the bowsprit.

Next morning, the sun rose over the table-flat marsh grass. I wore my Irish wool sweater and a warm watch cap. The weather was clear, windy, and cold. Steam rose from my coffee like fog. As soon as I could see the day marker in the main channel, I lifted my anchor and headed north.

For most of the morning, we motored through the last of the marshes, the current with us some times and against us at other times, the caprices of the various streams, rivers, and creeks too complex to calculate. Then we were crossing choppy Calibogue Sound and I was glad to put on my foulies to protect against wind and spray. We needed gas and I stopped briefly at a marina near the famous Hilton Head Island.

The island—named not for the hotel magnate, but for Captain William Hilton, who claimed the island for the British in 1663—has a rich history including its tremendous significance in the Civil War, when it was an important base for Union forces blockading Southern ports, particularly Savannah and Charleston.

Now, it was just a playground for the rich. With all that money in the neighborhood, you would think the marinas would be able to attract friendly staff, but, no, the pump was manned by a crabby old man who sniffed at my little boat, as if pumping ten gallons of gas into my little red plastic tanks was hardly worth his time. No doubt it was more profitable to decant hundreds of gallons at a time to the 1 percent, but I thought his behavior a poor introduction to South Carolina hospitality.

Little did I know.

We followed the ICW up the long west coast of Hilton Head (the second largest barrier island on the east coast) and then crossed Port Royal Sound which was wide open to the Atlantic and in none too friendly a mood that afternoon. By the time we headed up the Beaufort River on the other side, I was tired and looking for a place to anchor for the night. I thought I might try the anchorage off Beaufort, a city renowned for its well preserved antebellum architecture and scenic location.

As I dropped my anchor at the edge of a veritable fleet of pleasure boats, I could tell something was afoot in Beaufort. Upon landing at the dinghy dock (why don't all towns have dinghy docks?), I discovered I'd arrived in the midst of the city's annual Shrimp Festival.

We'd covered forty-four miles and I felt I'd earned my beer, barbecue, and leg-stretching walk through the old shipbuilding city. Little evidence of that history remained, except for a couple old shrimp boats. The party crowd seemed unhappy and even strangely hostile. I didn't let it spoil my beer, but I got out of there as soon as I could.

Over the next few days, I cranked out the miles. Nothing about the dreary South Carolina scenery distracted me from my mission to keep moving north. But gradually, something about the state lowered my spirits. For example, the boaters.

For hundreds and hundreds of miles, I'd been exchanging friendly waves with passing boaters. There were exceptions, sure. I, myself, had a policy of never waving to a power boater who didn't have the decency to slow down a little for a smaller boat. But in general, boaters are a friendly crowd, and saluting passing boats is an ancient courtesy maintained the world over.

Not in South Carolina. Day after day I waved my hand off, and never received a wave in return. They seemed a surly lot, these

South Carolinians, and it was getting me down. Perversely, I kept waving and that didn't help.

Worse, none of them slowed down when passing. Time after time, a monster wake would nearly pitch me out of the *Blue Moon's* cockpit and my friendly wave would turn into a waving fist (and occasionally something worse.) One mini-destroyer insisted on driving in my lane, despite the rules of the road. The only rule that applied in South Carolina, apparently, was *might makes right*.

"It's road rage!" I told *Cabin Boy*, after regaining my feet. "It's the only way to explain it!"

As always, weekends brought out the biggest jerks. During the week, the tide of manic weekend boaters receded, leaving a few surly fishermen, the occasional sailboat scurrying south for the winter, and me.

One afternoon, I forget exactly where, I stopped for gas. The marina had one of those fuel docks I yearned for: a long, empty dock, right on the waterway, seemingly easy to tie up to, and easy to leave. Making things trickier was the two knot current flowing under the dock. Tying up would not be easy for a single-hander. Since there didn't seem to be anyone on the dock to help, I let the *Blue Moon* drift a bit downstream while I hung a couple fenders overboard and led the forward dock line back to the cockpit. Then, motoring upstream a bit faster than the current, I slowly approached the dock and—at the appropriate time—stepped off with bow and stern lines in hand. In a few seconds, the boat was moored securely.

"That was rather neatly done," I said to *Cabin Boy*, "though I shouldn't say so myself." I looked around. The lack of an appreciative audience sapped some of the glory out of this minor triumph. Where was everyone?

A ramp led from the dock up to the boat yard. I climbed the ramp, and then wandered through the yard, looking for someone, anyone, who could sell me some gas.

A full quarter-mile from the dock, I finally located a small office near the front gate. I knocked, walked in, and approached a small man behind the counter who appeared to be engrossed in a newspaper.

I might add that I was dressed from head to toe in foul weather gear, including sea boots. It had been chilly and wet on the water, but the boat yard was hot under the warm, fall sun. I was sweating profusely under all my gear.

"I need some gas," I said.

"Uh-huh," he said, not even looking up.

I waited a bit, sweating, giving him time to work his way through the next sentence (it was a long one, with big words, I figured), but when he flipped the page, I reminded him of my presence.

"Gas?" I said.

"No gas."

"No gas?"

"Done for the summer," he said.

"Why didn't you say so?" I asked. "And why the heck don't you put a sign up on the dock?" I'm afraid I didn't actually say, 'heck'.

He just shrugged. He might as well have said, "Because we like watching New Yorkers trudge a quarter-mile for nothing."

"Excellent service," I snapped, and walked out.

It takes a fair bit of abuse to get me angry, but that chap had done it. I trudged back to the dock, started the engine, untied the dock lines and—not without some trouble—got underway again.

I was still annoyed when I realized I'd left the fenders dangling overboard. Leaving *Helmo* to steer, I went forward, muttering the whole time about miserable South Carolina. I'd just pulled the second fender aboard when we ran aground. Bump, bump. I jumped back to the cockpit and threw the engine into neutral as we skidded to a stop atop the third bump.

We were perhaps 300 yards downstream from the gas dock.

Blast. Moving my weight forward always threw the *Blue Moon*'s course off a bit. *Helmo* always straightened us out, but this time the channel had been too narrow and we'd run aground before *Helmo* could react. I knew about this problem. It wasn't *Helmo*'s fault. I'd just been too angry to think.

Blast, blast, and double-blast.

I put the engine in reverse and tried backing off, but it didn't work (backing off never works unless you go aground very, very slowly.) There was nothing to do but wait for the tide to lift us off. Luckily, it was coming in fast. I glared at the still-deserted marina dock, made a cup of tea, and settled into the cockpit with a good book.

But I couldn't focus on it. I was too busy worrying. If this marina was done for the season, could others be far behind? What would happen if I couldn't buy gas or ice or tie up for the occasional night? Could the whole ICW really shut down for the winter?

I was still worrying over this problem when I felt the keel lift off the mud. I jumped up, started the engine, and maneuvered us back into the main channel.

It was even more important to keep going now, I thought.

"Miles and miles to go before we sleep tonight," I told *Cabin Boy* grimly, but he was already napping. Lucky boy.

That night we anchored in the lower South Santee River. I noted in my log, *"this area is really deserted… didn't see another boat for an hour before reaching this anchorage."* There was an island in the middle of the river. I anchored in a few hundred yards short of the island, in ten feet of water. Except for the channel leading back to the ICW, we were surrounded by shallow water, but there was plenty of room for two or three boats to swing.

I knew it wasn't a great anchorage as soon as I dropped the hook. A swift current flowed upstream, because the river was a tidal estuary, and the current was controlled by old man Atlantic, not the forces of gravity. It would reverse every six hours or so with the tides.

So I made double-sure that the anchor was dug in, and then settled down to enjoy the sunset and the splendid isolation of the anchorage. But I kept a wary eye on the current and set the anchor alarm on my Garmin GPS, just in case.

An anchor alarm is a feature that practically every GPS provides, even my simple Garmin. When turned on, the GPS will beep if your boat drags more than, say, one-hundred feet. This sounds great in theory. In practice, it has problems.

JOHN ALMBERG | 217

If you make the alarm distance too small, the darn thing turns into a nervous Nellie, waking you up every time the boat swings with wind or current. If you make it too large in a restricted anchorage like a river, you can easily be aground before the blasted thing goes off.

Having spent several restless nights with Nellie, I tended to set the alarm distance too high. I could live with going around on a river bank, but if King Neptune tried to drag us out to sea in the middle of the night, I wanted to know about it.

Thus prepared, I went to sleep.

In the middle of the night, the alarm went off. In seconds, I had the hatch open and my head out in the cool night air. It was black as a coal mine. I couldn't see either river bank, or the island. I was totally disoriented. Which way was I looking? Upstream, towards the ICW, or downstream towards the island? Had the current reversed yet, or not?

I finally thought to look at the compass. Downstream. The island was somewhere over the transom, then. I still couldn't see it.

I looked at the GPS again. We'd only moved 150 feet. Probably because we'd swung from one side of the anchor to the other with the current. Nothing to worry about.

I reset the alarm, and went back to sleep.

This happened several times throughout the night. Each time it was pitch black out. Each time we'd only moved 110 or 150 feet from the previously set location. No biggie, I thought. Not dragging, just swinging.

Eventually, I tired of the game and turned the alarm off.

I awoke well after sunrise. I was tired. My eyes were itchy. It had not been a good night. The morning was chilly. I kept the hatch closed, made a cup of tea, checked my email, and finally wandered up on deck.

"Oh, blast," I said.

The shore was ten feet off, on the starboard side. Which shore, I wasn't sure. The whole scene was changed from last night. For a moment I was disoriented, then the view snapped into place. The shore was the island; we were close to it. The anchor must have dragged. I looked at the anchor line to see where it lead.

Oh, no... The anchor was practically on the island. It was in the water, but just a few yards off the tip of the island. How could it have gotten there? Had the *Blue Moon* gone ashore during the night? Or drifted into the north channel, where the chart showed four feet of water? How had we not gone aground? Were we, in fact, aground now?

I grabbed my long boat hook and used it as a sounding pole. It hit the bottom with a thud, in about four feet of water. The *Blue Moon* did not seem to be moving. Blast. We *were* aground, and the current was flowing out. If I didn't want to spend half the day exploring the charms of tiny, barren Grace Island, I had to get us out of there, fast.

Once again, I went through the fire drill of rowing the kedge out to deep water in *Cabin Boy*. Would I ever learn? Why had I ignored the anchor alarm? What could I have done differently in the dark? I didn't know, but surely I could have done something.

With the kedge out, I thought about getting the main anchor up. I couldn't get it with the *Blue Moon*, so I grabbed the anchor line and pulled *Cabin Boy* over to the anchor. We were right over it. I stood up in the stern and tried to break the anchor out by brute force. No good. It was really dug in. I would have put *Cabin Boy's* transom under water before the anchor broke free.

Dang! How could the anchor drag up and down the river all night, and then be stuck like glue in the morning?

Nearly resigned to spending the next few hours aground, I rowed back to the *Blue Moon* and climbed aboard. As I did so, she heeled to my weight.

Was she floating? I rocked her by moving my weight back and forth.

Yes, she seemed to be floating!

I looked towards my main anchor. Could I get it? I really didn't have a lot to lose. Maybe...

I went forward and picked up the main anchor line. I pulled on it. We moved forward; we were definitely not aground. I pulled some more, and we inched towards the anchor.

JOHN ALMBERG | 219

"Never faint heart won fair lady," I muttered, grimly.

I continued to pull in the anchor line, letting out the kedge line when necessary, until we were right over the anchor. It broke free and came up covered with black, smelly mud. I left it dangling over the bow and turned my attention to the kedge.

In a few moments, I'd hauled us out into deep water. It seemed a miracle, but apparently the water was deep all around the island. If we'd been aground earlier, we'd lifted by the time I got the kedge out. It was all very mysterious, but I was thrilled to be floating in deep water again.

"Next time," I told *Cabin Boy*. "Next time we have any doubts, we're putting out two anchors!"

* * *

That afternoon, I was fed up and ready to quit. We were struggling up Winyah Bay against a two knot current, wasting buckets of gas going nowhere. I cursed the current, cursed every powerboat that rushed by as if we weren't there, and cursed myself for getting us into this voyage in the first place.

Of course, by now I knew the symptoms: I was hungry because in all the dashing about I'd forgotten to eat, and I was tired from being awoken 149 times by the anchor alarm.

In short, I had that edgy, jaded feeling that only a good walk, a good meal, and some friendly human contact can cure. Probably all solo sailors get this feeling. Probably it's a natural result of doing something hard, alone, for a bit too long. But there was something else. Something about South Carolina just rubbed me the wrong way. I told myself it was just my overactive imagination, but then some power boater would swerve out of his way to swamp us with his wake. And never a friendly wave. Oh never.

"I just need a decent meal," I told *Cabin Boy*. His stern look reminded me that we needed to get north as fast as possible.

"Yes, yes," I said. "But we have time for a bit of lunch while we wait for a fair current. No point wasting gas."

Thus armed with a handy rationalization, I studied the chart, looking for a place to stop. We were just a couple miles south of the city of Georgetown, SC. It looked easy to reach. Claiborne Young devoted an entire chapter to the town: "*Sitting astride the confluence of Winya Bay and Sampit River, present-day Georgetown constantly calls to mind its storied past. Long the most important South Carolina port north of Charleston, the town retains the character of by gone years alongside a new spirit of success. Fortunate cruisers who make Georgetown a port of call will find a quiet, beautiful, and historic town waiting to greet them.*"

That sounded good enough for me. An hour later, I tied up at one of the downtown marinas, took a blessedly hot shower, and set off in search of a restaurant that didn't specialize in all-you-can-eat fried food.

The Spanish had tried to settle the Georgetown area as far back as 1526, but their colony was a complete failure and most of the 500 original colonists died before the remainder did the sensible thing and sailed back to Spain. Two hundred years later, the English had better luck. William Swinton laid out the town and a few years later the colony was sending vast quantities of lumber and dye back to England. By 1738, the colonists were building ships and it looked like Georgetown's future as a major port was all but assured.

But Charleston had a better harbor and eventually captured the majority of the seagoing trade. Georgetown stayed a relatively minor port, which actually helped spare it from the worst ravages of the Civil War.

I read all this in a guidebook while wandering around the city's historic district. The waterfront was charming and main street was lined with the sturdy brick buildings found in cities up and down the east coast. In many ways, it reminded me of my home town of Huntington, NY.

But whereas Huntington (birth place of Walt Whitman and Ralph Macchio, former home of John Coltrane, Jack Kerouac, and Antoine de St Exupery) was a bustling village of eighteen thousand, Georgetown—a larger city with half the population—seemed empty. Deserted, almost. 'Depressed' was the word I wrote in my log.

Only a few people wandered the empty sidewalks, so I was a bit surprised when I was nearly trampled to death by a small herd of old folk.

There were just four of them: two couples, the men bald, the women with stiff, grey helmet-hair, all enormous. They were dressed loudly like tourists, but apparently had not come to Georgetown for the quaint shops, historic buildings, or interesting northerners. It was lunch time. A silent bell had rung, and nothing, but *nothing*, was going to stand in the way of these famished folk and their lunch.

That was my mistake. As I strolled down the sunny side of main street, looking into store windows, reading menus, and enjoying the feel of solid ground under my feet, I'd let down my guard. I wasn't keeping a weather-eye out for zooming power boats or stampeding senior citizens. So by the time I spotted the flying gray phalanx, it was too late to take evasive action. All I could do was try to stay on my feet as they rushed past me on both sides like a herd of water buffalo. In aggregate, they outweighed me by several tons, and as the ground rumbled under my feet, I savored the irony of such a death, on such a voyage.

But then the stampede swept by and I was in the clear again, blessing my lucky stars.

"Excuse me!" I called to their broad backs. But of course they paid me no mind. Lunch beckoned and this was no time for social niceties. I watched them hip-bump through the door of the greasy cafe I'd recklessly blocked.

I brushed the dust out of my clothes. What was wrong with these people? Or was it me? Perhaps I was invisible. I poked myself in the chest. No, I didn't seem to be.

As much as I hated to judge an entire state by a relative handful of people, I couldn't help myself. I was fed up with it. I'd grab some lunch, get back to the *Blue Moon*, and head for the border. If I kept hard at it, I could be over the state line by tomorrow. Hopefully, North Carolina would be an improvement.

I must have looked as mean and snarly as a native as I stomped up the street, so when a pretty girl said, "Good morning!" it came as a shock.

She was twenty-something, with red hair, an open face, and a ready smile. She turned a key in a lock, opening the door of a small shop.

"Is it?" I said.

"Yes, definitely," she said. Her laughing eyes seemed to mock my snarl.

"You know," I said, "you are the first person I've met in South Carolina who's said hello to me."

"No!" she said. Her surprise sounded genuine.

"Oh, yes."

"But South Carolina is such a friendly state!"

That made me laugh bitterly, but I caught myself before I said something really rude.

"Then I've been darn unlucky," I said.

"Well," she said, shifting her key to her left hand and holding out her right. "Let me be the first to officially welcome you to the beautiful and friendly state of South Carolina."

We shook hand, rather formally, her lips pursed in an ironic smile, but the press of her hand melted away my anger. I felt rather foolish.

"Thank you very much," I said.

"Don't mention it. And I hope you enjoy the rest of your stay." She turned to go into her shop.

"By the way," I said. "You don't know of a decent restaurant?"

* * *

It was a modern and chic little restaurant, with large windows and good jazz playing in the background. The service was friendly and efficient—a combination I had not yet experienced in the south. The food was made from fresh ingredients, simply prepared: a steak salad with blue cheese dressing for the main course, and an apple and pecan crisp with cinnamon ice cream for desert. Best meal I'd had in months.

I walked out of that restaurant with a new feeling for South Carolina. The sun was shining, the air was fresh, and the ICW glinted blue beyond the waterfront.

It wasn't such a bad place, after all.

* * *

That evening I anchored in beautiful Jericho Creek. It was rather narrow, with trees and vines overhanging the water on both banks. Alligators peeped out at me from under the still water. Exotic birds called 'time for bed' from the trees. We could have been anchored in a small river in Africa.

That night, as I lay half-sleeping in my bunk, I heard a dolphin breathing—just breathing—outside the porthole. Unlike other nights, when I might have jumped up to see it, I just listened. It was sublime.

The next morning, we headed up the Waccamaw River. The landscape had changed for the better, in my eyes. A forest of Atlantic white cedar, live oaks, and loblolly pine grew on both banks. These were tall, substantial trees, not the low, scraggly trees that my eyes had gotten used to further south. The river was narrow in places so that we cruised in shade, out of the harsh glare of the sun. I wrote in my log that this was the first time that we'd been able to cruise in shade for the whole voyage. It was delightful. Almost blissful.

The trees were really beautiful, and would be even more beautiful when the leaves began to turn, which they soon would.

The guidebook warned of a new hazard—floating logs—but though I kept a good watch for them, I didn't see any.

We pushed up the Waccamaw—one on the most beautiful stretches of the entire ICW—all morning, and then anchored at the top of the river for lunch. I studied the chart as I ate. It was roughly thirty-five miles to the border. Thirty-five miles that ran through a canal on the back side of Myrtle Beach. There were no anchorages for the entire stretch.

We had seven hours of daylight yet. If we could just average five knots, we could make it. But many bridges blocked our way. If they held us up too long, or if the current ran against us, we could be stuck in a no-anchor zone when night fell.

It was risky, but I was determined to reach North Carolina as soon as possible. We'd go for it.

The first bridge—the Socastee—opened quickly and we flew through. The current was with us. Five miles or so later, the GPS said we were making 6.8 knots over the ground as we passed under the rail road bridge, on the outskirts of Myrtle Beach.

We sped down the arrow-straight canal, hitting seven knots for a while—almost scary fast—which was good, because there wasn't much to look at. The Great Recession had evidently hit Myrtle Beach hard. Enormous McMansions lined the ICW, but most of them were empty, standing alone on empty, bulldozed plots, not a tree, shrub, or child in sight. Stark reminders that a pretense of wealth (and lack of taste) often cometh before a fall.

We anchored in the Calabash River just before dark. We were a mile or so short of the North Carolina border. There was lots of rude boat traffic on the river, but as I rested in the *Blue Moon*'s cockpit and watched a splay of blood-red fingers fade in the western sky, the last few powerboats flew past, the whine of their engines sounding like mosquitoes fading into the darkness. We'd done fifty-two miles that day: not a bad run. I raised a toast to South Carolina, both good and bad.

On balance, I was happy to say good bye.

CHAPTER 19

NORTH CAROLINA

Who is the happier man, he who has braved the storm
of life and lived or he who has stayed securely on shore and
merely existed? – Hunter S. Thompson

"North Carolina!" I said to *Cabin Boy* as we crossed over the state line. "Hallelujah!"

We were fifteen days out of Jacksonville, but it had seemed longer. Much, much longer.

Three states down and five to go. How long would it take to reach New York? That depended on King Neptune. How many more of his tridents would we have to catch? But it felt like maybe we were over some sort of hump. I'd fixed or worked around most of the *Blue Moon*'s kinks. I'd learned many new tricks. And I was fit. The *Blue Moon* had worked her magic: the weight I'd mysteriously gained at home over the summer had melted away again, and I was back in fighting trim. Our daily distance was still ragged—fifty miles one day, twenty the next—but on average we were doing better and better as time went on.

Most importantly, I was back in 'the groove'. This is what I called the mental state my voyage required. At the beginning of each leg, I had to get back into this groove, and it was a painful process. It was a matter of letting go of shoreside comforts like hot water, dry clothes, comfy chairs, and the companionship of friends and family. Letting go, too, of the shoreside pace: the restless, technology-driven pace of the typical American. Go faster. Do more. More of whatever—it hardly mattered what. The craziness of the typical New Yorker, in other words.

That mind set just didn't work on the water. I *couldn't* go faster, and worrying about it didn't help. It would have been a real problem if I had not been able to let go, to adapt, but I found I could. The go-go fever always abated over the course of two or three days and gradually I'd adapt to slower pace of the *Blue Moon*. I'd get into the groove. The groove that allowed me to think not of tomorrow, but of now. And that made all the difference: outside the groove, the voyage seemed impossible; inside, I knew it wasn't.

"It's just a matter of time," I told *Cabin Boy,* confidently. He seemed to mutter grave warnings about Hubris, but I waved them away.

"Superstitious nonsense!" I said. Then I knocked on wood. No sense taking chances, after all.

We were cruising down the ICW towards Cape Fear. The North Carolina coast had been curving more and more towards the east, and now we were headed almost due east. Naturally, the wind blew right on our nose, so we were motoring. We had the current with us and we were making 6.3 knots. Yes, things were going our way.

This being a Friday, the weekend power boaters emerged from creeks and rivers like a swarm of angry bees, buzzing who-knew-where at breakneck speeds. North Carolinians seemed a friendly lot—certainly an improvement over their surly southern cousins—but they suffered from some of the same delusions.

For instance, they seemed to think that a friendly wave—or even a half-hearted one—made up for swamping the *Blue Moon*.

"It doesn't!" I shouted at their swiftly vanishing sterns.

A friendly wave is nice, but it's a pleasantry hard to appreciate when your boat is rolled on its beam ends or pitched into the trough of a four foot wake. A wave is more polite than the implied gestures that were common south of the border, but really, slowing down is better.

As I said, North Carolinians seemed a friendly lot. And intelligent. More than one turned around to check his wake after roaring past us, realizing too late that they should have slowed down. Many even spread their hands in a regretful "Sorry!" as I piloted the *Blue Moon* through the maelstrom he'd left behind. I did appreciate the sign-language apology, but really, slowing down is better.

Don't get me wrong. Many did slow down. And I never failed to wave my thanks, even when I knew they'd probably gun their engines a moment too soon and leave us pitching and tossing in their wake, as they vanished around the next bend.

They at least meant well, most of them, and that was an improvement.

At Cape Fear, the ICW turns 90 degrees to port and heads up the mighty Cape Fear River. As we approached this turn, I consulted tide and current charts and determined that we would arrive just in time for the 2-2.5 knot current to turn against us. Since there wasn't enough time left in the day for the ten mile run up river against this adverse current, I decided to stop at a little town right off the mouth of the river: Southport.

We passed through the narrow entrance, into a small, round, land-locked harbor. It could not have been much more than one hundred yards across. There was room for perhaps three boats to anchor, so I anchored off the center of the basin, leaving room for a couple more boats. But I needn't have bothered. No other boat tried to anchor while I was there.

Anchor down, I surveyed my surroundings. The shore was so close, I could see people's faces, and even hear them talking. The east side of the harbor was lined with restaurants, their outside tables beginning to fill up with the Friday night crowd. To the north was what looked like the old center of town, with quaint homes sheltering under tall shade trees. To the west was a small, somewhat rickety-looking marina. To the south, a low marsh protected the basin from the river and the ocean beyond.

The slanting rays of the late afternoon sun lit the town with a warm glow and deepened the colors of the dockside restaurants. The happy sound of clinking glasses drifted across the anchorage and made me want to get ashore as soon as possible. I tidied up on deck, changed into shore-going clothes, and rowed to the dock of the aptly named Fishy Fishy Cafe. The restaurant looked like a typical beach-shack type place. I expected the usual variety of fried whatever and hamburgers, but the chicken with a lemony wine sauce was excellent. I was liking Southport.

After dinner I walked around the well-preserved little seaside town and found a couple of old wooden boats along the waterfront. They were on display in a small roped-off area. A handmade sign said the 1st Annual Southport Wooden Boat Show would be tomorrow, Saturday.

"I guess I've already seen both boats," I said. A good effort, but hardly worth missing my tide for. I didn't give the 'boat show' another thought.

The next morning, a couple of guys rowed out to check out the *Blue Moon*. They asked if I'd come especially for the boat show. I told them I was just passing through, and it was pure luck I was there that day. They wanted to know, would I like to participate in the show? I hesitated a moment (*must catch that tide… must catch that tide…*), then said, sure!

They guided the *Blue Moon* into a slip in the middle of the show. Overnight, two dozen wooden boats had sprouted from nowhere. Most were small boats on trailers: lovingly crafted jewels, gleaming with varnish and fresh paint. Their owner/builders—shy craftsmen, mainly—stood proudly beside them.

I spent a couple hours standing on the dock, answering questions and giving tours of the *Blue Moon*. Then I walked around the show, talked to all the builders, and even played a small part in a TV news report, filmed by a local reporter. The video is still available on YouTube as of this writing: http://youtu.be/-iBA-r7XEpc

In short, the 1st Annual Southport Wooden Boat Show was a great success and I was happy to participate. Well worth missing my tide for. There would be another one in the morning.

There's a lesson there, somewhere…

* * *

The next morning, I had to get up early to catch the tide. Sunrise was officially at 7:25, but by 7:15, I had my anchor up and was motoring out of Southport.

Twenty minutes later, I logged 8.4 knots over the ground as we rode up the Cape Fear River on the back of a ferocious current. We flew past buoys that looked like speedboats heading down river, leaving creamy white wakes behind them.

There were enormous ships plying the river, including a Yang Ming freighter from China, its deck piled high with steel containers, each big enough to hold the *Blue Moon*. I gave it a wide berth.

We soon turned off the Cape Fear River, taking Snow's Cut to Myrtle Grove Sound. By then the day was hot and sunny. We ran up the coast in a man-made channel with barrier islands between us and the Atlantic. The water was calm, we had plenty of gas, and I stuck with it all day. By the time we anchored in Mile Hammock Bay, just north of the New River, we'd put sixty-seven miles behind us—a new record.

Mile Hammock Bay (who names these places?) was a large and well protected anchorage. There were half-a-dozen sailboats anchored there, all headed south, all cheerfully visiting each other by dinghy. Before I could tie up my sails, a friendly couple from Maine motored over and invited me on board their yacht for cocktails. I'd rarely run into real cruisers on my voyage, but whenever I had, I'd gotten the same treatment: the husbands wanted to know all about my little ship, and their wives were never happy unless I had a drink in my hand and 'a little something' to eat.

"It must be hard to cook on that little boat," they always said, with a motherly look.

And they were right about that.

That night, I heard what sounded like gunfire. I told myself that was crazy, and went back to sleep. Next morning, while planning the day's sail, I realized we'd been anchored within the bounds of Camp Lejeune US Marine Base. At dawn, a pair of green helicopters roared over the anchorage. They were so loud, *Cabin Boy* nearly jumped out of the water.

I really needed to limit his coffee intake.

I'd gotten up early to rig my depth sounder. I'd somehow managed to navigate a thousand miles of narrow channels without one so far, but the further north I went, the shallower and narrower the ICW got. I'd bumped the bottom once yesterday, seemingly right in the middle of the channel, and had idly thought, "I wonder if I should install that depth sounder…"

The magic words having been spoken, I got to work.

I'd had a depth sounder in my kit since Jacksonville, but hadn't been able to get it working. An electronic depth sounder has two parts: the numeric display and the transducer. The transducer is the part that transmits the sound wave and listens for its bounce. Mine was supposed to be powerful enough to shoot its beams right through the bottom of a boat, but was apparently thwarted by the sound-absorbing ability of an inch and a half of Douglas Fir. Experiment as I had, I could not get it to work.

But last night I'd had a brain wave. I removed the broomstick from my deck mop and lashed the transducer to its end with some tarred marline. A long waterproof cable led from the transducer, up the broomstick handle, and then to the back of the display, which was also connected to the *Blue Moon*'s 12 volt battery.

I hooked all this up, then gingerly lowered the transducer at the end of the pole into the water. Instantly, the display came to life and showed the reading 9.0.

"Wow!" I said to *Cabin Boy*. "I think it's working!"

I lowered the transducer about a foot and watched the reading tick down to 8.0. It did indeed seem to be working. I then lashed the pole to the *Blue Moon*'s stern so that the transducer was about a foot under water. It had to be tightly lashed so it could resist the five knot current that would flow under the *Blue Moon*'s keel when we were moving. This took a bit of trial and error fiddling, but when we motored out of Mile Hammock Bay, we had a working (if odd looking) depth sounder. I would soon need it.

We spent the rest of the day steaming up wide-open Bogue Sound. It was one of those stretches where it looked like there was plenty of sailing room, but just beyond the narrow marked channel, the water was only two feet deep. There was too much wind and wave for *Helmo*, so I hand-steered most of the way. By the time we anchored in Spooner's Creek, I was dog tired. We'd made thirty-four miles. Not bad for a late start.

The next day, we gassed up in Moorehead City, then headed up the Newport River to Core Creek and the cut to Adam's Creek. In Adam's Creek, I felt a change come over the environment. I couldn't put my finger on it, but I suddenly had the feeling that the South was behind us. The trees looked different: taller, hardier, as if they could stand a bit of snow without whining. And instead of the ubiquitous white plastic powerboat, we followed a little two-masted sailboat—an old wooden sharpie, by the look of her.

Not that we got close enough for a good look. We were motor sailing and making a good five knots, but we could not catch up with that white-feathered will-o'-the-wisp. We chased her right out of Adam's Creek, but finally she turned south onto the Neuse River, while we headed across the Neuse to Oriental—the self-named 'Sailing Capital of North Carolina'.

By the time the sun was lowering in the west, I'd tied up at a marina in Oriental, washed my laundry (yay!), and taken a shower (yay! yay!). Oriental is a tiny town with about 1,000 people and 2,000 boats—surely a sailor's heaven. I spent the evening walking her docks, admiring the fleet of working shrimp boats. Darkness fell all too quickly, forcing this sailor to take refuge in the nearest pub.

The next morning, I was just cleaning the grime off the *Blue Moon*'s deck when a guy with a big smile and a raggedy old bush hat stopped by. Now, I happened to be wearing my own bush hat—a Tilley that I would not trade for anything—but this guy's hat looked like it had more mileage on it than mine. A lot more mileage. But it was his smile you first noticed. It was the kind of smile that instantly breaks down barriers and turns strangers into friends. It was, in other words, a *traveler's* smile.

I'd been practicing this smile myself for many months. One of the great things about traveling alone is the opportunity to meet people you would otherwise never get to know. This is much harder to do when you travel as a couple, or as part of a group. Two or more people create a bubble around them that's hard to break into or out of. The lone traveler might start out in a bubble, but he soon

The Blue Moon in Oriental, NC

tires of his own company and looks for ways to break out. A big smile, I discovered, is just the sledgehammer you need.

Needless to say, thirty seconds later, Bernie Harberts was walking all over the *Blue Moon*, snapping pictures while we interviewed each other.

Bernie had a good reason for interviewing me. He was a reporter for TownDock.net, Oriental's online newspaper. The job consisted mainly of hanging around the town dock, which was a magnet for sailors traveling up and down the east coast of the US. He wrote up their stories for *The Shipping News* column in the paper, which is why he was interested in me and my story.

I interviewed him for an even better reason. A few direct and personal questions from me revealed that Bernie was that most exalted of creatures: a travel writer. As a young man, he'd sailed around the world in a thirty-five foot steel cutter, and written about his voyage. Then he traded in his boat for a mule and pony and walked across America, from Oriental to San Diego, and written about his walk. He was about to set off for Tasmania to bike across that far away island.

That seemed like an ideal life to me, and more to the point, I'd long ago learned to value other people's experience; so while he interviewed me, I picked his brain.

I really liked Bernie's DIY approach to travel and publishing. With social media replacing advertising, print-on-demand technology replacing publishers, and Amazon replacing bookstores, a writer could—if so inclined—control the whole process. That appealed to me, and I was glad to meet someone who'd actually done it. There are a lot of talkers in this world, but few doers. Bernie was a doer, and I'm sure I got more out of our mutual interview than he did. I left the Oriental town dock with an incredibly optimistic glow, and a new resolution to practice my traveler's smile.

At the time of this writing, Bernie's interview is still online at this link: http://tinyurl.com/gqx85th

* * *

Happy families are all alike, meaning they make for boring stories. So, too, for happy sailing days. The next morning saw me sailing down the Neuse River with a fair ten knot breeze. The air was cool, but the sun warmed me as I lounged in the cockpit, while *Helmo* steered a steady course down the miles-wide river.

For once, I was more captain than crew. I listened to the radio, navigated, and wrote in my log. Just a few boats dotted the horizon, mainly under sail, none of them close enough to upset our smooth progress. Water chuckled under the *Blue Moon*'s bow, *Cabin Boy* slept at the end of his painter, and all was good with the world.

These conditions held all the way up Pamlico Sound and up the Pamlico River to the Pungo River, where we had to take refuge for a half-hour because of a passing thunderstorm. But that hardly slowed us down and as the day drew to a close, we were on the Alligator River/Pungo River Canal. This man-made canal was arrow straight and fairly narrow. The guide books showed only one place to anchor on the whole stretch. As the sun sank into the trees, I worried about finding it. We were in the middle of a wildlife refuge, and the night, when it came, would be black. I needed to find that anchorage. But when we reached it, just before dark, I didn't like the look of it. It was hardly big enough for a rowboat. I doubled back for a second look, and cruised slowly past the entrance.

"What do you think?" I asked *Cabin Boy*.

He thought it looked full of snags and fallen trees. I agreed with him. For once, the guide books had let me down. Or perhaps I was looking up the wrong creek. I didn't have time to make sure. The sun was already down and night was falling. I had to find another place to anchor.

In a bit of a panic, I turned north again. The canal was less than one-hundred yards wide and bordered by grassy verges The man-made banks were straight and featureless, for the most part. The occasional creek entered the canal from one side or another, but they were too shallow for the *Blue Moon*. Boats didn't normally travel the ICW by night, but I couldn't just anchor in the middle of the channel. Tweaking the nose of Fate like that was sure to bring the blunt bow of a barge down on me.

A half-mile north, the Alligator River crossed the canal several times. At each crossing, the canal widened a bit. At one intersection, I thought there was just enough room to tuck into for the night. It would get us out of the main channel, anyway. Just barely, but...

I didn't like it, but sometimes you have to settle for 'good enough'. I wanted to get the anchor down before it was fully dark. I just about managed it. In fact, I set two anchors—the main anchor (or bower) off the bow, and the kedge off the stern. Setting two anchors kept us snugged up against the muddy bank, and out of the main channel.

That was the night of the great Mosquito Massacre. As soon as the anchor dropped, we were attacked by a hundred million mosquitoes. I quickly hung my brightest anchor light from the forestay to distract them, then rigged the mosquito net over the cabin top.

Too late! The cabin was already filled with the buzzing bloodsuckers. There was nothing to do but kill them, one by one. This took the best part of an hour and by the time I was done, the cabin's white paint was spattered by the blood of 10,325 ravenous insects. I would have felt sorry for them, but it was my blood on the walls.

As I celebrated victory over the insect kingdom, a forty-five foot sailboat passed by, doing five knots through the dark, dark night. My anchor light burned as bright as the moon, so there was no danger of them hitting us, but I could hear the crew talking as they swished by.

They must have been steering by chart plotter, because visibility in that black night was close to zero. I marveled at their foolhardy and unseamanlike behavior, which was oblivious to floating logs and other obstructions. To this day I wonder if they made it.

The next morning we motored out of the canal and onto the Alligator River, which was several miles wide. As the sun rose, so did the wind, and we were soon sailing again. This gave me time to do some planning.

We were approaching Albermarle Sound, the largest fresh water sound in the United States: fifteen miles across, and about eighteen feet deep. I didn't like Claiborne Young's description of it in his *Cruising Guide to Coastal North Carolina*:

> *There is perhaps no other major body of water in North Carolina that has been so consistently overlooked by pleasure cruisers. This is largely because Albemarle Sound has the dubious reputation of having the roughest inland waters on the entire eastern seaboard. It is quite true that winds from most any quarter tend to funnel up or down the sound's entire length. This long wind fetch, coupled with the Albemarle's relatively shallow depths, can quickly form violent seas that can daunt the heartiest captain and crew. Always consult the latest weather forecast before venturing on the sound's wide waters.* — Cruising Guide to Coastal North Carolina

Sunny day, light breeze… could conditions be any better? I decided to go for it.

The crossing did not start well. The mouth of the Alligator

River shoaled, but the twisting path through the shallows was clearly marked by six or seven buoys. If I'd kept my mind on my navigation, I'm sure we would have had no problem, but my attention was distracted by a sight you don't see often—a large sailboat with all sail set, seemingly going nowhere.

This sight was surprisingly disorienting. For a moment, I couldn't understand what I was looking at. Then I realized they were aground. There was a woman on the foredeck, struggling with something—perhaps the roller furler, or perhaps the anchor. The captain stood by the wheel, looking manly and probably shouting unhelpful orders. An all too common scene, and one that I never could understand. Surely it is easier to teach a woman to steer than it is to get her to manhandle a heavy anchor or sail on the foredeck.

"Tsk!" I said to *Cabin Boy*. "I will never put Helena in that position. It's disgraceful!"

I had just decided to give the captain a piece of my mind, when the woman on the foredeck began to wave frantically at us.

"What is she waving at?" I wondered. Did she want to be rescued from her cruel and incompetent captain? Did she expect me to give them a tow? Their boat was twice as big as mine. I didn't think...

"Oh blast!"

A bump on the keel brought me back to my senses. The woman wasn't just waving at me, she was waving me *off*! I was running straight on to the same shoal that they were stuck on. Now I could just hear her voice.

"What?"

She yelled again.

"Go this way!" She pointed to her starboard side. "You're headed into shallow water!"

The next few moments flashed by as the *Blue Moon* bumped over shoals. I held my breath, and tried to steer into what I hoped were deeper waters. In seconds, we were past them and through the worst part. By the time I thought to wave my thanks, we were too far away.

Almost immediately, I second-guessed my decision to cross

the Albemarle that day. As soon as we cleared Long Shoal Point (no doubt how it got *that* name) the wind felt heavier and the seas picked up. I wondered if I should leave it to another day.

Normally, of course, the simple act of wondering would have decided the issue. But I did not want to risk running through those shoals again. Besides, the *Blue Moon* could handle a bit of wind and wave. She was a blue water boat. The Albemarle was just an over grown stream. What could go wrong?

I gave the tiller to *Helmo* and went below to put on my full weather armor and to make a strong cup of tea. The wind was on the beam, which made working down below a bit rough, but I got my warm drink and stuffed my pockets with portable food. I wasn't sure when I'd be able to go below again.

Over the course of the next two hours, the wind blew harder and the seas kicked up higher. In the middle of Albemarle Sound, the waves were five to six feet. Nothing the *Blue Moon* couldn't handle, but I was glad I'd donned my foul weather gear, because spray flew everywhere.

Then, just to add interest, storm clouds began gathering on the northern shore. For the next hour, I watched one ugly black cloud after another race across the Sound. Some of them looked like real trouble so I put a reef in the main, just to be sure. This was not an easy task with the *Blue Moon* rolling through the crossing seas and the wind gusting violently. I'd read stories about men taking an hour to put in a reef and wondered why it had taken them so long. I now knew why: everything takes longer when you have to hold on with two hands and need two other hands to haul down stiff and stubborn sail. But somehow, eventually, I did it, and the *Blue Moon* rode much easier under the reefed main and staysail.

There were gray curtains of rain hanging all around us, but like the black clouds, they passed us by. The visibility must have been miserable in those storms. I was happy to be in the clear.

The path across the Albemarle was well marked and after a four hour crossing, we approached the shoals that guarded the mouth of the North River. I didn't fancy crossing shoals in a gale, but as we bore down on the northern shore, the waves abated, even if the wind didn't. I fired up the engine, just in case we went aground, but the channel through the shallow bit was straight and well marked. We sailed through into the North River with no problem.

Now the wind was right on our nose, blowing straight down the river at what I estimated to be thirty knots. I was exhausted and night was coming fast. I needed a place to anchor, but there was no protected anchorage on river until it narrowed and turned around Buck Island. In the lee of Buck Island, I thought we might be able to anchor with some shelter from the waves, if not the wind, so I took down the sails and we motored straight up the river for another hour.

Buck Island was a low, sandy island with a few scrub trees. As I suspected, it offered no protection from the wind, but the water was six feet deep right up to the shore. I nudged the *Blue Moon* in as close as I dared, and dropped the anchor.

As I had hoped, the island blocked enough of the waves to provide a safe anchorage. Up above, in the rigging, the wind blew like stink. But down low, where it counted, the surface of the water was barely ruffled. We'd be fine, as long as the wind didn't swing around and put us on a lee shore. I'd have to keep an eye on that.

We'd covered fifty-five hard miles that day. I issued the crew a double ration of rum, gave the captain the same, set an alarm for two hours, and slept like the dead.

CHAPTER 20

SAILBOAT COUNTRY

*"Ships are the nearest things to dreams that hands have
ever made, for somewhere deep in their oaken hearts the soul
of a song is laid." - Robert N. Rose*

Around midnight, I climbed out of my bunk to take a look at
the weather. The only light came from the lantern swinging on the
forestay. Beyond the short cast of its beam, the world was misty
black, with Buck Island an even blacker line, just visible off the
bow. The wind blew hard enough to scare me, though we were
still in the lee of the island, which meant we were okay. The wind
was like the big bad wolf, huffing and puffing to blow my watery
house down, but with the island protecting us from waves, the
wind alone couldn't hurt us.

Nevertheless, I got the kedge down, just to make sure we didn't
drag. Then I went below, reset my alarm, and went back to bed,
hoping for a bit more sleep; instead, I lay awake for a long time,
hearing and feeling the wind pull at the rigging, trying to work
us off the island where his friend, the waves, could give us a good
roughing up, but in this the wind was frustrated.

Next morning, the wind still blew at thirty knots, with stronger
gusts. We'd been lucky so far, but it was time to move.

I studied the chart. On the other side of Buck Island, the North
River narrowed and twisted its way up to a canal. There was a marina on the canal, which looked like a good place to wait out the
storm—if we could reach it. I finished my breakfast, then climbed
on deck. There were those two anchors to get up.

"They must be dug in good," I told *Cabin Boy*.

They were, but I'd mastered a simple method of freeing anchors from the clutches of the most gripping, sucking mud, even with the wind blowing like stink: I'd pull in the anchor line by hand (one of the benefits of having a small boat) until it was straight up and down, then tie it off to the sampson post. Then I'd slowly motor the *Blue Moon* ahead a few feet. This never failed to tip the anchor out of the mud. Once broken out, the anchor was easy to haul it in.

With both anchors up, we motored around the west end of the island where we met the full fury of the wind and waves, right on the nose, of course. There was no hope of sailing up that river, so it was all up to the engine. It always made me nervous to depend so much on a mere machine, so I sang Gilbert and Sullivan songs, loudly and defiantly, into the wind. Nothing keeps a fellow's spirits up like a bit of G&S.

We had ten long miles of that evil river, but eventually we worked our way up to the canal—the North Carolina Cut. Once there, trees on shore blocked the wind, the waves died away, and we were safely in the arms of the narrow canal. I don't mind saying I was relieved.

An hour later, we tied up at one of the two marinas in Coinjock, NC. I took a shower, had a meal in the restaurant, and spent the rest of the afternoon chatting with other sailors who had taken refuge from the storm. They'd all come from the north, off stormy Currituck Sound. We debated whether the Currituck or Albemarle Sounds had been the more treacherous passage. Obviously, I argued for the wild Albemarle, but since the *Blue Moon* was the only boat heading north, I was out-voted.

"Heading up to the Chesapeake?" one of the old gaffers asked me.

"Yes, and then through the Chesapeake and Delaware Canal, down the Delaware River, and up the coast to New York."

He sucked air through pursed lips and shook his head. "A dangerous bit of water, that C&D canal."

"Really?"

"Loads of ship traffic out of Baltimore goes through that canal. It's jammed with all manner of tankers, container ships, and freighters."

"Sometimes they close down the whole canal to let a big one through," another sailor piped in. "You just have to tie up to a barnacle-encrusted pile and wait."

"The worst are the tugs and barges. Act like they own the whole canal. Saw a fifty foot yacht crushed to matchsticks by one of them, once."

"And if they don't run you down, they leave you spinning out of control in their wake. Makes you an easier target for the next one."

"No…" I said. "It can't be that bad."

The old gaffer and his friends looked slightly offended by my plain disbelief. "Well, see for yourself," he said. "Don't say we didn't warn you."

By the next day, the storm had blown itself out. The morning was clear and calm, and I motored up the flat and easy Currituck Sound, thinking those other sailors were a pack of liars and exaggerators. No doubt they thought the same of me.

The town of Great Bridge in the Commonwealth of Virginia provided that rarest of rarities: a *free* dock to which you could tie up for the night. I don't know why more towns don't offer this marvelous service, but they don't. In fact, this was the first free town dock I'd come across and I never did find another. It was a rickety old thing, grey and splintery, with a few missing planks, but it was free, empty, and within walking distance of a grocery store. My pantry was bare, so I tied up and headed into town.

By the time I returned, night had fallen and every inch of that decrepit old dock was occupied by cruisers, both sail and motor. The light shining out of many companionways and portlights was a cheery, welcoming sight. After stowing my groceries, I strolled down the dock with a bottle of Mount Gay rum, looking for someone sociable. A beautiful steel ketch flew the Dutch flag. I slowly walked along her side, admiring her high bulwarks, no-nonsense rigging, and teak decks. She was a real ocean-goer and looked ready to head off to Greenland or Cape Horn tomorrow.

I hailed her captain and was soon invited on board by the Breukers. Jan was a compact little man, well north of seventy, with white, short-cropped hair and vivid blue eyes. Christina had plump, red cheeks and an easy, throaty laugh. If Santa and his wife got in shape and went cruising, they'd look just like the Breukers.

Jan broke out the glasses while Christina showed me around her home. It was the warmest, coziest cabin I'd ever seen, with flowered, deep-cushioned sofas, pictures on the walls, and books in bookcases. The kitchen (it wouldn't be right to call it a 'galley') was larger than the whole *Blue Moon* and looked like it could turn out a better meal than I'd eaten in a long time. But it wasn't a mere houseboat. Everything was secured in its proper place by a screw, or a strap, or a hatch, or some other ingenious device. If the boat turned upside down, nothing would fall out of place. A non-sailor might not have noticed, but I could see that this was a real sea-going boat.

"This boat looks like she could go anywhere," I said, as we settled onto the comfy sofas.

"Yes, and she has," said Jan. "Since 1978, she's been on every ocean of the world."

"Brazil last year," said Christina, "and this summer, Maine. Very beautiful."

"Now we are headed to New Orleans for the winter. And then, maybe back to Holland in the spring."

"And it's just the two of you?" I asked.

"Ja, just the two of us," Christina laughed.

"But…" I stopped, not knowing how to ask the obvious question without sounding rude.

"How do we do it at our age?" Jan asked. He leaned in towards me, his eyes piercing. "I will tell you something," he said in a low voice. "Sailing… like we do… it is the secret to eternal life!"

I sat in Jan and Christina's gorgeous salon and, for a few stunning moments, felt he was dead right.

Then they both laughed at me and Jan poured another round of rum.

* * *

Chesapeake. *The* Chesapeake.

Unlike most bodies of water, like New York Harbor or Albe-marle Sound, it's always *the* Chesapeake. For me, it promised the best sailing since the west coast of Florida. Everyone I talked to said it was fantastic: open water, moderate tides, hundreds of sheltered anchorages in many rivers and creeks, two shores to sample... the list of recommendations went on and on.

And for the first time, I was promised, there would be more sailboats than powerboats. The Chesapeake was sailboat country, and not by accident, I was told...

When the Earth's Architect finished the construction of North America (so the story went), she suddenly realized there weren't enough good places to sail. This was 35 million years before the first sailor was due to be born, but the Architect was thinking ahead. Clearly, this lack of sailing ground was a defect in her design.

"No matter," she said. "Easily fixed!"

Choosing her spot carefully, she flung a giant meteor down into the middle of the east coast of North America (accidentally obliterating a species of talking dinosaurs) and—whammo—the Chesapeake was dug.

"Perfect!" she said. "If I do say so myself. And if I don't, who will? Ha, ha, ha!"

But before I could reach this sailor's paradise, I had to sail through the largest naval base in the world: Norfolk. Four miles of waterfront, seven miles of pier and wharf space, this naval station supported seventy-five ships, and was the home port of my late Uncle Frank, when he was a Navy fighter pilot.

I found the prospect of sailing through Norfolk both exciting and intimidating. It sounded worse than sailing through New York Harbor—another challenge I worried about whenever I had a few spare moments. The southern approach to Norfolk was guarded by at least six bridges and one major lock. Once within the bounds of the naval station, pleasure boats dared not stray into the many restricted areas, or they would be blown out of the water by trigger-happy sailors in gunboats.

Or so everyone said.

There was no point leaving too early, since several downstream bridges would be firmly closed for the morning rush hour, so I caught the 9 a.m. opening of the Great Bridge Lock and began my passage of Norfolk.

I was an old hand at locks, by then, and thought I knew most of their tricks. But somehow, I didn't trust them. Locks were usually set in bucolic, park-like settings, and this one was no exception. Tall trees lined its approach, and children and old gaffers fished from its embankments. I knew the drill and had the necessary dock lines prepared, but always I felt uneasy when puttering in between those high concrete walls, hearing those steel doors close behind me.

There was a large sign on the bank that told the distances—via the ICW—to various destinations.

To the south, it said, Coinjock was just 37 miles away; Southport, 310 miles; Savannah, 575 miles; and Jacksonville, a long 734 miles.

To the north, Norfolk was a mere 12 miles; Cape Charles, 50 miles; Washington, 209 miles; and New York, 452 miles away.

452 miles… a mere 10 days—if I could somehow average 45 miles a day. That didn't seem likely; 20 days was more realistic; 30, if problems appeared. But in the big scheme of things, New York wasn't so far away. Maybe we were almost home…

"Let's not get ahead of ourselves," I told *Cabin Boy*. "Just take it one step at a time. First, let's see if we can get through this lock without getting swallowed up by a giant whirlpool."

We followed three boats into the lock for the north-bound opening. There was plenty of room in the enormous lock, so I picked a spot midway between the lock gates, to be as far as possible from any whirlpools. I needn't have worried. The difference in water levels was so slight that the water barely stirred around us. No whirlpools.

We followed the other boats out of the lock and proceeded down the Elizabeth River towards Norfolk. The banks remained leafy and green for a few more miles, then began to look more and more industrial. Pretty soon, there wasn't a leaf, or blade of grass, or bunny rabbit to be seen, just grim warehouses, steel tanks, and iron jetties.

Just north of Newton Creek, a railway bridge and a highway bridge crossed the river side by side. Neither had more than ten feet of vertical clearance. The highway bridge opened every hour on the half-hour. The railroad bridge was normally left open, but closed for trains. I arrived twenty minutes before the highway bridge was due to open, but as I slowly motored towards the closed bridge, I realized the railway bridge was also closed, meaning a train was expected. The guide book said the highway bridge would not open on time unless the rail bridge opened first.

"No problem," I told *Cabin Boy*, who was beginning to look worried. "I'm sure the train will go by soon."

We crept down the narrow, hemmed-in channel towards the twin bridges. One or two boats already waited. A bit of a current wanted to pull the boats under the bridge, so we had to keep moving to stay in control. I wish there was a standard method of waiting for bridge openings, and maybe there is in some book, but on the water, every captain seems to have his own method.

Sailboats have the worst time of it. A sailboat's deep keel makes it more susceptible to current, so they drift down on a bridge faster than powerboats. At the same time, sailboats have to keep moving forward through the water—like sharks—to maintain steerage. For these reasons, sailboats tend to circle slowly in front of closed bridges.

But to say sailors used a uniform system would be to exaggerate. Most circled counter-clockwise, since this helped them stay in their proper lanes. I say 'most'. Some—the largest, of course—seemed to think the Rules of Navigation were suspended in the proximity of closed bridges, at least for them. They circled clockwise, or across-wise, or in a nervous zig-zag pattern.

Powerboaters had the most control over their boats, and so were the most casual about bridges. They never join the sailboat carousel, choosing instead to use their various thrusters to maintain a single position—usually blocking the sailboats. Or they just drifted downstream, talking loudly and drinking beer, getting closer and closer to the bridge, until you're sure they'll be swept under, when they suddenly notice the bridge towering over them, and zoom off at high speed through the rest of the fleet.

The result was usually chaos.

Not trusting my own boat handling skills, and never liking to mix with large fiberglass boats that could easily slice the poor *Blue Moon* in two, I usually hung back from the mêlée. But this time I was one of the first arrivals at the bridge. As we waited, more and more boats—some of them quite large—gathered like logs in a jam. There was not much room to maneuver in the narrow river, and my careful, counter-clockwise circling was quickly disrupted by the game of *Dodge 'Em* which soon commenced.

I was monitoring the bridge tender on channel 13, hoping to hear some news about the train which had not yet appeared. But all I heard were the repeated—and increasingly hostile—calls from the milling fleet. Bridge tenders tend to be friendly and patient people, used to dealing with the boating public, but if there was a tender on that railroad bridge, he or she was silent. Perhaps the poor public servant had died, leaving the bridge closed, in which case it might be weeks before anyone in authority noticed. Or perhaps she was fed up with impatient boaters. The smoked glass windows in the tender's steel box high above the river were like dark, blank eyes, revealing nothing. Meanwhile the cacophony on channel 13 was becoming abusive. I'd had enough.

I worked my way back through the fleet, heading up river, out of the throng. Though the *Blue Moon* was one of the smallest boats in the pack, with her long bowsprit and *Cabin Boy* trailing behind, we needed almost as much space as the forty footers. Once free of the others, I was able to breath again. I resumed my orderly counter-clockwise circling, gladly allowing new-comers to pass me.

Eventually, of course, the train did hove into view. It slowly clattered across the steel bridge, and after it had passed, first the railway and then the highway bridge opened. The two angry fleets (yes, another group of boats waited on the far side of the bridge) passed each other in the narrow gap, with the usual near-misses and shouts, some boats going too fast, and some too slow, but eventually we all got through. I was happy to be the last.

"Thank you," I radioed to the invisible and silent bridge tender.

"You're welcome," came the cheerful reply.

After turning Money Point and cruising down the Gilmerton Bridge Reach, we passed through another railroad bridge (thankfully open) and entered the naval base. Grey-clad aircraft carriers, cruisers, and destroyers lined the channel; docks and derricks towered overhead; gigs and patrol boats whizzed back and forth across the channel; and an army of sailors, boatbuilders, and dockworkers swarmed over all. No one seemed to take any notice of the poor *Blue Moon*.

As we cruised past a formidable looking ship that was not an aircraft carrier (that was as far as I could classify it), I wished I had my Uncle Frank on board to explain what I was looking at.

Captain Francis Almberg was a carrier pilot who'd been awarded the Distinguished Flying Cross "for heroism and extraordinary achievement while participating in aerial flight as a Pilot attached to and serving with Attack Squadron ONE HUNDRED NINETY-TWO (VA-192), in U.S.S. TICONDEROGA (CVA-14), on 25 January 1967 in the Republic of Vietnam." He'd once been an integral part of this hive of activity and I'm sure he could have brought the unfolding scene vividly to life for me, but even without his expert commentary, there were so many interesting things to see, it was hard to know where to look.

I was careful to stay in the main channel. Each ship was ringed by floating booms meant to keep the unauthorized out. If the booms and pointedly-worded signs weren't a broad enough hint, grey patrol boats cruised back and forth, ready to blast intruders out of the water.

So I kept to the channel, snapping pictures all the time, and all too soon we were through and out onto the famous Hampton Roads.

Here, I made a mistake. There are a number of anchorages in the Hampton Roads area. They all sounded pretty good, so it was hard to choose between them. I'm sure I chose the worst one.

The guide books called it the Mill Creek anchorage, which is deceptive on a number of levels. First, 'creek' sounds like a narrow and protected body of water. The anchorage was neither narrow, nor (as I discovered) protected. Second, the anchorage wasn't even in Mill Creek.

The anchorage was on the north side of Hampton Roads, just west of Old Point Comfort at the very mouth of the Chesapeake. Sailors, said the guidebook, are advised to proceed past the marina and to anchor in ten-to-twelve feet of water in open space. The road traffic will die down at night, the book said.

Road traffic? Well, the anchorage was in the middle of a city, but as long as it quieted down at bed time, what did that matter?

The entrance to the anchorage was wide and easy to enter. I caught a glimpse of the marina with its thicket of masts. We were in sailboat land, now, for sure. The anchorage was big enough for two dozen boats, but was nearly empty. The double-yellow lines on the chart were now explained. They indicated two elevated highway bridges. The bridges stood on narrow trestles far above the anchorage. Between the trestles legs was water. Very open water.

When I arrived, the wind blew from the north. To the southwest, clearly visible between the trestle legs, Hampton Roads stretched to the horizon, perhaps a twenty mile fetch. If the wind shifted to the southwest during the night...

"But what is the chance of that?" I asked myself. "It's been blowing from the north for days."

Reassured by this impeccable logic, I anchored the *Blue Moon* close to the northern shore of the anchorage. Up on the bridges, the afternoon rush hour had begun, but the noise didn't bother me. I'd had plenty of silence in the past few weeks. Meanwhile, I was worn out by all the excitement of the last few days. I cooked a hot meal, read a bit, and sipped a bit of rum. The sunset was spectacular, and I'd soon be sailing up the Chesapeake. What more could you ask?

At 2 a.m., I was nearly rolled out of my bunk, onto the floor. The next moment, I was wide awake, with my head outside the companionway hatch. The wind had shifted to the southwest.

One-to-two foot waves rolled in under the trestle legs. The concrete bulkheads that had sheltered us from the evening's north wind had turned into a black and greasy looking lee shore.

The *Blue Moon*'s captain roared out his orders and, in short order, her crew had the engine running and the anchor up. In a few more moments, we were leaving the black bulkheads behind and heading for the lee of the small man-made island near the mouth of the anchorage. There, the willing crew dropped anchor and played out plenty of scope, never suspecting that the captain of the *Blue Moon* was, even then, berating himself...

"'What is the chance of the wind shifting to the southwest?'" he mocked himself. "Ha!"

He'd worried about that long fetch to the west, but had ignored his own gut. Such an incompetent captain deserved to be woken up in the middle of the night. Deserved worse! But his poor crew didn't deserve such treatment! Not the ever-suffering, never-complaining, loyal crew of the *Blue Moon*.

The captain suffered in silence, then retired to his cabin, waking at every wind shift, cursing himself for his carelessness.

"Never just wonder," he reminded himself. "Do!"

* * *

By morning, the wind had turned back to the north with a vengeance. I listened to the weather radio as I made my breakfast. "Winds... North winds 15 to 20 knots with frequent gusts to 25 knots... Seas 1 to 3 feet increasing to 4 to 6 feet by afternoon. Rain... Visibility 1 to 3 nautical miles..."

The sky looked dark and stormy; the anchorage unprotected, isolated, miserable. I really didn't want to waste another day and night there. I was becoming obsessed with the need to keep moving north.

I studied the guidebooks and charts, looking for a better anchorage to the north. Progress would be slow against that wind, so I didn't look too far. If I could make my way out onto the Chesapeake and go north just ten miles, there was a protected anchorage in Chrisman Creek, just off the Poquoson River. It seemed worth a try.

I put a reef in the main before lifting my anchor, then motored out of the so-called Mill Creek anchorage. But as soon as we rounded Old Point Comfort, I knew it wasn't to be. Out on the open Chesapeake, the wind blew thirty knots, and the wind had piled up four foot seas. To the north, the sky looked black and ominous, promising worse conditions in the afternoon. It was Albemarle Sound all over again. No doubt the *Blue Moon* could have bashed her way north a few miles, but only at a high cost to my reserves of strength. It just wasn't worth it.

"Not today," I told *Cabin Boy*, reluctantly, and turned around. Such was my focus on traveling north that I hadn't bothered to look for more protected anchorages to the south. Later, I learned there was a much better anchorage in Willoughby Bay, not far away. I returned to the awful Mill Creek anchorage, picked the safest, if not most comfortable spot, and dropped my anchor.

I spent most of the afternoon staring gloomily at the grey waves out on Hampton Roads, and then had a thought.

Back in Southport, a fellow named George had given me a lift to a grocery store. Along the way, he'd told me about a new fangled way to get wind forecasts. Something about GRIB data. "You can get an app for your iPhone," he said. "Best thing since sliced bread for wind forecasts."

I was doing this voyage, in part, to get away from computers, so I'd just filed the information under 'slightly interesting', but in that gloomy anchorage in Hampton Roads, I suddenly found it more than just interesting.

I installed the app he recommended and spent the rest of the afternoon trying to understand how it worked. The main screen showed a map of the southern Chesapeake, with colored arrows showing the direction and strength of the wind. Supposedly it was blowing from the northwest. I stuck my nose out of the hatch... that seemed about right. I closed the hatch again.

If you pressed the 'play' button, the map began to change like a video, showing how the wind would change in speed and direction for the next five days. Only it stepped through time in six hour intervals, so it was a bit jerky and hard to understand what you were looking at. As far as I could make out, the wind would swing into the south sometime during the night.

I looked out the hatch again. There was no spot in the anchorage that was sheltered from both the north and the south. "So now we know it's going to be a nasty night," I told *Cabin Boy*. "I'm not sure that helps." I closed the app, and shut the hatch.

After another rough night which indeed forced us to move yet again, we motored out of Mill Creek into a south wind. If anything, Hampton Roads was worse than it had been the day before. Sharp, confused seas seemed to be rolling in every direction. The sky looked nasty, but I was determined to anchor somewhere else that night. Somewhere north.

We passed through the gap below Old Point Comfort at the same time as a big steamer. I worried about the steamer's wake, but oddly enough, we'd never been discomforted by a really large ship. This was no exception: any wake it made was hidden in the confused seas.

"If it's bad here, what will it be like out on the Chesapeake?" That was the obvious question that worried me, but I soon had my answer. We rounded Old Point Comfort and headed north. That put the wind on our port quarter and suddenly we were flying free with the wind.

It was a tumultuous sleigh-ride, up and down four-to-six foot waves, but with the wind behind us, the *Blue Moon* was in her element. We made up the ten miles we'd lost yesterday in less than two hours. As the day progressed, we flew up the coast. At the same time, the wind veered more and more to the west, just as the GRIB app had predicted. By late afternoon, we were hard on the wind. We had to tack the last few miles into Jackson Creek, but we made it before dark. I dropped the anchor into a narrow, protected anchorage on the creek, nearly fifty miles north of Hampton Roads. After days of being tossed about by wind and wave, the calm anchorage was a bit of heaven.

The north wind blew hard again the next day, so I stayed holed up in Jackson Creek. I rowed ashore, borrowed a bike, and peddled the narrow lanes and small towns in the area. I needed the exercise.

Then the weather broke and for the remainder of my time on the Chesapeake, the weather was mild, sunny, with a south wind pushing us forty or fifty miles north every day. I had my choice of beautiful anchorages, both on the eastern and western shores, and at that time of the year (late October), the anchorages were mostly empty. It truly was a sailor's heaven.

On the 26th, I got an early start, hoping to make it all the way to the north end of the Chesapeake. The morning was grey. We cruised through a fleet of tall freighters anchored outside Annapolis. Their crews must have been sleeping late, because all the ships looked deserted, except for one young man who waved at us as we sailed by.

For a while, I watched a grey Navy patrol boat cruise a parallel course to ours, a mile or so to the east. For the first time, I understood why the Navy loves that color. The boat was exactly the color of the mist and the low shoreline behind it. It blended in almost perfectly.

The boat looked ominous and dangerous, and I guessed it was meant to look that way. I didn't like when it altered its course and headed towards us. I knew patrol boats—whether Navy, or Coast Guard, or Fish & Wildlife—were manned by young American boys and girls who were invariably friendly and helpful, but there was something about their boats that made me nervous. The boats were not friendly looking. Quite the opposite, in fact. They looked like predators.

Eventually, the boat crossed our bow with several hundred yards to spare. I waved, but no one waved back. Whatever their mission, I was glad to leave them behind in the mist.

Awhile later, outside of Baltimore, we were overtaken by a very grand topsail schooner that not only passed us easily, but sailed a circle around us, which impressed *Cabin Boy* and I immensely. It wasn't until she was footing away from us that I could read her name and we realized she was the *Blue Moon's* big sister—*The Pride of Baltimore II*. Also designed by Tom Gilmer, *Pride* was a Baltimore Clipper—ships that are legendary for their speed. No won-

Cabin Boy's big sister, the Pride of Baltimore II

der she was able to sail circles around us. She must have been out
for a day sail with some happy tourists. All too quickly, she sailed
away from us, back into Baltimore Harbor, but that brief encounter was a highlight of our voyage up the Chesapeake.

By late afternoon, we were in the northern reaches of the
Chesapeake. The eastern and western shores, which had seemed
like different worlds farther south, drew closer and closer together.
They rose from the low, grey lines of distant shores, into tree-clad
hills dotted by white cottages and farms. We were leaving the low-
lying South behind, and entering the rock-ribbed North. I was
glad of the change.

We were headed up the Elk River, which led to the entrance
of the Delaware and Chesapeake canal. Oddly, I had turned on
the weather radio—odd, because this is something I almost never

did. I got most of my weather information from the Internet. I didn't like the harsh sound of the robotic weather service voices, or the loud squelch of the radio. I always seemed to miss the part of the broadcast that applied to my area, and had to listen to the broadcast over and over again until I got it. Downloading the text version of the forecast and reading it on my phone was easier and faster. But for some strange reason, that day I had the radio turned on, and as the late afternoon declined towards evening, the announcements grew more and more dire.

As usual, I only caught snatches of the broadcast: *A strong low pressure system passing through the region... Thunderstorms... Sustained winds of 35 to 40 knots with frequent gusts to 50 knots... 6 foot seas...*

Snatches, but I got the gist. There was trouble coming. I had already taken down the sails in preparation for anchoring in the Bohemia River, about a mile north. Grey clouds gathered in the south. Jagged bolts of lightening sizzled on the horizon. I gave the engine full throttle and hoped we would make it before the storm struck.

My goal was Veasy Cove, on the south shore of the Bohemia. The wind was still a mild breeze. The river was calm, with barely a ripple playing on its surface. Veasy Cove looked a green haven, with lovely homes nestled under tall trees, and long green lawns leading down to the water.

I didn't waste any time looking at the view. I picked a spot with plenty of room and put down my 35 lb. storm anchor in about six feet of water. I gave the anchor plenty of scope, backed the *Blue Moon* to dig it in firmly, and set about 'battening down the hatches', securing everything on deck against the oncoming storm.

When everything was lashed down or stowed away, I broke out my foul weather gear, made some hot food, and sat in the cockpit to eat, watch the sky, and await the onslaught.

Nothing. Not a drop of rain, not a gust of wind. No six foot waves, no lightning cleaving the *Blue Moon*'s mast in two. Nothing.

I passed the time measuring the height of the *Blue Moon*'s

mast. According to the calculations in my log, the height from the water to the top of the mast was 27 feet, 3 inches. Call it 28 feet with a margin of safety. According to the cruising guides, the height of my mast would soon be vitally important. But where was that storm?

Eventually, I gave up and went to bed. My log says: "Light rain, no wind, a very quiet night."

For once, I wasn't complaining.

CHAPTER 21

DELAWARE CHALLENGE

"Take long walks in stormy weather or through deep snows in the fields and woods, if you would keep your spirits up. Deal with brute nature. Be cold and hungry and weary."
— Henry David Thoreau

The longer I sailed on my voyage, the more obsessed I became with currents: finding current data, understanding it, and using it to my advantage. By the time I reached the head of the Chesapeake, I'd long since discovered the raw data was easily available on the Internet. NOAA—the National Oceanic and Atmospheric Administration—issued current predictions for thousands of locations up and down the coast on their website.

Understanding the data was harder. On the following page is the table for Chesapeake City on the Chesapeake and Delaware Canal, for the month of October, which I pondered with my sleep-deprived brain on the morning of the 28th.

If I understood the data, I needed to hit Chesapeake City around slack tide—7:50 a.m.—and then ride the flood through the rest of the canal.

But Skipper Bob's *Anchorages along the Intracoastal Waterway*, which I really trusted, had its own recommendation:

Eastbound vessels should give some consideration to the tidal current at the head of the Delaware Bay. Near the C&D Canal and Reedy Island, it can approach 3-4 knots. Obviously, a slow boat will have a better time with the tide if it is going out when you transit this section. Because the tide is literally a wave rolling up the bay, you cannot carry a fair tide for

Chesapeake City Bridge, 0.45 n.mi. E of
Predicted Tidal Current
October, 2010
Flood Direction, 092 True.
Ebb (-)Direction, 273 True.
NOAA, National Ocean Service

Day	Slack Water Time h.m.	Maximum Current Time h.m. / Veloc knots	Slack Water Time h.m.	Maximum Current Time h.m. / Veloc knots	Slack Water Time h.m.	Maximum Current Time h.m. / Veloc knots	Slack Water Time h.m.	Maximum Current Time h.m. / Veloc knots
1	0129 +2.0	0544	0739 -0.8	1004	1319 +1.8	1613	1930 -1.6	2317
<snip>								
28	0331	0527 -0.8	0750	1103 +1.9	1352	1709 -1.8	2050	
29	0010 +2.3	0419	0621 -0.8	0848	1201 +1.9	1454	1810 -1.7	2146
30	0103 +2.2	0507	0714 -1.0	0951	1301 +1.9	1605	1913 -1.6	2247
31	0156 +2.1	0553	0805 -1.0	1059	1403 +2.0	1725	2015 -1.5	2348

All times listed are in Local Time, Daylight Saving Time has been applied when appropriate. All speeds are in knots.

Chessapeake City Current Table

October - Reedy Point

Date	Day	Time	Height	Time	Height	Time	Height	Time	Height
10/01/2010	Fri	12:01AM LDT 1.0 L		05:15AM LDT 4.9 H		11:43AM LDT 0.8 L		05:34PM LDT 5.9 H	
<snip>									
10/28/2010	Thu	02:59AM LDT 4.9 H		09:30AM LDT 0.6 L		03:08PM LDT 5.9 H		10:46PM LDT 0.7 L	
10/29/2010	Fri	03:56AM LDT 4.9 H		10:30AM LDT 0.6 L		04:09PM LDT 5.8 H		11:42PM LDT 0.7 L	
10/30/2010	Sat	05:00AM LDT 4.9 H		11:36AM LDT 0.6 L		05:18PM LDT 5.8 H			
10/31/2010	Sun	12:40AM LDT 0.5 L		06:07AM LDT 5.1 H		12:45PM LDT 0.5 L		06:28PM LDT 5.7 H	

All times are listed in Local Standard Time(LST) or, Local Daylight Time (LDT) (when applicable). All heights are in feet referenced to Mean Lower Low Water (MLLW).

Reedy Point Tide Table

six hours as you go down the bay. Instead at 6 knots, you only get about 3.5 hours of fair tide when eastbound before the tide switches. The ideal time to depart Chesapeake City for a slow boat is 1 hour before high tide at Reedy Point. This will put the tidal current with you as you go east on the C&D Canal. Then before you reach the east end, the tide will switch against you, Finally, as you break out into the Delaware Bay, you will have the tidal current with you and building speed. You will carry a fair tide for the worst part of the trip down the Delaware Bay before it switches against you part way down the bay.

According to the tide tables, the next high tide at Reedy Point would be at 3:08 p.m., meaning I should pass Chesapeake City (at the beginning of the canal) around 2 p.m., which meant I'd have the current *against* me in the canal. That made no sense to me.

I sat in my cabin through two cups of coffee, trying to reconcile these two conflicting pieces of information. It seemed so clear: if I picked the right time, I'd have an almost two knot current with me; if I timed it wrong, I'd have the current against me. The other cruising guides insisted that underpowered sailboats *must* catch the right tide, or fight the contrary current the whole way. The very thought of fighting the current through a canal jammed with cargo ships, tankers, Seawaymax container ships, and barge-pulling tugs filled me with dread. I hadn't forgotten that conversation back in Coinjock. I still didn't believe that pack of liars, but there was no sense taking chances.

In the end, I decided to trust the NOAA current table, which seemed unambiguous. The Skipper Bob advice, I figured, was for bigger boats that could easily fight the two knot current in the canal, and then be set to fly down the Delaware Bay with the current behind them. But that didn't work for me. If I tried to fight the current through the C&D, it would be dark by the time I hit the Delaware. By then it would be too late to proceed: I had no intention of trying to sail down the infamous Delaware Bay in the dark, current or no current.

So, first decision made: I'd to pass Chesapeake City at slack water, around 7:50 a.m. But what about ship traffic in the canal?

Dozier's *Waterway Guide to Chesapeake Bay* agreed with the marina bar gloom-and-doomsters that sharing the canal with big ships could be a bit tricky:

> *Cargo ships and military vessels... pass through the canal. Ships of this size—among the largest—require powerful bow-thrusters to keep them on course in the C&D's close quarters... Huge surges roll well ahead and astern of these leviathans, and the troughs left behind can send large and small yachts wallowing....*

Yikes.

The canal had its own dispatcher who controlled traffic using flashing red and green lights at both ends of the canal. If the lights were flashing green, that meant small boats could pass through. But if they were flashing red, we'd have to wait until 'the leviathan' emerged. Considering the length of the canal (seventeen miles), the wait could be hours. But it seemed there was nothing to do but to go up and see the lights for myself.

I got under way and headed up the Elk River towards the mouth of the canal, about five miles away. The scenery was lovely with the trees on the surrounding heights just starting to turn color, and lush farms and beautiful homes adorning both banks. It was a scene from the past and it was easy to remember that this had once been an important colonial waterway. Wooden boats—not too different from mine—had been plying these waters for over 400 years. A bit more imagination removed the traces of European settlers and left the original natives paddling their elegant canoes up and down these very same waters.

It really was a beautiful section of the ICW, and one of the few I could imagine living on. Someday I must come back here, I thought.

By the time the entrance to the canal hove into view, I was stripping off my foul weather gear. The morning mist had cleared off and the sun was hot on the back of my neck. The wind was still, the water flat, and the *Blue Moon* glided over its surface leaving barely a ripple.

I had to get quite close to see the dispatcher's flashing lights, and was relieved to see them green and not red. The coast was clear. I glanced back to check on *Cabin Boy*. He was tucked up close under the transom, to keep him out of trouble.

"You ready?" I asked.

Super-tankers... fierce currents... smashed to matchsticks... best day of my life!

I took that as a Yes, and headed on in.

Naturally, after all that worry and preparation, the C&D turned out to be a wide, placid canal with plenty of deep water and leafy banks. I'd picked my time correctly, and we had the current with us the whole way. We averaged 6½ knots, peaking at nearly 7½ knots. The day turned hot and half-way through the canal I stripped down to shorts and T-shirt—the first time I'd done that for a couple of weeks.

And—slightly disappointing, though it was—we didn't pass a single freighter or aircraft carrier. The only boat I saw on the canal was propelled by oars and manned by two boys in straw hats.

In short, we'd been lucky. We had an easy, quick passage on a lovely fall day. But it was the last bit of luck I'd see for a while.

* * *

We emerged from the eastern end of the C&D feeling triumphant. We'd carried a fair current through the whole canal and had cleared Reedy Point just after 12:30 p.m. There were a good six hours of daylight left—plenty of time, I thought, to reach the Cohansey River.

For hundreds of miles I'd been told that the Delaware—both river and bay—were ugly, ill tempered, and notoriously short on anchorages, but as I turned south onto the Delaware River, the day was warm, the sky blue, and the water flat. The doomsters had been wrong about the C&D, and it looked like they'd be just as wrong about the much-maligned Delaware.

"Just another case of sailor exaggeration," I assured *Cabin Boy*. The river was two miles wide, so I handed the tiller to *Helmo*, and ducked down below for a snack. If our luck held for a bit longer...

"Just one more warm, flat day, and we'll be across the Delaware Bay and into New Jersey," I shouted encouragingly out the companionway door.

The Delaware River descended twenty miles from the C&D to the mouth of the Delaware Bay. From there, it was another thirty miles, straight across the bay, to Cape May. It seemed eminently do-able.

I was only down below for three or four minutes, but by the time I climbed back into the cockpit, snack in hand, two large freighters had appeared on the river. They were both heading up the river, towards Philadelphia, and they were moving fast. We were well outside the shipping lanes, but I edged a bit more towards the Delaware shore, giving them all the room I could.

Considering their tremendous speed, I could not help noticing ours. Though the engine was pushing us through the water at 5.5 knots, the shore line hardly seemed to be moving. I checked the GPS and confirmed that we were making just 3.5 knots over the ground. Clearly, we had a 2 knot current against us.

That made sense, I admitted, grudgingly. The current table predicted 2 knots peaking some time around 2 p.m.

I did some swift calculations: It was twenty miles to the Cohansey. At 3.5 knots it would take roughly six hours to reach the Cohansey. That was cutting close, but not too close, and reaching the Cohansey was worth the effort, I thought.

There was only one other place to anchor between the C&D and the Cohansey river, and that was at Reedy Island, just five miles south of the C&D. If I played it safe and anchored there for the night, we'd lose a whole day. *Another* whole day.

"That," I said, "isn't something I'm ready to do without a fight."

As we cruised down river, I watched our speed over the ground (SOG) slowly drop, from 3.5 knots, to 3, to 2.5, to 2, and finally to 1.7 knots.

Impossible, I thought, but the flat, ugly shore of Reedy Island seemed almost motionless. How could we have a four knot current against us?

I re-calculated our arrival time at the Cohansey. At this rate, we'd be lucky to get there by dawn, assuming we had enough gas for eleven hours of motoring, which we did not. It was time for Plan B. We'd have to anchor for the night behind the abysmal Reedy Island. I pulled out my chart.

The anchorage was protected by the island itself, and by a dike which extended far to the south. The dike was a low stone wall which submerged at high tide. The only entrance to the anchorage led through a pass in this wall, marked by two buoys. On the chart, the entrance looked narrow and, with the cross current, dangerous. But with no other option, I girded myself for battle.

By the time we reached those buoys, hours later, the sun was low on the horizon and the dike was completely submerged. Only the two markers showed where the dike lurked—just inches below the water—like a recumbent dragon, ready to tear the bottom out of the unwary boat.

The two markers appeared to be motoring downstream at three knots. Both threw up large bow waves, though they were securely anchored to the rocks.

I did not fancy shooting that narrow, rock-bound passage with a three knot cross current, but the sun was going down and it wouldn't be an easier job in the dark. I sucked up my courage, said a little prayer to the god of outboard motors, and headed for the gap.

By now, I knew how the *Blue Moon* handled in cross currents, so I headed in crabwise—that is, angled into the current, to cancel out the drift. By using the gap as a range marker against the shore-line, it was fairly easy to steer a line straight through the center of the entrance, but it was nervous work. I breathed a sigh of relief when we passed through and left the flags behind us.

I anchored close to the Delaware shore to get protection from the westerly winds predicted by the evening forecast. The current behind the island was fierce, so I put down my 35 lb. storm anchor and gave it plenty of scope. It was the first and only time I would anchor in the state of Delaware.

Yes, it was windy. Yes, the current was scary fast—if I somehow fell off the boat, I'd have been swept upstream away from the *Blue*

Salem Nuclear Power Plant, across the river from Reedy Island

Moon at a running pace. But what really worried me that night was the ominous silhouette of the Salem nuclear power plant, just across the river on the Jersey shore.

In marina bars throughout the Chesapeake, I'd heard stories of giant, mutant crayfish that stormed small boats at night, taking their captain and crews prisoners, carrying them down, down, down to their glowing, undersea kingdom, never to return...

Was it yet another case of sailor exaggeration? Or were the stories—told in hushed, slightly inebriated voices—true? There was no way of knowing, but the water *was* abnormally warm.

As the sun went down, I scattered tacks on the deck, closed the hatches, and went to my bunk with an uneasy feeling.

* * *

So, the tacks worked and I wasn't devoured by mutant crayfish after all. But sometime during the night someone—or something—made off with summer. It felt cold, really cold, when I reached out of my warm sleeping bag to shut off the alarm. It was still dark. Slack water would be at 6 a.m. and I wanted to be heading downstream before the tide turned. Just the thought of bucking that Delaware current again was enough to get me moving.

My little one-burner stove was soon hissing under a pot of water for my morning tea and porridge. It warmed up the cabin a bit, too. I checked email as I ate, wondered if it was too early to call Helena (yes), and then ran out of excuses. I cracked open the companionway hatch. The starry sky glowed pink in the east. The *Blue Moon* tugged gently at her anchor, swinging to the slight breeze, instead of the current. Nearly slack water.

I rolled back the hatch, letting the night air pour in. Man, it was cold. Hard to believe I'd been in shorts, yesterday.

In a few minutes, I had the engine running and the anchor line straight up and down. In another minute, the anchor dripped mud from its roller as we steamed through the narrow gap in the dike. No wind yet, but the forecast called for a 10-15 knot NW wind later in the morning. Perfect for a fast run down the bay. With a good tailwind and a strong current flowing with us until noon, I hoped to make Cape May by late afternoon.

By mid-morning, the promised NW wind filled in and I soon had the sails up. We ran down wind at five knots. A bit chilly, but great sailing. I sneered at the cruising guides for again exaggerating the difficulties. This was going to be a snap.

A half hour later, I was wondering if I should get the sails down. *While I still could.* The wind had increased to fifteen knots. Just an easy breeze for the *Blue Moon*, normally, but in a few minutes it had kicked up the worst following seas I'd ever seen. Tall, fast, and breaking, they were already giving *Helmo* fits.

Studying the chart, my heart sunk. We were still in the Delaware River, really. Just at the mouth of the Bay. The wind blew straight down the river, in the same direction as the current. When the current reversed, later in the day, the waves would get even worse. I decided I did not want to be on the water when that happened. As much as I wanted to keep going, King Neptune would have his way. Luckily, the one and only port of refuge on the whole

Delaware Bay—the Cohansey River—was still downwind of us. I'd been eager to put it behind me all morning, but now I was glad we hadn't. It would have been hell beating back to it.

So I made for the Cohansey, studying the chart to avoid the many shoals between us and the narrow inlet. I was hand-steering by now, surfing down seemingly enormous waves. The bottom of the Delaware was a series of ridges, with the depth going from deep to shallow and back again. The waves seemed to ride up over these ridges, and cascade down their sides. It was this, I theorized, that caused the water to buck up so much. No wonder the Delaware had such a foul reputation.

As we approached the river, we had to turn more to the north, putting the wind and waves hard on our port side. The *Blue Moon* didn't seem to mind, but I was getting knocked around like a pea in a can. I didn't often wear my safety harness in the cockpit, but I had it on that day, on a very short tether. Even if we got knocked down, I meant to stay in the boat.

By now, there were two other sailboats in view. We were all headed madly for the Cohansey. One boat was a half-mile ahead of me. He was a big one, maybe forty-five feet, and he was motoring without a stitch of sail up. It made me queasy to watch him rolling gunnel to gunnel. I was glad we still had the main up. At least it steadied us a bit.

The cutter behind us had all sails up. She was streaking along, a couple miles back, but I could only see her when we were on top of a wave. And sometimes I could only see the top half of her mainsail when she was in a trough. That's how big the waves were.

I kept my eyes on that big boat in front of us. I hoped she knew where she was going. With all the waves and spray, I couldn't see anything of the river's entrance. I knew it must be there, but I couldn't spot it—not until the big boat was nearly at the inlet.

I watched him pass through into the Cohansey. We weren't far behind. As we passed between the entrance buoys, the depth sounder flashed 4.2 feet. A bar across the inlet? A rock in midstream? The wreck of a fellow sailor? Whatever it was, we flew over it with a few inches to spare and shot into the wide, deep, almost miraculously calm Cohansey River.

Welcome to New Jersey!

I dragged down my wet sails with shaking hands. Now that we were out of danger, the adrenaline wore off quickly. I was exhausted. Sails loosely tied, I headed up river, looking for a quiet place to anchor.

There's an old English proverb that says, *"An yll wynde blowth no man to good."* Apparently, this was a bit gloomy for Sir Walter Scott, who completely reversed the proverb's meaning with his own version: *"It's an ill wind that blaws naebody gude."* Stranded by a very 'yll' wind on an isolated river in southern New Jersey in early November, I wondered which version of the proverb applied to us.

I had originally intended to follow the cruising guide's advice and anchor in the Cohansey River, just above the two marinas that lie in a crook of the river's northern shore. The cruising guides warned of strong currents and advised mariners to "set two anchors before retiring below for cocktails," but after being knocked around by the Delaware, setting two anchors sounded like too much work. I was tired.

"Besides," I rationalized, "My supply of grub is getting dangerously low."

So I slowly cruised past the two marinas, checking them out.

The first was crowded. Every inch of dock space was full, even the fuel dock. There were no people in sight on that damp, cold, grey day. No parties in progress, no bikinis, just a silent line of white, plastic boats.

The second marina was nearly deserted. The empty 'T' dock seemed to beckon to me. Sure, it looked a bit rickety, as if its planks had been laid down in the 1960s; sure I knew the old saying about empty restaurants; but was that Frank Sinatra? His voice floated tinnily over the water, sounding like a ghost from the past...

> *...The way your smile just beams.*
> *The way you sing off-key.*
> *The way you haunt my dreams.*
> *No, no - they can't take that away from me...*
>   *-- Ira Girshwin*

JOHN ALMBERG | 267

How could I resist that? I headed into *The Marina That Time Forgot*…

It *was* Frank's voice that beckoned across the water, and by the time I'd tied up, I'd also heard Tony's, Ella's, and Dean's voices. This marina had a soundtrack. A jazz soundtrack.

"How cool is that?" I asked *Cabin Boy*.

Still clad in high-performance long undies, foulies, and sea boots, I trudged up to the office to register with the old salt who kept the marina humming, so to speak. A man of few words, but friendly and welcoming, he quoted me the cheapest dock fee I'd heard in 1,500 miles. That alone made me warm to the *The Marina That Time Forgot* (*TMTTF*, for short), since it looked like I might be there for a few days.

Outside the office, I watched a few dockyard guys assemble a floating crane out of rusty steel beams, bolts, and blocks. Like playing with a full-sized Erector Set. It looked dangerous to me, but they seemed to know what they were doing.

We chatted for a bit, then one of the crew offered me the use of his own car to run into town for supplies. That was another first. I was starting to like New Jersey.

I accepted his offer and drove into town for a week's groceries. Once I had them stowed away in the *Blue Moon*'s fo'c's'le, I settled down to do some planning.

By this time, I'd discovered another feature of my GRIB app— the graph view. Not as sexy as the map view, but more useful. It displayed a graph of the wind direction and speed for the next few days, which was far easier to read than the flickering map view. "Pick the right weather…" I muttered as I looked at the forecast.

That's a phrase you read a lot in cruising guides: "Pick the right weather to cross _____". Fill in your favorite nasty bit of open water. But picking the right weather isn't so easy.

First, you need to know what the right weather is. Before heading down the Delaware, I thought a lovely NW wind, blowing me straight down the bay, would be the ideal weather. What could be better than a 'fair wind'? Isn't that what sailors dream of?

In most cases, yes, but not on the Delaware, as I'd discovered.

And that was important. To pick the 'right weather' you needed 'local knowledge'. Another favorite phrase of cruising guide authors.

Well, I now had local knowledge, learned the hard way. I now believed that the 'right weather' was a moderate (10-15 knots, say) northerly breeze. This would put the wind on my port quarter, and minimize the fetch across open water, since I'd be sailing in the lee of the northern shore for most of the way.

I'd worked all this out in my head while walking around the grocery store. Okay, fine. Ideally, I wanted a north wind, or even a northeast wind. But I couldn't just order up a north wind from the weather service. How long would I have to wait for it? The GRIB forecast was not encouraging. It predicted northwest winds for the next few days, which meant stormy seas out on the big D, as I was starting to call it.

"Blast..."

I couldn't wait forever. The weather was already turning cold. I only had so many days left before I'd have to pack it in for the winter. I needed to keep moving.

I went out in search of more 'local knowledge'. "Pretty nasty out there," said the old salt who ran the place. "I'd stay right where you are." "Looks like it will keep blowing like this for the next few days," said the young salt who ran the gas pumps. Another sailor, looking pale and shaken, tied up his boat next to mine, just before dark. "Worst water I've ever seen," he said. "Like sailing in a cocktail shaker."

Looked like I wasn't going anywhere soon.

I spent the next day walking around Olde Greenwich. Discovered that the Boston Tea Party wasn't the only one: they had had one in Greenwich, NJ, too. In 1774, the Cohansey River was one of the few deep water ports between the Atlantic Ocean and Philadelphia. With the bigger colonial towns in an uproar over the tea tax, the dastardly Brits had snuck a load of tea ashore in sleepy Greenwich. But the local patriots were having none of that. They burned the tea during the night of December 22, 1774, a year after the Boston Tea Party, and commemorated the party with a pretty grand monument in the center of this very small town.

It didn't seem like Greenwich had grown much since the 1700s. The main street, called "Ye Greate Street," in the tradition of all things olde, is lined with beautiful, well preserved, colonial-era homes. Adorned with satellite dishes, of course.

In keeping with the importance of sea trade to the village, there was also a pretty terrific Maritime Museum. Or so the brochure said. Unfortunately, it was closed.

Oddly enough, the most fascinating building in town, for me, was a small, log-walled, grain storage shed, built in 1650. It was supposed to be the oldest agricultural building still standing in the US. Pretty darn interesting, if true, but I couldn't figure out how they got untreated logs to last over 400 years... Hmmm.

Back at the marina, I poked around the boats laid up for the winter. Found a small, flat-bottom cruiser wedged in between a bunch of tired-looking, production fiberglass boats. It was a fun find, but once I'd admired her lines and snapped a few photos, I thought I'd done Ye Olde Greenwich to death.

I wanted out of there.

That afternoon, the wind was still blowing hard from the northwest. The GRIB forecast was for more of the same. There was a hint of snow in the air. I wondered if I'd be stuck forever—if I'd been shunted through a worm hole in time and space into *The Marina That Time Forgot*. I was in a bit of a panic about that, for a minute or two.

I whiled away the evening catching up on laundry and taking hot showers and climbing up onto the highest deck in the marina, leaning out over the railing, holding my phone up, trying to find the exact spot that gave me one bar of cell phone service. I managed to call Helena, who cheered me up for a few minutes, but then the call dropped, and try as I might, I could not find that bar again.

Weary but clean, I trudged back to the *Blue Moon*. It was late, nearly midnight, but I had no reason to get up early. I read a bit, sampled my new stash of snacks, and eventually gave up and snapped off the light. But before I went to sleep, I checked the

Oldest Agricultural Building in the USA

GRIB forecast one more time.

I sat up in the dark, studying the bright screen. Something had changed. Instead of 15-20 knot NW winds for as far as the eye could see, the wind dipped down to five knots tomorrow morning, and then swung into the north. The next day looked even better, with calm winds forecasted all day. Go tomorrow, or wait for 'better' weather the next day? I dithered over this question, but only for a few moments. In this business, you have to grab your chances. Sometimes they are fleeting.

I set my alarm to ring an hour before dawn, determined to leave the dock the moment I could make out the markers.

The Cohansey was glassy when I cast off my dock lines the next morning, but a good breeze had set in by the time I got to the Delaware, almost an hour later.

As predicted, I had the wind on my quarter and I put up all my working sails to make the most of it. We made hull speed most of the way down the Bay, with just the right amount of wind to keep us moving fast.

Also as predicted, the north wind did not kick up the same sort of vicious chop that I'd seen two days before. In spots, where the current rolled over undersea hills, the waves stuck their heads up two or three feet, but that was no trouble for the *Blue Moon*.

"Pick your weather," I told *Cabin Boy*. "That's the secret," and he agreed. Interestingly, in this case, technology—in the form of the GRIB forecast—had trumped local knowledge. It was a small detail I'd remember in the trying days to come.

By mid-afternoon, we were across the Bay and heading into the Cape May canal. The cruising guides had warned against 'monster' ferries, which supposedly crushed all small boats that dared to cross their path, so it was with some trepidation that I crossed the bar into the mouth of the canal, but the monsters were asleep in their berths as we slipped by.

As we entered the canal proper, three large powerboats swept by. "Back in the land of rude powerboaters," I muttered. But I was so happy to be across the Delaware and back in the ICW that I found myself waving cheerfully after the demon boaters, as we wallowed in their wakes.

We were on the New Jersey ICW. In the home stretch. Of course, NJ ICW was notorious for its dangerous shallows, but surely they would be a snap after the miserable Delaware Bay.

Right?

CHAPTER 22

NEW JERSEY

The sea is for sailing… strenuousness is the immortal path… sloth the way of death. —H.W. Tilman

I have a problem writing about New Jersey. Which, of the 147 miserable experiences should I tell you about? I can't possibly write about all of them. Even if I did, you'd think I made half of them up. So I will pick one or two of the more believable incidents, and hope you can imagine the rest.

New Jersey taught me a new rule. It's a lot like the rule that I made up while building *Cabin Boy*. That rule was *Make Mistakes Slowly*. In other words, since mistakes are inevitable when building a boat, it's better to make them in slow motion (with hand tools) than in fast forward (with power tools).

My new rule is *Run Aground Slowly*. I discovered this maxim by doing the opposite, several times, during my first day in the infamous NJ ICW.

Until I got to Cape May, I had prided myself on grounding only three times in the 1600 miles from Steinhatchee, FL. All three times, I did something wrong, like cutting a corner or trusting *Helmo* too much. But no mistakes are required to run aground in NJ—except for the primary one of believing the ICW in that state is a navigable waterway.

My first grounding was typical: It was the day after we'd crossed the Delaware. The morning was cold, windy and miserable, but I was on my way home and we were making good time, doing 5 or 5½ knots. The ICW was straight and well marked. I was headed right down the center line. My depth sounder showed six to eight feet, with the occasional deeper patch. Plenty of water for the *Blue Moon's* four foot draft.

All of a sudden, I felt the telltale bump that every sailor dreads. Before my hand could move to the throttle, we bounced another half-dozen times, finally coming to a rather abrupt stop.

"Blast and botheration," I said. Or something to that effect.

Luckily, I'd read the cruising guide, which was unequivocal in saying that prudent sailors, in boats drawing four feet or less, should always travel on a rising tide. (By the way, there is a sign over the entrance of the NJ ICW that reads *"Abandon all hope, ye who enter here in boats drawing more than four feet."* The sign itself has a thirty-five foot vertical clearance.) So, twenty minutes later, we floated off and were on our way again. After running aground two or three more times, I gave up counting. Clearly, the game was different in NJ. It wasn't *if* you were going to run aground, but how hard and for how long.

Over the next couple days, I learned to keep a sharp eye on the depth sounder, and on the signs that are often visible if you are watching for them: a certain kind of ripple, just below the surface, or the finger of marsh that points to a shallow spot.

If the sounder suddenly started showing five feet and trending lower, I'd slow the boat down to a crawl until I'd cleared the shoal. Sometimes I'd be lucky and glide over the shallow spot. But if there wasn't enough depth, I'd just nudge the shoal and be able to back off and try a different spot.

Usually, there was a deeper part of the channel I could get through if I looked hard enough. Except for one really bad place where I just had to anchor, eat my lunch, and wait for the tide to rise another foot.

This made for slow going, but I didn't complain. At least I was making steady progress north. The weather was miserable, with hard winds from the N or NW. According to the weather service, those winds were kicking up six to nine foot seas on the ocean, just on the other side of the barrier island. Even if I'd had enough nerve to venture out, we never could have beaten north against that wind and those waves. Even big sailboats were bottled up in Cape May. It was only the *Blue Moon*'s relatively shallow draft and short mast that allowed us to squeak through the ICW. Otherwise, we too would have been stuck in Cape May, waiting for a turn in the wind that might not come until spring.

Meanwhile, we made our slow peregrination through an interesting, and surprisingly beautiful part of the world. We had heavily populated barrier islands to the east and the rural mainland to the west. In between, the ICW wound through a wide swath of channels, marsh grass, windswept isles, and lonely anchorages. This was the famous New Jersey Shore, and it ran one hundred miles or more up the coast. And that November—weekdays, anyway—I had it practically to myself. Just me and the odd fisherman. And considering how cold it was, I thought them very odd indeed.

After a few days, I thought I'd got the hang of the tricky waterway. I was feeling pretty confident, not to say cocky. It was the middle of the afternoon. The hard north wind had finally dropped, but had been replaced by rain and fog. We wound our way through an exceptionally wide expanse of shallow bays, fog-draped islands, and marshland. We might have traveled a thousand years into the past. The only sign of civilization was the occasional red or green buoy that marked the thin trail of the ICW.

But the ICW wasn't the only trail through this wilderness. Other trails meandered off to other places. Some eventually wandered through inlets to the Atlantic; others led into rivers or harbors. These side paths crisscrossed the ICW, making it easy to get confused. This was particularly true when the fog or rain closed in, and I could only see the closest marker. Sometimes, I couldn't even see those.

The first time that happened, I nearly panicked. I was in a narrow, shallow channel. A few feet away, I knew, the water was only a foot or two deep. But the black water told no tales. Without the markers to show where it was, the channel disappeared. Instantly. In this kind of situation, you either anchor and wait for the visibility to improve, or pull out your GPS chart plotter.

When I started my voyage, I considered chart plotters (which I could not afford) a luxury, not to say a cheat. But then I'd upgraded my first-generation iPhone to a 3GS with built in GPS. With the addition of the Navionics app, I was able to hold a mini chartplotter in the palm of my hand.

This was not a luxury in the NJ ICW where it was often impossible to tell where the channel was. In these situations, a chart plotter—even a tiny one—could keep us moving north in the foulest of weather.

So there I was, motoring at a stately four knots, visibility one-quarter mile, with low grassy islands all around me, playing the keep-the-red-arrow-inside-the-channel game on my iPhone. This was a pleasant pastime at four knots. The red arrow showed my location; the head of the arrow showed my direction of travel.

In fact, the game was so easy that it hardly required any conscious thought. As we traversed a fairly wide, open stretch of water, my mind was far away. I can't remember exactly where it was… perhaps home with Helena, perhaps with the Swallows and Captain Flint, in the far north of Scotland (I was reading Arthur Ransome's *Great Northern?* at the time.) So it was rude shock when I abruptly ran aground, a half-mile from the nearest visible shore.

Now, I don't mind going aground in protected water, surrounded by grassy islands, but it's no fun at all getting stuck in the middle of a bay, with a couple miles of fetch in several directions. It's all too easy to imagine the nasty chop that would pick up in a hurry if the wind started to blow. That's why I made it a rule to only travel on a rising tide in the NJ ICW. And to cruise at a reasonably slow speed, so I wouldn't run fifty feet up a sand bar if I hit one.

In fact, with the tide in my favor, I was able to back off this shoal in a few minutes. Then, paying attention this time, I tried to resume my course. Slowly.

Bump! Aground again, even though the chart plotter showed I was smack in the middle of the channel. This had happened before, of course. Channels get shoaled up, or they move, or the chart isn't exactly right.

Yes, hard as it is to believe, sometimes the chart isn't as accurate as the GPS. The mistakes are rare on a highway like the ICW, but they do happen. I'd found one or two other mistakes the hard way, but this was different. Those other mistakes had been in well marked channels. Here, I was in the middle of open water. The next channel marker was at least a quarter mile away. I could just see it through the fog and drizzle.

At least, I thought that was the next channel marker. As I looked around, I noticed there were quite a few around me. I tried to match up the markers I could see with the ones marked on my screen. Something wasn't quite right…

Now that I was looking around, I noticed there seemed to be more real markers than virtual ones. That was odd, but I knew the Coast Guard sometimes added markers to show where a channel had shoaled or shifted. There was a red and green pair quite close by, maybe fifty yards away. They looked shiny and new. I figured they were new markers that showed where the channel was. They were more or less in the right direction…

Yes… That must be right.

I carefully motored towards the new pair. No problem. I passed between them, and then looked towards the next red buoy. There were no other markers between me and the buoy, so I guessed the idea was to head right for it.

Bump! Aground.

Worse, I was lost.

Not lost in the sense that I didn't know where I was. I had a GPS that told me exactly where I was. But I was utterly disoriented: what I was seeing with my own eyes did not match what I was seeing on the chart plotter.

Fog made the problem worse. A line of buoys doesn't just tell you where you need to go, it often tells you from which direction you need to approach, at least roughly. That single red buoy was surrounded by shoals. Of the 360 possible lines of approach, only two were right. But which two? Without other buoys to orient me, I didn't know.

The best thing to do when lost or confused on the water is to anchor. Nothing could be easier than anchoring where I was, in five feet of water. I dropped the hook, went below, and made a cup of tea. Some people might have had a stiff drink, but I find a strong cup of tea clears the mind better.

After the first brain-clearing sip, I did what I should have done a long time ago: I pulled out the old-fashioned paper chart. Within a few seconds, I realized my mistake. I was in the wrong channel. Instead of being in the ICW, I was in a cross-trail that led to a river. I wasn't far into it, just a couple hundred yards. But between me and the buoy I was aiming for, the water was one foot deep. I could have nosed around all day and never found a way through.

I carried my tea and chart up on deck and looked around. There were the two buoys clearly marking the wrong channel. And there, a couple hundred yards back was the previous green buoy, where I'd made the wrong turn.

I hoisted my anchor, went back to the green buoy, and cruised past the red one without a bump. Even then, it was hard to understand how I'd gotten so utterly lost in such a simple situation. Upon reflection, I think the problem was a matter of scale.

The GPS chart plotter is excellent for showing what I will call, for lack of a better word, the detailed picture. You can zoom in as close as you like and see where you are in the channel within a few feet.

What it does not show well is the big picture. As you zoom out on a chart plotter—particularly a small one—you lose much of the detail. I normally kept both chart plotter and paper charts on deck, so I'd always had the benefit of seeing both the big picture and the detailed picture simultaneously. But since it had been a rainy day, I'd left my paper chart below to keep it dry. It only took a moment's inattention to turn into the wrong channel. My zoomed-in GPS showed I was in *a* channel. What I didn't see, until I could see the big picture on my paper chart, was that I was in the *wrong* channel.

If this sounds confusing, it's because it was confusing. I'm telling the story as I remember it, and as I *believe* it happened. I can't say for *sure* how it happened. This is my best guess. People who are lost can rarely say how they came to be lost. That's the nature of the thing. You only know you are lost when you are.

But I do think I am right about the big picture vs. detailed picture thing. It's not that one is good and one is bad. It's that you need both.

I'm just lucky that King Neptune taught me this lesson in so gentle a way. Just a few soft bumps on a rainy afternoon, and a little confusion. It could have been worse.

A few hours later, he taught me another important lesson. Ordinarily, I think two lessons in one day is excessive, but King Neptune must have realized he was running out of time with me. It was late in the day, and I was hurrying along, trying to reach my planned anchorage before dark. Not surprisingly, there are relatively few anchorages in NJ. There just aren't enough places with water deep enough to anchor. But my usually reliable cruising guide promised an anchorage behind Mordecai Island: in *"5 to 6 feet of water, with enough room for 5 to 10 boats."*

That sounded great, so it was with high hopes that I turned into the Liberty Thoroughfare behind Mordecai and began looking for this enormous anchorage. The channel was narrow, and the shore was lined with docks and boats. But where was the anchorage?

I spotted a small cove.

"That must be it," I thought. The chart showed blue, with no depth markings, just a note which said that buoys are not charted because they are frequently shifted in position.

Buoys? What buoys? During the summer, the channel into the cove was probably marked by a line of markers. But it was November, and all the local buoys had been pulled for the winter. The way in to the anchorage was unmarked.

"Blast!"

It was already getting dark. I had to do something, so I tried to feel my way in. I picked what looked like a likely spot, and slowly nudged my way towards the cove. Bump. No good.

I tried several other places, but no luck. If the channel to the cove was still there, I wasn't going to be able to find it. The Thoroughfare itself was too narrow to anchor in. I had to face it, the

Mordecai Island anchorage was a bust. I needed another place to spend the night.

I dropped my anchor and went below to study my charts and guides. There was a marina right around the bend. I called to see if they were open and thank goodness they were. The dock master said to come on over and he'd guide me into a slip. When I got there a few minutes later it was nearly dark, but the dock master was true to his word. He stood on the dock and waved me into a slip on the south side. That would give me the best protection from the north wind that was picking up again, he said.

The marina was my least favorite kind, with a long dock with barnacle-encrusted pilings marking out the slips. Ideally, you'd back your boat into the slip, tie up stern-to the dock, with bow lines led to a piling on either side.

Unfortunately, these slips had been designed for sixty footers, because even the first of the two sets of pilings were too far back for the *Blue Moon*. Also, with the wind that was blowing, I couldn't back into the slip—the *Blue Moon* was not fond of backing up in the best of times and I deemed the possibility of backing past two sets of pilings to the dock to be effectively impossible.

So I had to go in bow-first, tie up to the dock and to the short finger pier, and then use *Cabin Boy* to run stern lines back to the out-of-reach pilings behind us. It was quite a fiasco, with the be-wildered (and cold) dock master watching helplessly. However, we were eventually secured and I was happy to have a berth for the night.

After thanking the helpful dock master, catching up on some laundry, and walking across the street to a lively restaurant, I hit my bunk for some sleep. I wanted to get an early start in the morning.

During the night, the winter-like wind shifted from the north to the northwest, and proceeded to blow hard. The marina was well protected from every wind, except from the northwest. The wind blew straight across the two mile wide Little Egg Harbor and soon kicked up 2-3 foot waves that rolled straight into the marina. In the middle of the night, I made an entry in my log:

5 Nov 2010 - Lots of pitching & rolling in slip. Had to adjust lines several times because some of them chafed half-through during the night. Amazing how fast a half-inch line can chafe through in these conditions. Doubled-up the ones taking the most strain.

I got very little sleep that night. All I could think about was getting out of there. But when the sun came up, and I stood on deck surveying my position, I realized that was not going to happen.

A 15-20 knot wind blew across the slip. 2-3 foot waves rolled in from the same direction. And a fast current from the south ripped under the violently pitching, rolling boat. Only the web of eighteen dock lines I'd put out overnight kept her from slamming into the dock and finger pier. To escape, I'd have to slip this web and back past two sets of barnacle-encrusted piles without scraping all the paint off my starboard side, or getting pushed sideways in the slip and getting pinned up against a pile, dock, or another boat.

This was galling, because I could have predicted the problem. The GRIB forecast had been for northwest winds, but I hadn't checked them before I'd pulled into the marina. Hadn't even thought to check them. Being in a marina wasn't like anchoring, where one had to anticipate bad weather. Marinas were supposed to be safe havens. Who ever heard of 2-3 foot waves in a marina? Not I! So I hadn't checked the forecast. Neither had the dock master, apparently, or he would have led me to a more protected slip, but I couldn't blame him. I was the captain of the *Blue Moon*. It was my responsibility. My fault. Another of King Neptune's lessons learned the hard way. Would they never end?

After resolving never to get trapped in a slip again, I spent the rest of the day figuring out how to escape. The forecast was for several days of strong NW wind. Even if I was tempted to stay put (which I was not), I was worried about winter closing in on me. I still needed to make the offshore passage from Manasquan Inlet to New York. That jump was not going to get easier if I waited. I had to keep going.

So my first thought was to use *Cabin Boy* to put an anchor in the channel outside the slip, slightly to windward. I could then warp the *Blue Moon* out of the slip, while keeping her under control and off the piles. The helpful dock master promised to assist with the dock lines.

The GRIB forecast, however, predicted a short dip in the wind speed at 5 a.m. the next morning. The narrow V-shaped forecast predicted a low of 5-10 knots at 5 a.m., picking back up to twenty knots, shortly after dawn.

If the wind actually dropped, that would be a terrific opportunity to escape from my trap without any risk at all. I couldn't expect the dock master to show up so early, so I'd have to handle all the lines myself.

"No problem," I told *Cabin Boy*. "That's our plan A."

If the dip didn't show up as predicted, plan B was to warp out as soon as the dock master appeared.

The next morning, my alarm rang at 4 a.m. I made a cup of coffee and took it out on deck. It was cold. The wind still blew from the northwest, but it had gone down during the night. There was a 2-3 knot current flowing from north to south, pushing me out of the slip. That was the right direction, but a bit faster than I wanted. The current would slow and eventually go slack around dawn. I'd wait until the current weakened, but would keep a close eye on the wind in case it started to pick up. Five o'clock still looked like the sweet spot.

I gradually removed dock lines, first the slack ones, then the doubled lines, finally getting down to the three lines needed to keep the *Blue Moon* in place: the port-side bow and stern lines, and a short, mid-ship spring line on the starboard side that held us against the current.

At 5 a.m. the wind was 5-7 knots, the NW swells had gone down to less than a foot, and the current was favorable, about one knot.

"It isn't going to get any better than this," I told *Cabin Boy*.

I fired up the engine, let it warm for a few minutes, and then cast off the starboard spring line. I warped us out as far as I could with the stern and bow lines, then cast off the lines and used the engine to back us out of the slip, first between the two inside pilings, then past the two end pilings.

Despite the still considerable pitch and roll, we got into the clear without touching either pile. I yelled something like "Yahoo!", but it was still pitch-dark and I had no intention of running the insanely shallow ICW in the dark. I dropped my storm anchor, dug it in, and shut off the engine.

We'd done it. We'd escaped the trap. My ship and my crew had performed beautifully. To say the captain was relieved would be an understatement.

I treated myself to a full cooked breakfast, with a fresh cup of coffee, eggs, ham, and toast; called Helena to tell her the news; and then waited for the rose-red fingers of young Dawn to appear in the sky.

It was going to be a good day.

We got underway at dawn and by 11 a.m. we had completed the most difficult section of the NJ ICW—the roughly ninety miles of narrow channels through shallow marshland from Cape May. As we passed between Sandy Island and Long Beach, the relatively wide and deep Barnegat Bay spread out before us.

Note that word 'relatively'. In fact, the Bay was only 8-10 feet deep, at most. The notoriously shallow Great South Bay off the south coast of Long Island was both bigger and deeper. But it was with a great sense of relief that I looked upon the open waters of Barnegat Bay. We were only thirty miles from the Manasquan Inlet and—with nearly seven hours of daylight left—I thought we had a good chance of reaching it. From there, it was just a short offshore hop to New York. I was almost home.

So easy did the afternoon leg seem, that my mind had already skipped past it. I was more worried about the 'hop' to New York. That's what the guides quaintly called it. The Intracoastal Waterway ended at Manasquan. The twenty-five mile hop to New York was decidedly extra-coastal. There was no protected route even for a small boat like the *Blue Moon*. The only way was outside, in the

North Atlantic, and from listening to the National Weather Service radio, I wondered if we'd arrived a week too late.

Just a few days before, I'd been sailing up the Chesapeake with a lovely southerly wind at my back. That Indian Summer weather had ended the day we'd turned into the Delaware River. Since then, we'd seen nothing but cold and nasty northerly winds, with a bit of icy rain thrown in for fun. If we had arrived a week or two earlier, the hop to New York would have been easy. I'd have been home by now.

"Too late?" I kept wondering. There was only one way to find out.

As we cruised into Barnegat Bay, the weather service issued small craft advisories for the next few days. A major storm approached. Seas on the Atlantic were already eight feet high, and the storm was still approaching. As I listened to the forecast, my cheerfully optimistic mood evaporated and was replaced by a grim realism. There was no question about making the hop in the next few days. The immediate question was, where should I hole up? Manasquan, or one of the many rivers off Barnegat Bay?

If I went up to Manasquan, I'd be near the inlet, ready to make the hop whenever the weather was right. But better protection was available in Barnegat Bay, where there were sheltered rivers with almost no tides.

I tossed this question back and forth as I sailed through the southern part of the Bay. I wanted to wait out the storm in a snug little harbor, but I didn't want to be a whole day's sail from the inlet. The weather was too changeable. Unless I was ready, on the spot, I could easily miss a one-day weather window. And one day was probably all I was going to get.

After a bit of dithering, I decided to try for Manasquan, but as I thrashed up the Bay, the weather got nastier and nastier. By the time I had reached the mouth of the Forked River, we were beating into the kind of short, nasty, four foot waves that made progress in the *Blue Moon* difficult. The wind was rising every minute. Suddenly, finding that storm hole seemed a lot more important than reaching Manasquan. I turned into the Forked River.

As soon as we shot through the entrance on a broad reach, I knew I'd made the right decision. While the wind was howling out on the bay, the river was a ribbon of calm. I quickly doused the sails and motored up stream.

The Forked River was literally lined with marinas and since everyone with an ounce of sense had already pulled their boats out of the water, there were plenty of open slips. I slowly motored up the river, shopping for a likely marina, and in the end, chose the last one: the State Marina. It was as far up the river as you could get, and seemed perfectly protected from the wind. I tied up, found the ranger in charge, and made the arrangements. He told me the *Blue Moon* would be safe from the storm in her berth, and that the tidal range in the marina was only six inches. That meant I wouldn't have to adjust the dock lines every few hours, even if the storm was raging. That gave me an idea.

I walked from the ranger station, back down the dock to the *Blue Moon*. The water was glassy calm and seemed like a heavenly refuge after the marina we'd escaped from that morning.

I made a pot of tea to warm up my chilled bones and ate lunch while considering my new plan. The more I thought about it, the more I liked it.

I called Helena on the phone.

"How would you like to pick me up?" I said.

"I'd love it!"

I was now only two hours away from home by car. I'd wait out the storm there. That was my new plan, and in my bone-chilling cabin, with a winter storm approaching, it seemed like a darn good one. Helena agreed.

I began to prepare the *Blue Moon* and *Cabin Boy* for the storm. There was much to do before Helena arrived, but one question kept nagging at me.

Had I missed my last chance to make 'the hop'?

CHAPTER 23

THE HOP

It is folly to complain of the fickleness of the wind.
— *Ovid, "Heroides"*

A funny thing happened on my long journey up the side of America: the farther I sailed, the more cautious I got.

This seemed odd, even to me. I'd accumulated an enormous amount of experience and practical knowledge. You would think I'd have gotten bolder as I went along, more confident in my abilities to pull through difficult situations. Instead, I found myself avoiding problems whenever possible.

And my self-confidence? Well, we'll soon see how that helped me.

After docking the *Blue Moon* on the Forked River, I had my first shore leave since Jacksonville. Suffice to say, I enjoyed every moment of it. After six weeks of being outside all day, every day, it was a relief to watch the storm blow from the warmth and comfort of home.

And blow it did. Through the Internet, I monitored the weather sensors on buoy 44065, at the entrance to New York Harbor. At the height of the storm, on 8 Nov 2010, the wind blew from the NW at 33 knots, with gusts up to 40 knots. Not a hurricane, but enough to worry my Uncle Marty, who called to find out where I was. He was relieved to discover I was safely at home.

Even after the storm passed, the wind kept blowing hard out of the North, gradually swinging from the NW to the NE. It was now winter on the North Atlantic and I was determined to wait for a wind that came from the southwest—a fair wind blowing off the shore, so the seas wouldn't build up too high. Yes, a southwest wind would be ideal, but as the days flipped by, I realized I might have to settle for good enough.

For months I'd been confidently telling everyone I'd be home by the 1st of November. Each time I did, Helena would pipe in with, "He means Thanksgiving," which showed a distinct lack of faith, I thought.

When the 11th of November rolled around, I was still at home, and it looked as though the wind would howl out of the North all winter. Helena and I started to talk about "final deadlines," and what we would do if the wind didn't ease soon. We decided December 1st was my drop-dead date. If I couldn't make the hop before then, we'd lay the *Blue Moon* up for the winter in the Forked River.

I was determined, however, to make every effort to get her home. I still had some faith in the GRIB forecast, which showed the weather improving over the next few days. The *Blue Moon* was still a day's sail from the Inlet, so I decided to sail her up to Manasquan, and wait for my wind.

At 4 a.m. the next morning, Helena drove me back to New Jersey, so I could get an early start. We arrived before dawn and quickly prepared our little ships for sea. I backed the *Blue Moon* out of her slip just as the sun came up, with *Cabin Boy* trailing behind. Helena waved goodbye from the dock and called out "Good luck!" After days of being home, I was definitely out of my sailing groove, and was severely tempted, then and there, to give it all up for the winter. But I steeled myself for the task, waved back, and pointed the *Blue Moon* down channel. Too soon, we turned a corner in the river, and Helena was out of sight. The crew was smart enough to stay out of the Captain's way for a while after that.

There was no wind and the Forked River was glassy smooth, but as the sun rose, so did the wind, and by the time we motored out of the river, onto Barnegat Bay, the wind was again blowing 15-20 knots, out of the NE, right on our nose as usual.

In those miserably shallow waters, the wind soon kicked up waves big enough to stop us cold when they struck the bow. Worse, riding over the steep waves pitched the outboard out of the water, making it race as though to tear itself apart. I slowed to half-speed, which reduced our progress even further, but lessened the strain on the engine. I could not afford to have it give out on me.

I made a note in my log: "Nasty, cold, and wet." But the further north we went, the closer we were to the windward shore, so the waves gradually dropped. In a couple hours, we were in the shelter of Goodluck Point, and the worst was over. A few hours more and we left Barnegat Bay behind. For good, I hoped. The ICW shrunk again into its usual narrow, twisting channel. The trees on shore blocked most of the wind. The sun came out and bathed the cockpit with warm rays.

"Just five miles to go," I told *Cabin Boy*. We were rapidly approaching the Point Pleasant Canal—the last ditch on the ICW. Glancing at the chart, I could see it was about one and a half miles long, with two lift bridges and no locks. Easy-peasy. It was a beautiful day and we were almost home. I cruised into the mouth of the canal without another thought.

Almost immediately, our speed slowed from five knots over the ground, to three. "Must be some current against us," I thought.

That was a bit annoying. I wondered if I should turn around. There was a small basin outside the mouth of the canal that would be a pleasant place to anchor and wait for the tide to turn.

"No," I thought. What did it matter if it took forty-five minutes, instead of fifteen minutes, to traverse the canal? It might be hours before the current turned. I was too irritable to wait. It just seemed like too much trouble. I kept going.

By a stroke of good luck, the first bridge was opening just as I approached it. A large powerboat approached from the other side. I opened the throttle to full and reached the bridge just as it opened fully. I passed under the span and waved to the bridge tender.

My handheld VHF radio crackled to life. Someone was calling to "the blue sailboat headed north," but I could not make out what they were trying to say. I picked up the radio. "This is the *Blue*

Moon, heading north. Can you repeat, please?"

With that transmission, I used the last few electrons in the radio's battery. It powered off before I could hear the reply.

I reached inside the cabin to push the dead handset into its charger, and in that small moment of inattention the current spun us 90 degrees to port, straight for the canal's concrete seawall. I corrected course just in time, and cursed myself for not having the sense to keep the VHF's battery charged.

I waved back at bridge tender and headed north, towards the next bridge.

What had he been trying to tell me? Probably something like this, which I later read in Skipper Bob's *Anchorages Along the Intracoastal Waterway*: "**Caution:** *There is a swift current through the Point Pleasant Canal approaching 4 knots on the ebb and flood. If you require the bridges to open, make arrangements with the bridge tender before you enter the canal. The canal is very narrow and there is little room to maneuver if the bridge is not open when you arrive.*"

The emphasis is Skipper Bob's, but I did not read those fateful words until later that evening, when it was too late.

Our speed over the ground decreased rapidly after the first bridge. Pretty soon, we were doing exactly one knot over the ground. Suddenly, a mile and a half seemed a long way. I was also worried about that second bridge. If my VHF didn't charge in time to make the call, I'd have to depend on the air horn to signal the bridge tender. Was it one blast, or two, to ask for an opening? The answer was in one of my books, but there was no chance to look it up. The canal demanded every bit of my attention. I'd never seen such bad current. It ripped past the seawall, throwing up white waves wherever a bit of the wall stuck out. Whirlpools and eddies tried to push the *Blue Moon*'s nose off her course, threatening to spin her around. I knew if I lost control, even for a moment, we'd be whipped around and perhaps driven into the dangerously close seawall. I kept to the middle of the channel and urged my trusty engine on: "Keep going, baby… keep going!"

In short, I realized I'd made a serious error. For over a thousand miles, I'd been trying to catch my tide and play the currents. In the one stretch of the ICW where it really mattered, I hadn't given a second's thought to planning. We were almost home; why plan? The crew silently cursed the captain for his poor seamanship.

Our slow progress gave the VHF battery time to charge, and by the time we reached the second bridge, I was able to call the bridge tender and ask for an opening. After calling him, it took another fifteen minutes of battling the current to reach the bridge, so I guess he had plenty of warning, after all.

It was then I realized how lucky I'd been. What if the current had been flowing with us, instead of against us? We would have flown through that canal at nine knots. There would not have been time to call the bridge and wait for it to open. The current would have swept us under the bridge, dismasting us, or worse. Just the thought of what might have happened turned my guts to jelly, and still does. No wonder they wanted you to 'make arrangements' before entering the canal. King Neptune had been gentler with this particular lesson than I deserved.

Eventually, we emerged safely from the fiendishly misnamed Point Pleasant Canal. The only thing pleasant about it was leaving it behind. As my heart resumed normal operating speed, we headed up the Manasquan River towards the Inlet. It was only a mile or so, but there were two more bascule bridges to wait for. There was plenty of boat traffic, too, even at that time of the year, including some large commercial fishing boats. Manasquan looked like the busy little port it was, serving as the main stopover for boats heading to and from New York City.

After passing under the railway bridge, I could just about see the inlet, a half mile away. But instead of heading out onto the North Atlantic, I turned north into narrow Crabtown Creek. After waiting for yet another bridge to lift—five in one day is more than enough, thank you very much—I cruised into the beautiful Glimmer Glass anchorage. I dropped my anchor in the middle of this tranquil pond (I was the only boat there), and thanked my lucky stars. For it was luck, not skill, that got us through that day.

The captain served a double ration of rum that evening, and the crew still grumbled for more. I checked the GRIB forecast again before hitting the rack: the forecast for the morning was still for light southwest winds—perfect for making the hop. My luck was holding. I went to sleep thinking, "We're almost home."

* * *

The next morning, I was up before dawn. The Glimmer Glass was a mirror, and a million stars glinted off its surface. The sky was clear and there wasn't a breath of wind. The storm had finally blown itself out. Today was going to be the perfect day to make the 'hop'.

I poured myself a cup of tea and congratulated myself for being the luckiest sailor ever. I dished up a double portion of oatmeal to get me through the long day, and flipped on the marine weather forecast. As I ate my breakfast, my mind was already offshore, trying to anticipate what it would be like 'out there' on the cold Atlantic. Exciting, but unadventurous, I thought. An easy, safe trip. So I was shocked when I heard the National Weather Service computer voice utter the words "Small craft warnings".

"That can't be right," I thought. "Must be talking about someplace else."

I listened all the way through the forecast cycle again. And then again. Until there was no doubt, whatsoever: the National Weather Service had clearly lost it. They were indeed issuing small craft warnings for New York Harbor and points south.

"They must be wrong," I said, indignantly, looking at the calm day right outside my door.

I remembered all the times the forecast *had* been wrong. I didn't blame the NWS. Weather was hard to predict, especially for specific locations. In Florida, I'd watched boats get pummeled by rain a mile away, while we were bathed in sunshine. In the Chesapeake, I'd wasted an afternoon waiting out a storm that never arrived. I'd waited days for this particular weather window. It might be the last one. If it was open, I could not afford to miss it. But I also couldn't afford to take chances on the open Atlantic. I had to be sure.

I called the Coast Guard to verify the forecast. Called them up in New York Harbor. Told them about my problem. Could the forecast be right?

"Yup," the young man said. "It's blowing like crazy here. You should stay put."

I hung up the phone. I still couldn't believe it. My old rowing coach used to say, "You don't know what the weather is until you are standing on the dock." Clearly, I needed to go stand on the dock.

I climbed into *Cabin Boy*, rowed ashore, and walked the mile to the inlet.

I stood on the northernmost of the two massive seawalls that guarded Manasquan Inlet. It was early morning by then. The wind blew on-shore, from the northeast, at fifteen to twenty knots. The seas were ten feet high and crashing violently onto the seawall, throwing up massive plumes of spray. The NWS hadn't lost it. A mile from my mirror-like anchorage, the Atlantic was a maelstrom.

Even if I had the nerve to brave that sea—which I didn't—with a 15-20 knot wind out of the NE and ten foot seas, tacking all the way, we'd be lucky to make one knot good to the north. That meant over twenty-four hours to Sandy Hook. That was too long. The *Blue Moon* might be able to take it, but I didn't think I could. By then, I knew my limitations all too well.

While I stood on the seawall, with other people fishing or walking or just marveling at the power of the sea, I watched a big sailboat coming down from New York. It was a sleek forty-eight footer, motoring without a stitch of sail up. It rolled, sickeningly, in those seas. When it was in the trough of a wave, only the tip of its mast showed.

I watched as the captain lined the boat up with the inlet. They were a half-mile offshore at that point. There must have been a strong cross-current, running from north to south, because as he motored in, the boat drifted south. South of the inlet there was a beach and the high seas had brought out the surfers. There were a dozen or more paddling around in their wetsuits, waiting for the perfect wave. Pretty soon, the big sailboat was in amongst them, much too far south of the inlet.

He must have noticed the current by then, but instead of turning around, getting some sea room, and trying again from a better angle, he chose to go for it. He motored straight towards the inlet, trying to get around the end of the south seawall, but all the time the wind and waves tried to push him onto the rocks.

Even then, he might have been okay. He could have aimed for the north sea wall, which would have given him some protection from the surging waves. But instead, he turned in close to the south seawall. As I watched in horror, the huge boat surged with the next incoming wave and came down within feet of the rocks. I didn't know whether to watch, or call the Coast Guard for help. But his engine saved him from his poor seamanship. The boat survived that first surge, then slowly pulled away from the rocks, looking small amongst the long waves.

I breathed again. He'd sure taken his chances. If his engine had stalled…

Later, I talked to some fishermen. They told me of a commercial fishing boat that had been wrecked not long ago in the inlet, with the loss of several crew members. It was not a good place to take chances.

I agreed. I wasn't going anywhere. Not that day, anyway.

* * *

Having decided to wait for the 'right' weather, I moved the *Blue Moon* to a marina right on the Manasquan River. It wasn't as peaceful as the Glimmer Glass basin—or as cheap—but when you're waiting in cold weather, it helps to be able to step ashore for food or a hot shower or a walk.

I hoped it wouldn't be a long wait. Every night, before hitting my rack, I'd study the next day's forecast, hoping for a fair wind. Every day, I'd walk to the inlet to inspect the sea and watch for boats. I saw a few flying south. I didn't see any fighting their way north.

Of course, big power boats went out nearly every day, but I didn't count them.

Each morning, the temptation to *just go for* it was strong. To get it over with, one way or the other. And this irrational impulse was leavened by the daily troop of dock watchers who came by to admire the *Blue Moon* and ask me where I was headed. When they heard I was waiting for a fair wind for New York, a certain number of them—actually, quite a large number of them—would sniff the air and say something like "Well, my brother-in-law, Tony, was out fishing yesterday, and he had no problem…"

So what's wrong with you, buddy?, was the unspoken question.

When I expressed interest in Tony's exploits, further bragging would reveal that Tony routinely thumbed his nose at danger from the bridge of his forty-three foot Egg Harbor SportYacht, with its twin 660 horsepower Caterpillar engines, but the difference between our two boats never seemed relevant to the dock watchers. Clearly, I was just a coward in their eyes.

I tried not to let it bother me, but it did. Whenever one of these dock watchers sniffed at me, the urge to *just go for it* spiked even higher. Luckily, my location in the marina provided a daily antidote.

I was berthed on a T-dock which was shaped just like it sounds. The stem of the 'T' was lined with berths, while the top was used as a fuel dock and for transient berths. Because of the heavy powerboat traffic on the Manasquan, I had insisted on an inside berth, so the poor *Blue Moon* wouldn't be dashed against the dock by every rogue wake. This was deemed highly irregular by the marina owner, but since the dock was deserted, he allowed me to tie up in the first inside berth, just on the other side of the fuel dock. This gave me many chances to talk to captains who had just come in off the ocean.

One example will suffice. Tom, a thirty-something professional man, sailed a forty-two foot Jeanneau out of Barnegat Bay. I will let him tell the story.

"This morning was bright and sunny and there was a great breeze blowing," Tom said. "I knew it would be one of the last sailing days of the season, so I thought we'd head out of Barnegat Inlet, sail around a bit on the ocean, and then head back in.

"As soon as we passed the end of the sea wall, I knew we were in trouble. The waves were huge and the wind was much stronger than it had been on the bay. The inlet is surrounded by shoals, and waves were breaking all around us. Terrifying.

"I wanted to turn around and head back in," he continued, "but the channel was too narrow—we would have ended up on the shoals for sure. So I just gritted my teeth and tried to keep her in the channel as we headed out. It wasn't easy with the wind blowing from the north and a wicked cross current. I didn't think we'd make it, but somehow we did.

"Once we were out in deep water, it was pretty rough. But after talking it over, neither one of us wanted to go back through that inlet. It was just too dangerous. So we decided to head up here, because the Manasquan Inlet is safer. We put up the reefed main and jib and motor-sailed the whole way."

"We both got seasick," his mate Joe piped in. They both shook their heads, as if remembering it. "Pretty bad. It was my first time on a sailboat."

"We work together in an office," Tom said. "I told him it would be a fun day. Well, he's seen the worst the sea can do. It can't get much worse than that!"

"Yeah," Joe said. "I thought I was going to die."

"But we didn't! Woo-hoo!"

They high-fived each other: two young men, just happy to be alive. I handed them a couple cold beers. Tom took a long pull of his, then eyed the *Blue Moon* on the other side of the dock and asked me where I was headed.

I said I was headed nowhere at the moment. Just waiting for some decent weather.

"Smart," he said soberly. "Smarter than us."

It was a long wait. That north wind blew for a week and a half. Helena came back and took me home again, and told me it didn't matter how long I had to wait, as long as I left before December 1st.

The north wind blew, and it blew, and it blew, while I waited in front of my fireplace, brooding.

And finally, on the 23rd of November, it stopped blowing.

***

It is easy to acquire the art of sailing a boat under favourable circumstances; but it is only after considerable experience that the sailor is able to do the right thing promptly in the various emergencies which he is sure to encounter. The tyro will soon discover that the more he knows the more he has left to learn, and if once he commences to acquire this knowledge of seamanship, he will be thirsty for more; and he will never weary of his favorite sport all the days of his life. — E.F. Knight, "Sailing"

E. F. Knight's *Sailing* is one of my favorite books. It's the book that John Walker consulted when, as a young lad, he had to sail the *Goblin* across the North Sea to Holland in a gale (in Arthur Ransome's *We Didn't Mean to Go to Sea*), and it's probably the book Ransome learned to sail with.

Knight says the science of sailing is "practically infinite," and I agree with him, particularly when it comes to weather. After many months of studying forecasts, and comparing them with actual weather, all I can do is quote the ancient weather proverb: "Believe it when you see it."

For many, many days, the wind blew from the north. And not just from the north, but from the Arctic: it was *cold*. North, north, north the forecast read, until I began to wonder if the needle was stuck, and the wind would never blow from the south again.

But then it began to veer from north to east, and then east to south. At the same time, the wind dropped from a howling thirty-five knots, to a less frightening twenty knots, with a corresponding drop in wave height.

Then, one afternoon, the forecast for the following day was, "S WINDS 5-10 KT... BECOMING 10-15 KT IN THE AFTERNOON. SEAS 2-3 FT."

I was excited, but ready for disappointment. The forecast could change so quickly. But it was the best forecast I'd seen for a long time, so the next morning, November 23rd, Helena ferried me down to Manasquan, hoping this would finally be the day.

She drove me straight to the inlet so I could climb onto the stone ramparts and see the enemy with my own two eyes. I half-expected to see Boreas with his army of the North still gathered at the gates, still assaulting the walls with their mighty battering rams, so it was a shock to see the enemy was gone, withdrawn to their chilly fortress far in the north.

"Gone for the moment, yes," I thought. "But they could return at any moment. There's no time to lose."

I climbed down and Helena drove me straight to the marina. There, we threw aboard stores for four days—all I'd need to get home, even in the worst case scenario, I hoped. While I unlashed the *Blue Moon* from her berth, Helena found a marina guy to top up my gas tanks. Clearly, she had been telling him about my voyage.

"You sailed up from Florida in that little boat?" he asked, handing me the gas hose.

"Sure did."

He shook his head. "Tougher than me."

"What do you think of the weather today, for heading up to New York?"

"Gonna blow hard from the south later this afternoon."

That matched my own thinking, but by the afternoon I hoped to be in sight of New York Harbor, one of the easiest harbors in the world to enter. It was late November. Boreas was taking a short break with his new girl friend. I wouldn't have a better chance than this.

"She's a tough little boat," I said.

"Looks it. You'll do all right."

Meanwhile, I could see that Helena had been decoding this grunting man-talk, and didn't like what she'd been reading.

"Is this safe?" she asked me, with one of those don't-even-try-to-lie-to-me looks.

That was the question. The question all these many months had led to. The question only I could answer. Was it safe?

I'd gathered all the information available: from the weather service, from local knowledge, from my own two eyes. Now it was time to weigh that information in the scales of experience—the experience I'd gradually accumulated along the way.

Stay or go? I looked at the clear blue sky. I'd been careful about picking this day. 'Prudent' was probably the right, old-fashioned word that Knight would have used. Maybe I missed a few marginal days when I might have made the hop. But *might* wasn't good enough for me. On this day, I was *sure* we'd make it. I knew it and I felt it. And that's what I told Helena.

I backed the *Blue Moon* out of her slip, with *Cabin Boy* trailing behind, and cruised past the fuel dock. My sweetheart waved from the dock. She looked beautiful in the silvery winter sun. I waved back, blew her a kiss, then pointed the *Blue Moon*'s bow towards the wide Manasquan Inlet. The Atlantic waited.

The day was perfect: sunny, and almost balmy at 55°F. The wind was calm and the monster swells were gone. The *Blue Moon* was ready for sea. She glided quickly over the near-flat water, as if she were eager to meet her mother again.

Since I expected following seas later in the afternoon, I'd tied *Cabin Boy* to the stern using a trick I'd read in Knight's *Sailing*. I had been using a long rope for most of the trip, but in the steep following seas I'd experience in Albemarle Sound and on the Delaware Bay, *Cabin Boy* had surfed down the waves and tried to ram us. *Had* rammed us twice, in fact, with a loud bang. It didn't seem to bother *Cabin Boy* with his stout oaken stem, but it made quite a ding in the *Blue Moon*'s transom and an even bigger ding in my nerves. I didn't like it.

Knight's idea, based on his own sailing in the North Sea, was this:

To tow the dinghy with two very short painters, one to either quarter of the yacht, while an iron half-hundred weight was lashed to the floor of the dinghy close to her stern. This weight steadied her so that she steered straight, did not yaw about, and did not run down upon the yacht. The short painters kept her nose right out of the water so that she could not be swamped. If a sea had filled her—it never did —it would have almost all run out over her stern again. -- E.F. Knight, "Sailing"

I didn't have a half-hundred weight handy, so I substituted one of my 6 gal. water jugs, which weighed about the same. I had the 'short painters' tied inboard, so I could adjust them as necessary. And one of the painters was fifty feet long. If Knight's scheme didn't work, I'd put *Cabin Boy* back on his long leash.

So my companions were ready. The crew was willing. And the captain? Was he able? I thought so, but there was only one way to find out.

We passed between the two stone breakwaters that guarded the inlet and cruised into the open Atlantic. The wind was light, maybe five knots from the blessed south. The seas were three feet high, but long and gentle. Absolutely no problem.

I headed towards the clanging #2M sea buoy. I wanted to get two or three miles offshore before starting my run up the coast. That sea room would put us outside the shallows and fish traps along the coast, but would keep us inside the Ambrose-to-Barnegat shipping lane, and the large ships that traveled it.

So first we cruised east, towards the sun and into deep water. By the time we turned north, the sea floor was fifty or sixty feet below us. The swells were much easier. It was good to be in deep water again. I'd had my fill of the shallow stuff.

I turned the steering over to *Helmo*, hoisted the main, staysail, and jib, and settled down for a long day's motor-sailing. It was thirty-two miles to the anchorage at Sandy Hook. At least six hours, which left plenty of time to spare, I hoped. With all the traffic around New York, I wanted to have my anchor down well before dark.

Meanwhile, there was the sky and sun, the rolling sea and swooping birds, and the flat, low-lying Jersey shore looking close in the clear air. I kept a good lookout and sent a few texts to Helena and the kids ("So far, so good!"). I was the only boat in sight, except for a swiftly moving container ship, far away on the eastern horizon.

An hour later, we passed the Shark River Inlet: the last inlet we could use before Sandy Hook. The fishermen were out in force, and it was comforting to have company for a while, but we soon left them behind.

Gradually the wind picked up and I killed the engine. We sailed along at hull speed on a broad reach. After weeks of motoring, the silence was fantastic. As the wind picked up, so did the seas, but more slowly than they do over shallow water; and they were long and gentle, rather than short and nasty. The GPS showed we were making 6.2 knots over the ground, meaning we had some current with us. King Neptune was making it easy for us for a change.

Off Monmouth Beach, there were plenty of boats again, mainly small fishing boats. They rolled in the gathering waves, making me feel queasy just watching them. The *Blue Moon*'s big mainsail kept us from rolling even half as much.

Then and there, I decided I do not get sea sick. When I first set sail from Steinhatchee, I wasn't sure. My grandfather was famous for getting ill. But watching those fishing boats roll, it suddenly occurred to me that I didn't. I hadn't felt sick for even a minute during the entire voyage, despite some pretty awful weather. It was a good feeling.

We cruised along the nearly featureless coast of Sandy Hook, with the Atlantic Highlands rising behind it. The wind blew steadily from the south, 10-15 knots. The seas continued to rise, but they were long and gentle, and didn't give *Helmo* any problems. I lounged in the cockpit, enjoying the sun, keeping watch. After all my worrying and planning, was it really going to be this easy?

I should have known better than to tweak King Neptune's nose with thoughts like that.

It started when we began our run into the Sandy Hook Channel—the entrance to New York Harbor. I kept us to the port side of the main shipping channel. Rather quickly, the depths shoaled from 50 feet, to 25 feet, to 17 feet. At the same time, those long, placid swells that had been rolling gently under our keel all day, rode up onto the shoals and showed their heads. Shallow water. I hated it. "If we ever make it to deep and lovely Long Island Sound," I told *Cabin Boy* grimly, "we'll never sail in shallow water again." Meanwhile, I had to deal with it.

The first thing I did was to relieve *Helmo* of duty. Knight's words in *Sailing* on the management of a yacht in a rough sea were still fresh in my mind:

> *When sailing a small yacht in a rough sea, certain precautions must be observed which we will describe as briefly as possible, for to handle a vessel properly under these circumstances requires a skill that cannot be imparted by books.*

Luckily, I'd had a bit of experience with rough weather. I just hoped it was enough.

> *To run before a high sea is dangerous, especially if the vessel is a short and beamy one, for a sea may strike the stern on one side and cause her to broach to; or again the vessel may be pooped, that is, a sea may break on board over the stern, filling the well and even swamping her.*

I looked around at the tall, peaky waves that now seemed to tower over the beamy little *Blue Moon*.

> *While running before the sea, steer with great care, so that every dangerous sea strike the vessel right aft, and not on the side, and be ready to meet promptly with the tiller any tendency to broach to.*

These were no doubt the very words that John Walker read when running before his North Sea gale from Harwich to Holland. And though his *Goblin* was a bigger boat, I guessed his seas were also higher. I concentrated on my steering.

I'd nearly forgotten *Cabin Boy*. The high, following seas were just the sort to send him careening into the *Blue Moon's* stern. Glancing over my shoulder, I could see him riding high and dry in our wake, keeping as steady a course as could be desired. Though it was only four miles from the mouth of the Channel to the tip of Sandy Hook, it seemed the longest leg of the trip. The *Blue Moon* was in her element, racing on a broad reach towards home, but I had to continually watch out for really large waves, bearing away to meet them stern on, and then turning back to the northwest towards the inlet. How had John Walker put it? So and back... So and back.

> *So and back... So and back... He sat there swaying with the tiller. Sea after sea rolled up astern, lifted the Goblin with a noise of churning foam, dropped her, and rolled on. Now and then in the darkness he could see the crest of a wave like a grey ghost as it passed close by. Once or twice he lit the big electric torch and flashed it over the side to get an idea of how fast the little Goblin was racing through the water. But mostly he was content to keep up that easy, rhythmical steering, to know by the feel of the wind that there was no danger of a jibe, and to look far ahead for that winking light... — Arthur Ransome, We Didn't Mean to Go to Sea*

And then, just as suddenly as the waves had come, they were gone. We had rounded the Sandy Hook itself, into Sandy Hook Bay and calm water. I turned south and headed for the anchorage behind the Atlantic Highlands breakwater. An hour later, I sailed behind the stone wall with a dying wind, maneuvered my way slowly through the empty mooring field, and dropped my anchor a hundred yards off the beach.

We'd done it. We'd made the hop. At long last. We'd conquered the mighty North Atlantic in winter, at least a little bit of it. I tried to feel the sense of achievement, the glory, that surely Amundsen, and Nansen, and Peary had felt. I puffed out my chest, and sang a patriotic song or two, but all the time I had my eyes on the towers of Manhattan, gleaming on the horizon in the dying sun, and somehow the celebration fell flat.

We weren't done yet.

CHAPTER 24

HELL GATE

When the tide rises on the eastern seaboard it sets into New York Harbor and, farther to the northeast, into Long Island Sound. At New York Bay it splits at the tip of Manhattan, one current pushing up the Hudson and through the Harlem River, the other entering the East River. Here, with the horizontal movement impeded by the opposite flow of the Harlem River and the narrowness of the channel up to the Sound, the huge basin of Hell Gate begins to fill.

The waters, like wild beasts, circle their confines, impatient for the chance to escape. The downcoming flow of the Harlem River is then stopped by the strength of the escaping currents and sent back up through Little Hell Gate and the Bronx Kills, and the channels to the west, like a sluiceway, is filled with swift seething water racing up to the Bronx shore.

This flow continues for hours, building up to a high tide along the East River shore. Then at a time when other waters would settle into slack, the downcoming tide, which has been delayed four hours by the distance and the drag of the Long Island Basin, begins its relentless drive and the struggle for mastery is on. Four hours after entering the sound this tide has changed the flow of the river which is now down the narrow sluiceway from the Bronx and down Little Hell Gate Channel into Hell Gate Basin, counterclockwise around Millrock and as far down the river as the upcoming tide will allow.

To this confusion of ebbs and flows, currents and eddies, add the rocks, reefs, and the freakish whims of the winds. At ebb tide the process was reversed, but no less confusing. —Claude Rust, "Military Engineer"

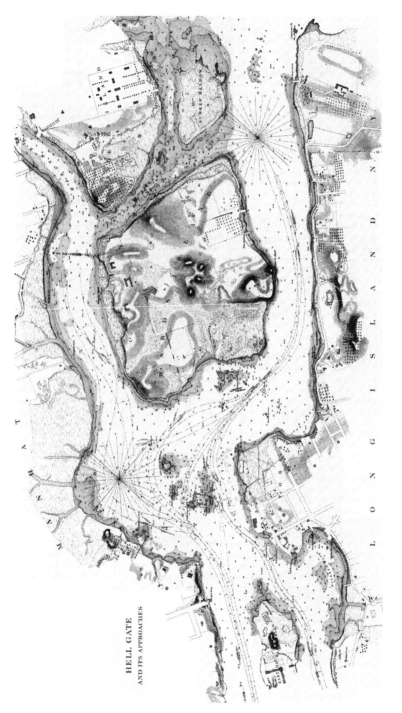

Chart of Hell Gate -- Wikimedia Commons

After dropping my anchor in Sandy Hook, I called Helena to let her know I'd made it and treated myself to a celebratory drink. But there was no time to relax. I had some decisions to make. A check of the forecast showed my weather window was closing fast. Tomorrow, Wednesday, looked good. But on Thursday, Boreas and his ruffians were due back in town. It looked like they planned to stay for the rest of the week at least.

Furthermore, Thursday was Thanksgiving. For months Helena had been saying I wouldn't be home until Thanksgiving. Call me small-minded, but I was determined to prove her wrong. That meant I had to reach Huntington Harbor by tomorrow. But standing between me and my triumphal arrival was the most infamous hazard to navigation in the entire western world: Hell Gate.

The East River connects New York Harbor to Long Island Sound. The alternative route is long and hazardous, particularly in winter: a one hundred mile offshore run down the south coast of Long Island.

The East River short cut attracted me for the same reason it's attracted mariners since the 1600s, regardless of the dangers, which were many.

Beside the particular danger of Hell Gate, there was the general hazard of sailing through the busiest port on the eastern seaboard. I'd been warned repeatedly about this part of my journey. When I'd wondered aloud in a Chesapeake marina bar if my passage through Norfolk had helped prepare me for New York Harbor, the gloom-and-doomsters had chimed in loudly: "Norfolk is nothing compared to New York!", "Like comparing grandma on a Sunday drive, to New York cab drivers!", "Those darn ferries hit forty knots!"

The cruising guides didn't help. They were unanimous in their warnings about New York Harbor: "Don't let the scenery distract you!", "This is serious water!", and "Pay attention!"

But the cruising guides and sailors agreed on one thing: if you didn't get run down by a ship full of Toyotas, or crushed by a tug, or cut in half by a speeding ferry, you were bound to get swallowed up by treacherous Hell Gate, unless you time it perfectly.

JOHN ALMBERG | 305

Hell Gate, brilliantly described by Claude Rust, is where the current flowing down the East River—long delayed by its passage through Long Island Sound—battles with the current flowing up the East River from the ocean. It was made infamous by its swift, reversing currents, standing waves, fog, and even whirlpools. Adding to the clash of currents, Hell Gate was studded with rocks and reefs with names like Pot Rock, Frying Pan, Heel Tap, and Flood Rock. The spot was cursed by mariners for sinking or damaging thousands of ships. According to the U.S. Army Corps of Engineers' *The Conquest of Hell Gate*, one in fifty ships trying to run the gauntlet of Hell Gate was either damaged or sunk in the 1850s.

Thankfully, the reefs and rocks are now gone, cleared by the CoE in a massive thirty year civil engineering project that culminated in 1882 with the largest explosion produced by man until the atomic bomb. The explosion that removed Flood Rock was witnessed by 50,000 New Yorkers, and described by the New York Times (in all caps) as "A COMPLETE SCIENTIFIC SUCCESS."

But even if many of the rocks were gone, the fast, swirling currents, and standing waves remained.

According to my cruising guide, the way to avoid these hazards was to enter the southern end of the East River precisely one hour after low water. One would then have a fair current all the way up the East River, through Hell Gate, and out into Long Island Sound.

As is so often the case, the ideal timing was impractical. Low water would occur at 3:21 a.m. and again at 4:17 p.m. Catching either of these tides meant running Hell Gate in the dark, something I wasn't prepared to do, particularly since fog was forecast for that night. But if I couldn't catch the ideal time, what should I do?

After puzzling over this question for an hour or more, with not nearly enough information, I decided the best plan was to hoist my anchor before dawn, cross New York Harbor at first light, and hit Hell Gate as early as I could. With a bit of luck, I'd pass through just before the tide turned, at 10 a.m.

I hoped I could get out onto Long Island Sound before the in-

The End of Flood Rock -- Wikimedia Commons

coming current swept me back down the river, but there was only one way to find out.

* * *

24 Nov 2010—Out of my bunk at 5:05 a.m. Still dark. Can't see the lights of the Verrazano Bridge, which were clearly visible last night. Must still be some fog up there. Made myself a good breakfast of hot oatmeal, boiled eggs, and an apple. Not sure when I'll have another chance to eat today. Sunrise supposed to be around 7 a.m., but I intend to be underway before 6. Hope I've left enough time to make Hell Gate before the tide turns. — Log of the Blue Moon

Before hitting my bunk last night, I'd carefully planned the day's voyage using all the information I had available. That included a cruising guide, a few iPhone apps that plotted tides and currents, several online bulletin board discussions on 'running Hell Gate', a complete set of paper charts, and an up-to-date copy of Eldridge Tide and Pilot Book.

I must confess that I am not comfortable using computer apps as my sole source of navigation information. Long experience with computers tells me that they are occasionally wrong (even NOAA warns about this); and—more importantly—it is oh so easy to misinterpret them, particularly when you are tired. That is, computer systems are highly subject to operator error, even when the operator is an expert.

So, like a good reporter, I liked to confirm the story told by my computer with at least one non-computer source. That might sound redundant, or even paranoid, but confirming my navigation with a second source of data gives me an extra dose of confidence. And sometimes confidence makes all the difference in an emergency. There's nothing more dangerous than second-guessing your own navigation when things go wrong.

I had an excellent source of printed information in the form of the *Eldridge Tide and Pilot Book*. This book, ubiquitous on the northeast coast of the US, traces its roots back to the 1850s when George Eldridge self-published a *Pilot for Vineyard Sound*. At the time, the number of ships sailing through Vineyard and Nantucket Sounds was second only to the English Channel, and no other information was available.

His son added tide and current tables (based on his own scientific measurements) for the same area in the 1870s, and then gradually expanded coverage of tides and currents up and down the east coast. It quickly became the indispensable book for professional and amateur mariners.

My cruising guide and the folks on the computer bulletin boards agreed that the best time to start up the East River was one hour after low water at the Battery (right near the mouth of the river), or around 3:21 a.m. Since Hell Gate was approximately six miles up the river, that would put me in Hell Gate at around 4:30 a.m. That was the ideal, presuming I was willing to run the gauntlet of New York Harbor in the dark, which I was not.

After studying the Eldridge current tables and maps, it seemed clear to me that it would be just barely possible to squeak past Hell Gate as late as 10 a.m. By 11 a.m. the tide would turn, and by noon the current would be flooding fiercely against me, but if I could squeak through by 10 a.m., I thought I'd be okay.

This went against all conventional wisdom, but it looked possible to me.

Just one problem: Hell Gate was roughly twenty-five miles from my anchorage in Sandy Hook. If I sailed at 6 a.m.—an hour before dawn—I'd have to average six knots over the whole course to make it. The *Blue Moon* could only do 5.5 knots under her own power. To make it on time, I'd need some current behind me.

Last night, that hadn't seemed a problem. According to my calculations, we'd have a fair current the whole way. Surely we'd be able to average six knots. But in the middle of the night, I had started to worry. Would I have enough time? There was no place to anchor in the East River, or even in New York Harbor. If I didn't make it, it would be a long sail back to a safe anchorage. I hardly ever fret, but that night, fret I did, until my unneeded alarm clock finally rang.

After my hurried breakfast, I rigged my hodgepodge of battery-powered running lights. We steamed out of the anchorage just before 6 a.m.

They say it never really gets dark in New York, but it was dark that morning. I pointed my powerful flashlight over the bow to pick out the numerous crab pots that had been so easy to avoid in daylight. Now they emerged from the dark just in time to steer around them. It was okay to dodge crab pots in the dark, but I didn't want to do the same with more dangerous flotsam. According to reports, New York Harbor was thick with containers fallen off ships, logs floating down the Hudson, and bodies dropped off bridges. I wanted some light for that kind of work.

I sipped my second cup of coffee as we cruised the four nautical miles up Sandy Hook Bay. Red and green buoy lights winked from all directions. I had the bay to myself, except for one or two fishermen in small boats and an ominous looking Coast Guard cutter. This ship seemed to follow us for a couple miles, and as usual, it made me edgy for no good reason. You see these Homeland Security ships on patrol in all big US harbors, now. I'd even been stopped by one when entering a port in Florida. I knew they had a job to do, but that morning I was on a tight schedule and didn't have time even for a friendly chat. I double-checked my running lights to make sure they were in order and held my course. After a while the cutter seemed to lose interest. It peeled off in another direction and sped away. I didn't regret seeing its stern light.

Meanwhile, we'd been making just five knots, which meant we probably had a half-knot current against us. As we entered New York's Lower Bay, with dawn's rose-red fingers just showing in the east, we were behind schedule.

The eight mile long Lower Bay is open to Atlantic swells from the east, and criss-crossed with shipping lanes with names like Swash Channel and Ambrose Channel. I followed the Chapel Hill Channel north, staying just outside the red buoys to avoid traffic. This didn't help. A steady stream of high-speed ferries buzzed back and forth between New York and New Jersey. They seemed to ignore the channels, preferring to veer as close to the *Blue Moon* as possible.

All the big ship traffic was in the Ambrose Channel—the main channel between the Atlantic and the Upper Bay. I found the speed of these ships disconcerting. You'd look over your shoulder and see nothing; a few minutes later, there would be a ship full of iPhones or whatever a mile away; in another few minutes, it would pass us. They were doing three or four times our speed and of course could not stop or turn out of the way to avoid us if we strayed under their bows. I wanted to stay well away from them, but at some point, we'd have to cross the Ambrose Channel. I was not looking forward to it.

Half-way up the Lower Bay, I still couldn't see the towers of the massive Verrazano Narrows Bridge. The bridge, and New York City beyond it, were still hidden in fog. But as we approached, the fog seemed to retreat north. Eventually, the bridge emerged from the grey, wet mist.

We were still sailing along the west side of the Ambrose Channel. There were no ships coming down from the Upper Bay, and just one ship entering the inlet far behind us. It seemed the perfect opportunity to dash across the mile-wide channel, so I turned to starboard and headed straight across the channel, towards the unfortunately named Gravesend Bay. I kept a wary eye on the ship that sped north towards us. It seemed to be moving at a frightening pace. If our engine should give out, my only chance would be to jump into *Cabin Boy* and row like hell. I told him to prepare himself for this emergency, then gritted my teeth and urged the *Blue Moon* ahead.

We reached the far edge of the channel just as the ship sped past us, creaming up an enormous bow wave. Man, those ships moved fast.

"Okay," I said to *Cabin Boy*. "Stand down."

He seemed to breath again.

We had the current with us by them, and as the flood squeezed through the Narrows under the bridge, we picked up speed. When we passed under the Verrazano Bridge, we were making six knots, at last. "Too late?" I wondered. It was already 8:30, and we were well behind schedule.

* * *

08:30 - just passed under the Verrazano-Narrow Bridge. SOG (speed over ground) about 6 knots. Thought we'd be doing more than that by now. Still pretty foggy. Lots of big ships anchored up ahead. Fingers crossed! — Log of the Blue Moon

Once you go under the Verrazano-Narrows Bridge, you enter the Upper Bay. It's fairly narrow—only a mile or two wide. From the chart and my knowledge of the city, I expected the shore to be blighted by industry, lined with warehouses, old ship yards, and scrap heaps. But as we cruised under the bridge towards the fog-bound city, the scene was surprisingly pastoral, with trees on shore in their autumn colors, the occasional white church spire poking above the tree line, and substantial houses that might have been there since colonial times.

The ship traffic was also lighter and easier to deal with than I feared. I stayed out of the ship channel, of course, hand-steering the *Blue Moon* in the relative shallows between the channel buoys and the Brooklyn shore. A large ship passed about every ten minutes. Some went north, some south, but they moved at a more stately speed than they had south of the bridge. We were far enough out of the channel to be safe, and close enough to enjoy watching them steam by.

I monitored Channel 13 as recommended. That was the channel used by the big ships and their handlers. I listened to the sound of efficient chatter going back and forth between the captains of ships, tugs, barges, ferries, and bumboats, but it was all jargon obscured by a sea of static. I hardly understood a word. I was glad no one seemed to be cursing at a small blue sailboat. I tried to stay out of everyone's way.

Starting from the southern tip of the Bay Ridge Flats, and going north, the main channel was an anchorage. Dozens of large ships slumbered at the end of their cables. A few small boats puttered quietly between them, but on important business, or early morning social calls, I could not tell. I cruised between the anchored ships and the Flats, out of traffic, but close enough to feel the enormity of the ships, to hear men laughing their foggy, early morning laughs, and to smell bacon frying, somewhere.

Meanwhile, I'd been keeping an eye on the north. Just when I'd begun to despair about sailing up the East River in fog, it lifted its skirts enough to reveal the southern tip of old Manhattan Isle. At the same time, the sun beamed across the horizon, lighting up Lady Liberty, who looked surprisingly small and vulnerable in the golden light. She basked in the glow as if enjoying the warm rays. Home had never seemed closer.

At the south end of Governor's Island, I had to choose whether to go up its west side, in the main channel, or its east side, in the Buttermilk Channel. The Buttermilk seemed to have less boat traffic, so I headed up the east side of the famous island.

Governor's Island is strategically placed off the southern tip of Manhattan. Its name dates back to colonial times when New York was a British naval base. The island, a mile south of Manhattan and close by the naval anchorage, was reserved for the exclusive use of the royal governor. Even back then New York was all about location, location, location.

The island was occupied by the American Continental Army at the beginning of the Revolutionary War. General Israel Putnam fortified the island with earthworks and forty cannon. During the Battle of Long Island, these guns kept the British Fleet out of the East River and covered General Washington's retreat across the river from Brooklyn to Manhattan. Stinging from this missed opportunity, the British recaptured Governor's Island and held the strategic point until the end of the war.

Cruising down the east side of this historic island, the fog burned off, and we got our first good view of Manhattan. It was 9:30. The sun came out and felt warm on the back of my neck.

"What a beautiful day!" I said to *Cabin Boy*, who was sticking close behind us.

After exiting the Buttermilk Channel, we passed the Battery and finally entered the lower end of the East River, but we were far behind schedule and still doing a mere six knots. Hell Gate was more than six miles away. We'd need to catch the last of the dying current to make Hell Gate before the tide turned against us. I was worried, but the view was terrific.

As we entered the East River proper, the current began to increase. By the time we cruised under the fabulous Brooklyn Bridge, we were making 6.5 knots. That was more like it, but it would still be 10:30 before we entered Hell Gate. Too late? Only one way to find out.

The lower reaches of the East River are spanned by three historic suspension bridges. When you visit New York City you can impress the locals by remembering their names. Just remember 'BMW': the Brooklyn, Manhattan, and Williamsburg Bridges. Each in turn was the longest suspension bridge in the world when they opened.

The first, the Brooklyn Bridge, opened in 1867 when traffic consisted of horse carts, pedestrians, and streetcars. The granite blocks that give the bridge its distinctive, solid look were quarried on Vinalhaven Island, Maine and delivered from Maine to New

York by schooner. The bridge was so revolutionary that when it opened people doubted its stability. Days after its opening, twelve people were crushed to death when a panicked mob fled from the gently swaying bridge. P.T. Barnum proved its safety by leading twenty-two elephants, including his star, Jumbo, in a much publicized parade across the span. When I sailed under it, the bridge was snarled in rush-hour traffic. We were making better time than the cars.

Once past the Williamsburg Bridge, we had a grand view of Midtown and the Empire State Building. We were approaching the southern end of Roosevelt Island. This island splits the East River into two narrow channels. I expected the current to pick up appreciably as it was squeezed through the main channel to the west. I was not disappointed. Our speed ticked up to 7 and then to 7.5 knots. That was more like it. The shore seemed to fly by at this dizzying speed, even though we were very near slack tide. I hated to think what it would be like when the river was in full flood.

With the boost from this current to help us along, we cruised past Blackwell Island Lighthouse at the northern tip of Roosevelt Island at 10:15 a.m. This was it. Hell Gate lay just ahead. I braced myself for the worst: standing waves, whirlpools, sea serpents, whatever. I was ready for it.

"Bring it on!" I rashly called to King Neptune. (Will I never learn?)

I was almost disappointed to find no standing waves, whirlpools, or even sea serpents. In fact, the infamous and much feared Hell Gate was more or less… a millpond. There was one swirly bit in the middle, but that was it. By sheer luck, we'd hit Hell Gate about a half-hour before slack water—probably about as calm as it ever gets. I whooped for joy. Hell Gate was the last major obstacle between me and home. All the tension of the last few days seemed to fall away, to be replaced by a huge sense of relief. We'd made it.

I turned around and took a celebratory photo of *Cabin Boy*. He looked suitably proud.

As I snapped this photo, my celebration was clipped short by the loud toot of a ship's horn. Turning around to see what the ruckus was, I saw the bow of a rather large freighter speeding towards us. The ship was coming round the bend into Hell Gate and moving fast.

Due to my premature celebration, we were on the wrong side of the channel, just north of Hallets Point. My hand twitched on the tiller, momentarily heading us for the right side, but then common sense took command. We did not have time to cut across the bow of the speeding ship, so I hugged the north side of the channel. To hit us, the ship would have to run up onto the shoals of Hog Back. Instead of endangering us, the rocks of treacherous Hell Gate were protecting us.

Luck—the dumbest form of dumb luck—was with us still.

Seconds later, the ship swept past. We cruised under the RFK bridge and crossed over to the correct side of the channel. We were through Hell Gate, but I didn't celebrate. King Neptune had taught me another lesson.

"Don't get cocky!" I told *Cabin Boy*. "We still have a long way to go."

Then I broke out a *Blue Moon* beer. I deserved a *little* celebration, anyway.

With attention thus enhanced by experience, we got through the rest of the East River. We passed depressing Riker's Island, the famous prison, home to some 14,000 or so unhappy souls, at least one of whom, I'm sure, had a bumper sticker in his cell that said, "I'd rather be sailing".

A while later, we passed under the Whitestone Bridge and I finally saw the sight I'd been awaiting for at least 1,000 miles: the Throgs Neck Bridge and the entrance to Long Island Sound.

For months I'd been urging us north thinking, "If only we can get to beautiful, deep Long Island Sound!", as if no storm or trouble ever ruffled its broad waters. I knew this was not true, but slowly I'd idealized the Sound until it had become in my mind the most perfect sailing water in the world. I longed to reach it.

And for once, King Neptune hadn't prepared an ironic twist for my story. When I sailed under the Throgs Neck Bridge, I wasn't met by a horrific line squall, or an out of control container ship, or even an uncharted rock.

In fact, I was met by the placid sea of my dreams.

And best of all, it was still early in the day—barely noon. There were still twenty nautical miles between us and home, but I thought we might just make it.

And if not, no matter! Unlike the many inhospitable places I'd been, on Long Island Sound there is a beautiful easy-to-enter harbor every five miles or so along the coast. I had my pick of anchorages. If darkness closed in before we made Huntington Harbor, we'd put into Oyster Bay, which was just minutes from home by car. But two things drove me on: First, the window of good weather I'd been enjoying since Manasquan (only two days ago!) was due to slam shut that very night with a vengeance. I might be stuck in Oyster Bay for several days, which would be okay, but I'd rather not.

And second, I still wanted to prove Helena wrong and arrive home before Thanksgiving, even if it was just by one day.

So we pressed on. There wasn't much wind, but I hoisted every scrap of sail and soon we were motor-sailing down the Sound at hull speed, and we even got lift from the current, though the tables said it should have been against us. A parting gift from King Neptune, perhaps.

We quickly passed City Island—historic home of New York City boat builders. On any other day, I would have been tempted to stop for a visit, but not that one. In turn, Manhasset Bay and Hempstead Bay flew by.

Then there was the long stretch to Oyster Bay. I put *Helmo* back in command and went below to heat up some soup and make a sandwich. It had been many hours since I'd been able to leave the tiller and I was starving. I poked my head out of the companionway every couple of minutes to make sure we didn't skewer a fishing boat with the *Blue Moon*'s long bowsprit, but we had the whole Sound to ourselves except for one sail, hull down, on the misty eastern horizon.

By the time we reached the entrance to Oyster Bay, it was getting dark. It was late November and the days were short. I hesitated for a moment, thinking, "Should I press my luck?" But only for a moment. These were my home waters. I'd sailed into Huntington Harbor many times in the dark. I had the one necessary ingredient for completing my sail, even in total darkness: local knowledge!

I urged my trusty Yamaha up to full speed—surely this was the time for the final push. And as we left Oyster Bay behind, I called Helena.

"I'm going to make it home tonight," I said.

"Really?" she said. I had kept her expectations low, just in case. "When? It's getting dark, isn't it?"

"I should be there in an hour."

"I can't believe it!"

And oddly enough, I didn't want that last hour to end. As we cruised down the coast of Lloyd Neck, our wake a wide 'V' behind us in the dying light, it was hard to accept that my once-in-a-lifetime cruise was coming to an end. We'd gone through a lot. It certainly had been a Big Adventure, and I was sorry to see it end.

But then we were headed down Huntington Bay behind a fishing boat, passing the big red #8 buoy that had marked the turning point of so many races, and headed towards the historic old lighthouse that marked the entrance to Huntington Harbor, where William Atkin had had his first boat shop, a hundred years ago.

We were home.

As I slowly cruised down the narrow and nearly empty harbor, I spotted a small black car on the harbor road, with Helena waving beside it. She'd come down as far as she could to get a first look at us.

Then, a little while later, as I slowly backed the *Blue Moon* into her winter slip for the first time, Helena was on the dock to take my line.

I stepped off the boat and kissed her.

"I told you we'd make it before Thanksgiving," I said.

Her eyes sparkled. "Happy birthday, darling."

In all the rush and worry, I'd forgotten. It *was* my birthday. And a happy birthday it was, too.

Cabin Boy departing Hell Gate

To learn more about the author,
please visit this book's companion website:
www.unlikelyboatbuilder.com

And if you enjoyed this book, please consider
writing a review on Amazon.com. Thank you!

CO-2
L-2019

Made in the USA
Charleston, SC
01 April 2016